DECEIVED

DECEIVED

THE POISONED FRUIT OF EVANGELICALISM

MARK A. WILIAMS, M.D., PH.D.

ISBN Paperback: 978-1-83663-234-4
ISBN Hardcover: 978-1-83663-235-1

Contact Copyright Holder at:

Mark A. Williams, M.D., Ph.D., All Things All People Publishing, P.O. Box 110793, Nashville, TN 37222, USA; Booking@atapmusic.com; +1 (615) 724-0131

Published non-exclusively by:

All Things All People Publishing, LLC, 8877 Meadowview Drive, Westchester, Ohio 45069

Dedication

To my wife, Darice Williams – My Life, My Love, My Friend: Your unwavering support empowers me to pursue God's calling in music, medicine, writing, and motivational speaking. You are my inspiration and strength.

To my children, Demarcus (and his wife, Miranda), Aaron, and Courtney: Thank you for your patience with my frequent musings on topics that may not always interest you. I pray that my words will resonate when you need them most, guiding you through life's challenges.

To my friends with differing political beliefs: I'm grateful for your understanding that our shared faith in Jesus transcends the fleeting noise of political ideologies. Your willingness to listen and share has broadened my perspective and informed many of my observations.

Above all, I thank God for His endless patience, for gently revealing my mistakes, and for always welcoming me back to His merciful embrace.

CONTENTS

PREFACE — 1

INTRODUCTION — 3

    The Call — 5
    Rebuke and Reprove — 11

JUDGEMENT BEFALLS AMERICA — 17

    The Prophetic Warning — 17
    Feed The Sheep — 20
    The Sermon Evangelical Pastors Forgot — 24
    For Misplaced Affections — 30
    For Love of Self — 39

MODERN-DAY PHARISEES — 45

    The World That Hates — 45
    The Nexus of Evangelicalism — 52
    The Leaven of Evangelicals — 60

THE UNSEEN CHURCH — 73

    Christian But Not The Church — 73
    Process Preempts Product — 80
    Jesus, The Liberal — 85

THE WAY THAT SEEMS RIGHT — 93

Ours is the Kingdom — 93
The Vulnerability of Passion — 101
The Ministry of Compassion — 110

THE ISSUES OF LIFE — 117

The Sanctity of Life — 117
The Shedding of Innocent Blood — 125
The Beginning of Life — 132

THE OTHER GODS — 141

Offering A Strange Fire — 141
Love of Country — 146
Nationalism and Fear — 156
The Cause of Capitalism — 167

THE FULLNESS OF TIME — 175

The Preference of the Prophet — 176
The Extinction of Truth — 189
The Rebellion Comes First — 205
Persecution Must Come — 221
A Nation Divided — 231

PREFACE

As a devoted follower of Jesus Christ and Gospel recording artist/worship leader, the message of the Gospel is of paramount importance to me. However, God's love is often conveyed in a manner far different from the example Jesus provided. This error frequently stems from the unbridled zeal of His messengers.

In their attempt to please God through good deeds, many people forget or completely disregard the method by which we attain salvation and favor with God – individual faith and personal profession. They begin a misguided quest to eradicate sin from the earth by exploiting the levers of democracy while abandoning the spiritual weaponry we were equipped with.

Clearly threatened by a flagrant and steep decline in societal morals, many Christians have determined that it is their mission to prevent the inevitable outcome predicted by the Bible. Motivated by good intentions, they preferentially employ political tactics to stifle society's decadence. While civic engagement is not contradictory to Christian faith, compromising values and using unscrupulous tactics to achieve legislative victories is.

Our legal system respects a doctrine called the "Fruit of the Poisonous Tree." According to this principle, evidence obtained through illegal means is inadmissible in criminal law. It is useless because of how it was obtained, regardless of how compelling it might be. This principle regrettably seems foreign to many Evangelicals, who presumably would hold themselves to an even higher standard of righteousness. Instead, they revel in their legislative accomplishments, no matter how unseemly the methods used to achieve them.

The blatant compromise and hypocrisy of self-proclaimed Ambassadors of Jesus Christ render the Christian message impotent. By mastering the ruthless strategies of a carnal world, they alienate the very people they are commanded to redeem. They oppress those they are called to liberate. Even the most casual observer of these offenses will readily reject their offer of the Gospel, not because they despise the good news but because the messengers have employed methods that distort the message.

In their fervor to eradicate sin, Evangelicals more deeply entrench lost souls in the cauldron of sin. The rejection of God's love is not motivated by impenetrable obstinance but rather by the repugnance of evangelical hypocrisy, which shuts their ears to the life-changing Gospel message.

In writing this book, I hope to reveal how the spirit that drove the Pharisees to enact oppressive laws is still alive and active today. It has redirected its attention to a relatively few but vocal and influential individuals who infect well-intentioned Christ-followers with the legalism Jesus referred to as leaven. They exploit seemingly honorable passions to enlist unrelenting support for good but misdirected and carnal causes. Through various biblical explorations and the example of Jesus, I expose the fallacy of this evangelical thinking. With great care, I demonstrate how the indoctrination of 'good deeds' blinds many Christians to the precepts of Christ. Prayerfully, the eyes of the deceived will be opened, for all who have a heart to receive.

INTRODUCTION

Few things deliver a more destabilizing jolt to your consciousness than realizing you have been lied to. Moreover, you've been deceived. The more prolonged and more consequential the deception, the more unnerving the revelation becomes. When faced with this reality, people respond in various ways. Learning of deception often thrusts an individual into a myriad of emotions and psychological responses.

Being lied to incite feelings of betrayal and hurt. The emotional disorientation leaves the individual questioning their judgment and the authenticity of their interactions with those they unworthily trusted. This betrayal casts shadows of doubt not only on past interactions but may also lead to challenges in developing future healthy trust relationships. *"Can I trust the veracity of what this person is telling me?"* they wonder. To prevent the emotional embarrassment, psychological harm, and, in many cases, the financial consequences of their previous misplaced trust, an individual devastated by the discovery of a lie may retreat into reclusiveness, presuming that a life of solitude or isolation might be more tolerable than the risk of trusting once again.

For some, the psychological burden of acknowledging deception is too great a price to pay. Consequently, they find it easier to never acknowledge the reality. It is sometimes more palatable for them to continue with the bliss of deceit than to do the hard work of recovering from it. If the relationship with the trusted one who lied to them is significant enough and the benefits that the relationship offered are substantial enough, a person may choose to move forward as if the deceit never happened in the first place. Only the individual lied to can determine how they will proceed after the discovery. Once your eyes have been opened, you cannot unlearn what has been learned consciously. You'll either deny its existence or manage the consequences.

There are some things that God never wanted us to experience. Chief among them is the knowledge of evil. When He created Adam and Eve, He gave specific instructions saying, *"You may surely eat of every tree of the garden, but of the tree of the knowledge of good and evil you shall not eat, for in the day that you eat of it you shall surely die"* (Gen. 2:16-17). Certainly, God wanted us to know good. In fact, after each thing that He created, the Bible says He acknowledged and established it as "good" (Gen. 1:10, 12, 18, 21, 25, 31). After creating mankind, God introduced man and woman to the good that He created. Of all the good God created, there was only one thing that man could not consume: fruit from the tree of knowledge of good and evil.

It wasn't that God didn't want man to know good; rather, He didn't want us to know evil. There is a certain bliss in ignorance. But an aspiration inherently resident within mankind compels him to be God, or at least god-like. The serpent in the Garden of Eden exploited this vulnerability to tempt the woman and the man, saying, *"God knows that when you eat of it your eyes will be opened, and you will be like God, knowing good and evil"* (Gen. 3:5). You and I don't have an insatiable desire to know evil; most of us would rather close our eyes to it and deny its existence. However, the temptation to be like God was sufficient to compel the disobedience of Adam and Eve.

Since that day, humankind has sought to acquire the power and control that has always been and should permanently reside in the hands of the omnipotent God. Even if we've chosen not to aspire toward omnipotence, from childhood, we all want to maintain an element of control over ourselves and often others. Most are just not honest enough to admit it. Frequently, that power is either obtained or exhibited through the tool of deception.

Deceit is the concealment or misrepresentation of truth. John 8:32 reminds us that the truth is made available to us and that it has liberating power. It is the truth that sets us free. Therefore, the implication is that we will remain bound without the truth. Thus, it can be surmised that the one who conceals or misrepresents the truth seeks to oppress. Oppression is a tool of hatred used to acquire and maintain power or control. Make no mistake about it: one who deceives you does not seek your liberty, despite their claims to the contrary. Rather, they seek to subjugate you indefinitely. Or at least until the truth sets you free.

Over the past ten years, the scales of deceit have gradually been lifted from my eyes. Now that I see clearly the deception perpetrated against the people of God for centuries, it becomes my charge to share the message with all who will hear and receive the liberating truth of the Gospel.

The Call

For most of my adult life, I paid little attention, if any, to current political affairs. I believed that as a citizen of the Kingdom of God, the world's affairs had little application to me. More importantly, politics held no eternal consequence or benefit for me. So, I paid little attention until the 2004 presidential election between George W. Bush and John Kerry. I vividly recall watching one of the presidential debates in which Bush was asked a question similar to ***"What do you say to your critics who say that you are only interested in pandering to the rich and large corporations?"*** Bush remained silent about the question, shrugged his shoulders, and donned a look on his face, which seemed to reflect the sentiment, ***"I know which side my bread is buttered on."***

Why that moment was so poignant to me at the time was not clear. However, it did strike me as curious that an individual who vociferously professed to be Christian would be blatantly biased toward the rich; in so doing, he'd forsake the poor. For the first time, I considered whether my faith should instruct my political position. This was obviously not a novel concept for many, as each year, one of the political parties seemed to strategically enlist the support of a group of religious leaders. In fact, it appeared that it didn't require much effort to secure their allegiance. Still, even recognizing this, I remained unenlightened about a ploy that evil spiritual forces devised to ensnare a gaggle of Christians.

It wouldn't be until the 2008 presidential election, Obama vs. McCain, that it would more substantively inform my vote. I listened intently to the two candidates' platform promises and evaluated which resonated most loudly with me. From that point forward, I determined that my vote would be given to the candidate who most closely matched my Christian values. What I didn't realize was that others did the same thing. However, their values were prioritized differently than mine. This realization kept me from becoming intolerant of those who professed the same faith in Jesus Christ that I did but who had political positions that varied from mine. It seemed innocent enough at that point. After the historic election of Barack Obama as the first African American president of the United States, I celebrated this feat that seemed up to that moment to be impossible. And into the recesses of my cerebrum went any consideration of political discourse until 2012.

The presidential primary season of 2012 was the first time I actually paid much attention to the primary candidates and how they differed. It was clear that Barack Obama would be the Democratic nominee, but who would the Republicans rally behind? For a period of time, I was stunned by the possibility that the nominee might be yet another African American man, Herman Cain. Imagine, a Black man born in Memphis, Tennessee, and reared in Georgia, who was a graduate of Morehouse College and the CEO of Godfather's Pizza, could actually be the Republican nominee for president running against the first Black president of the United States. That I loved Godfather's Pizza was simply icing on the cake. My mind was literally blown! Could this possibly be in

America? Could it be that the glass ceiling for Black people in America had finally been irrevocably shattered?

My enthusiasm was soon quelled when Cain announced the suspension of his campaign amid sexual harassment allegations. Assuming the favored position and eventually clinching the nomination was a Mormon, a purportedly moral man named Mitt Romney. Reverberating around the Republican public sphere was the mantra, "Character Matters." I agreed! The lack of moral turpitude should be disqualifying for any leader who seeks the highest office in the land. As much as I was disappointed by the suspension of the Cain campaign (admittedly, primarily for proud racial reasons), I understood the necessity of it.

Republicans proceeded to capitalize on the "Character Matters" campaign, shunning the Obama administration's efforts to advance civil rights protections for homosexuals. Perhaps most offensive to many conservative Republicans was a decision Obama and the Attorney General made to no longer enforce the Defense of Marriage Act's (DOMA) provision that defined the existence of marriage as only between a man and a woman. This eventually led to the Supreme Court's landmark decisions holding the Act unconstitutional. Infuriated by this seeming attack on morality, as defined by conservatives, Republicans became even more allied to the "Character Matters" mantra. The campaigns and political discourses revolved around the "assault" that Obama and Democrats had allegedly launched on Christian values. Despite the valiant effort to defeat Obama, Romney and conservatives would succumb to the monumental task of persuading Americans that their way was the righteous way.

Again, I agreed that character and morality mattered. Much like my conservative brothers and sisters, I was personally displeased by some of President Obama's and elected Democrats' socially liberal policies. I remained pleased that Republicans had still held their ground, insisting that leaders should at least set the moral temperature for the country and, more importantly, reflect it. This optimism persisted until 2016 when it became apparent that Donald Trump would be the forerunner and eventual Republican nominee.

While I had no consternation about most secular individuals pledging their support for him, I was confounded by White Evangelicals' overwhelming allegiance to Donald Trump. Only four years earlier, they were devoted to the "Character Matters" narrative. Their commitment was so resolute at that time that they abandoned their support for Herman Cain for sexual harassment allegations, which were fewer in number than Donald Trump's. Worse yet, Donald Trump's past and current moral turpitude became increasingly evident as the campaign progressed. It seemed that the worse he behaved, the greater support he gained. This fidelity was evident also to Donald Trump himself, who suggested that he could shoot someone on Fifth Avenue and not lose a single supporter, not even an Evangelical. This type of inscrutable loyalty seemed to embolden him to be even more offensive in his campaigning.

Several racially offensive comments were repeated and defended by Donald Trump, in addition to a barrage of accusations of sexual harassment, misogyny, and a long history of unscrupulous business practices. Still, none of it seemed to dampen the enthusiasm for his candidacy. *"How could this be?"* I thought to myself. How is it that a man as marred as Donald Trump could secure the endorsement of evangelicals – religious leaders, well-versed in scripture and well-established in their ministerial calling? How is it that this support could be unassuaged by even an admission by Trump that he had never asked God for forgiveness – a claim that he doubled down on in a subsequent interview when he was given a second bite at the apple? I was dumbfounded!

At this moment, God opened my eyes to see the appeal. The "Character Matters" approach in the past had failed them, and they perceived that the values they held dearly were severely threatened by the prospect of another four years of Democratic control of the Congress and/or White House. This was coupled with the promise by Donald Trump to appoint conservative judges to federal courts and, most importantly, the Supreme Court of the United States. He understood the colossal priority that evangelicals placed on overturning the Roe vs. Wade ruling. Finally, conservatives and evangelicals had someone who offered the promise of the golden egg conservatives have sought for decades. While others have promised in the past, their exercise of diplomacy and subscription to the "give a little to get a little" ideology rendered them a less reliable choice. In Trump, they found a bull in a china shop who was willing to do whatever was necessary to win.

It soon made perfect sense to me. Donald Trump's bravado was not repulsive, as one would have presumed. Instead, it seemed to attract even religious leaders who would never muster the courage to speak such profanities or vulgarities. Donald Trump became the mouthpiece and the muscle for conservative evangelicals. He had given voice and strength to a group of people who felt they had been ignored and bullied for decades.

At that time, I served as a worship leader and elder at a wonderfully diverse church. Unbeknownst to me, many evangelical pastors had determined that they would become much more affirmative in their support for Donald Trump's candidacy, even if it meant risking backlash from their congregations. In their minds, the stakes were too high, and the opportunity was too promising for them to allow this moment to pass. To reassure them of their passionate support for Trump, many referred to prophecies that either directly mentioned that Trump would become president, vaguely referenced him peripherally, or incompletely defined his character. Armed with this conviction, they threw their full-throated support to ensure Trump would become the 45th president of the United States. My pastor was one of them.

I recall a Facebook post my pastor made asserting that our vote in the 2016 presidential election would be a direct reflection of how our hearts and values aligned with God's. Although the assertion troubled me initially, I was reassured by the belief that each political party is imperfect but also has some platform goals that mirror Christian principles. I moved on and gave it no additional thought until election week.

On Sunday, two days before election day, my pastor made a bold proclamation from the pulpit. He said, ***"This year, there's only one Godly candidate. The guy I voted for would do well if he just keeps his mouth shut."*** It became immediately evident to this diverse congregation who he thought was the "godly" candidate, as there was only one male: Donald

Trump. The message was also heard loud and clear by other congregants of this diverse church. The message was unmistakable that my pastor thinks: 1) Donald Trump is either godly or a godly choice, 2) Hillary Clinton is an ungodly option, and if I vote for her, I am making an ungodly choice, and/or 3) If I vote for Clinton then my heart and values do not align with God's. Needless to say, this disrupted the peace within the congregation. As much as 40% of the congregation likely disagreed with his assessment and certainly disapproved of his public proclamation.

Over the ensuing days, and after Donald Trump won the election, I received numerous calls from congregants who were hurt by and angry at the accusation of their pastor. As an elder, I was charged with the duty of helping to maintain peace in the congregation. It became necessary that I speak with the pastor. During a very memorable and heated conversation with the pastor about his accusation, I finally realized just how passionate and committed to the cause of Pro-life policy many evangelicals are. With unyielding conviction, he shouted at me, "I cannot vote for someone who believes in killing babies!" At that moment, my eyes were opened. My confusion was resolved. I accepted that this noble, but still carnal (expounded upon later) cause is righteous to many, and to them, it was worthy of great sacrifice.

From that moment on, the Lord began revealing to me how a great deception that seeks to ensnare Christians and eventually help usher in the persecution Jesus foretold would befall Christians. By no means do I suggest that the deception is exclusive to evangelicals. It is a deception that seeks to entrap all Christians regardless of political persuasions. However, it has its strongest hold on the group of Christians who identify as "Evangelical."

From the time of Donald Trump's nomination as the Republican presidential candidate until this date, the Lord placed a prophetic burden on me to open the eyes of the blind. I knew that the fulfillment of this mandate would potentially cause friction with my pastor, especially if I remained in a leadership role as an elder and certainly in the visible role as a worship leader. I greatly respected my pastor for never asking me to refrain from the public rebuke, which I believe God charged me to make. While I personally felt he had no real authority to make such a demand, I knew it was his strong preference that I stopped. Consequently, I voluntarily stepped down from my positions and, to this day, continue to speak the word I believe God instructs.

Rebuke and Reprove

Admittedly, as my quest began, I saw a more political bent to my admonishments. But that was because of my perception. Our experiences and limited knowledge often influence perceptions. As more revelation comes, perception evolves. In hindsight, and as God revealed more of the deception to me, it became clear that politics was merely one tool of the deceiver. If permitted, he would use that tool to keep my eyes and the eyes of those who would otherwise hear closed. The more I matured, the less politically influenced my understanding became. Because of my transformation, I can clearly understand why those I pray would hear the message might initially reject it. Political persuasions have become so pervasive that they demand, in many cases, absolute allegiance and dismissal of anyone who does not align with its precepts. *"He who has ears to hear, let him hear"* (Matt. 11:15).

Since 2016, as the Lord provided revelation pertaining to the deception of Christians, I posted it on social media, most often on Facebook. There are many criticisms that can be offered for the dissemination of these truths through this media. Perhaps it is not the most effective mechanism, but it is the method I believe God instructed me to use – at least until the writing of this book. Often, the posts would be long and perhaps more appropriately referred to as a blog. It seemed that only a few people would bother to read it. At times, I wondered if and was even advised that it might be more palatable if they were recorded in a video. Certainly, I would reach more people this way. However, this method was not the instruction God gave me. At the time, I didn't understand why. It seemed that the more people that would see these warnings, the more they would likely heed them. But the Lord said, "No."

I continued to write my long posts and endured the jovial taunting of friends telling me they stopped after the first two or three paragraphs. To an extent, I was disheartened by this. The Lord reassured me that my charge was not to force the message but to make it available to those who would readily consume it. There were a faithful few who would be thirsty enough for revelation truth that they'd read it in its entirety. Still, others would vehemently disagree and post opposing arguments. My charge was not to persuade them but to provide scriptural support for the proclamations. Without fail, the rebuttals offered by those who rejected the warning would be centered around what we might consider common sense, cultural norms, or American perspectives and rights. I do not discount the influence of either of these, but the word of God is not constrained to respect the ordinance of man. Often, the Lord's instruction is contrary to man's ways. God's thoughts and ways are much higher than ours (Isa. 55:8-9). That which makes sense often doesn't make faith. In these dialogues, I've learned to discern between motives birthed from humanism and those birthed through faith.

> ### *The word of God is not constrained to respect the ordinance of man*

In this journey, I had become disturbed by the finding that trusted religious leaders would employ carnal justifications for their convictions. The Lord reminded me that even Peter, who walked with Jesus and witnessed things and accomplished feats that no other man has, was still susceptible. In Matthew 16, Peter has a great revelation of who Jesus is and professes that he is indeed the son of the Living God (vs. 16). Jesus commended this great revelation that was apparently uncommon and not shared amongst many others who have walked with him. Despite having this great revelation, Peter still processed the will of God through his human or carnal perspectives.

Jesus attempted to warn his disciples that he must go to Jerusalem and suffer many things from the elders, chief priests, and scribes. He warned the disciples that he would be killed, and on the third day, he would be raised. The Bible says, *"Peter took him [Jesus] aside and began to rebuke him, saying, 'Far be it from you, Lord. This shall never happen to you.' But he turned and said to Peter, 'Get behind me, Satan! You are a hindrance to me. For you are not setting your mind on the things of God, but on the things of man"* (Matt. 16:23). In this dialogue, Jesus reveals how vulnerable we are to processing things through our carnal perspectives, and in doing so, we hinder the plan of God.

As will be discussed in greater detail later, God has a purpose in allowing even the most unthinkable of atrocities. If we surmise, using our human or cultural perspectives, that He would want us to subvert or prevent the atrocity, we might easily hinder the plan as Peter would have done had he not been rebuked by Jesus. My social media posts represent such a rebuke of the presumed "noble" causes (at least by human standards) that seem to be motivated by honorable but carnal passions.

I'm sure you can readily see how those who remain stiff-necked and unmalleable might easily be offended and turned away from such a rebuke. And you would be correct. I have been unfriended by those who chose not to hear. Some chose not to read it in its entirety. And some quietly peruse the posts and comments to interrogate the truths and discern the lies. I am certain many have become more enlightened and resolute in their convictions to remain on guard against the deception that looms in the weeds. I pray that through the posts and this publication, some will read, repent of their transgressions (as I have), and resolve to guard against future susceptibilities.

A dear pastor friend of mine urged me to consider a method other than the public rebuke of evangelical Christians. He asked a question that pierced me. I am grateful that he felt obliged to challenge my process and cause me to inquire of God concerning my own motive and method. He asked, "How many souls have you won through your posts?" I earnestly considered his question and rendered the question to God. Have I missed the mark? Moreover, could my public rebuke of evangelicals be a deterrent to those who would otherwise enter the Kingdom?

Certainly, that is not my goal and, in fact, would be counter-productive to the goal. The Lord reaffirmed his mission and method to me. He reminded me that the 'lost,' those who have not yet come into the knowledge of Christ, are not blind to hypocrisy. In fact, they are very sensitive to it. When people see those who profess Christ behave and support things contrary to their profession, they readily identify it as hypocrisy. The loudest religious voices in the political and public spheres are those of Evangelicals, particularly White Evangelicals. The specific distinction of White Evangelicals is not racially motivated but rather a reference to a group of politically influential individuals with a unified goal and strategy. This will be explained later. Nonetheless, they have wrongly but effectively co-opted the "moral authority" title in this and other nations.

Many other Christ followers have not disparaged the cause or love of Christ in public. Still, they are not nearly as visible, vociferous, or influential as a political group as White Evangelicals. The perception of Christian faith has been tainted by the behaviors of a boisterous few. The reason these Christ followers have allowed the message to be apprehended by the evangelical movement may be multi-fold and may even be a part of God's ultimate plan. **But, there needs to be a faithful remnant that proclaims, "Repent for the Kingdom of God is at hand!"**

***Our goal is to make disciples,
not to recruit believers***

My pastor friend has such a heart for lost souls that I appreciate his concern for their well-being and his passion for evangelism. I realized, from our encounter, that the commandment of Jesus was for us to *"Go therefore and make disciples of all nations, baptizing them in the name of the Father and of the Son and of the Holy Spirit, teaching them to observe all that I have commanded you"* (Matt. 28:18-20). Our goal is to make disciples, not to recruit believers. Even as part of Jesus' personal ministry, there were many who believed and were named disciples but also turned back (John 6:66). Our charge is to build the

Body of Christ, full of Believers who have determined that no matter what, they will not turn away from the truth and liberty they gained through the knowledge and acceptance of Jesus Christ. That's discipleship!

Paul instructs that God "... *gave the apostles, the prophets, the evangelists, the shepherds and teachers, to equip the saints for the work of ministry, for building up the body of Christ, until we all attain to the unity of the faith and of the knowledge of the Son of God, to mature manhood, to the measure of the stature of the fullness of Christ*" (Eph. 4:11-13). This is often referred to as the five-fold ministry. There are people whom God ordained and equipped to be effective evangelists (not evangelicals). These people, like my dear pastor friend, are passionate about evangelizing the lost. They are very much needed for the edification of the Body of Christ. Similarly, the prophets, teachers, apostles, and shepherds/pastors are vital. When each member works according to his calling, the Body of Christ can be effectively edified.

I will no longer be guilted by persons bound by religious tradition who would assert that if I'm not evangelizing, I am spinning wheels and am of little value to the Body of Christ. I believe I am called to boldly speak and prophesy to those who would profane the crucifixion of Christ by relegating carnal endeavors to a righteous status. Through dreams and revelations, God provides me with insights and mandates that I share them despite the threat of castigation.

CHAPTER 1

JUDGEMENT BEFALLS AMERICA

The Prophetic Warning

Among the most impactful of all the dreams the Lord has revealed to me is one that occurred in 2005. Following is the contemporaneous publishing of that prophetic warning:

Blessed is the nation whose God is the Lord... But woe unto America for your atrocities perpetrated against God. The Lord is, in this very hour, commanding us to repent and to return unto righteousness. For the Lord says to this land, "Soon, I will visit you with my judgment. I shall release my angel of judgment upon you. And he shall come swiftly and with great fierceness." "There shall be no escaping my hand of judgment," declares the Lord. "I have sent my prophets to be a rebuke unto you, and you have resisted them. I have released the winds of my fury, and you have still not turned unto me. You trust in the wealth and the wisdom of flesh and not in me, the God who has given you the ability to attain wealth. Once more, I send my prophets unto you, and you'll not heed their rebuke. Swiftly and fiercely will I, therefore, visit thee with the angel of my judgment? None shall resist him. Your systems shall fail to alert you of my arrival, for I will come swiftly and without warning. I shall visit thee with the judgment with which I visited Pharaoh, whose neck too was stiffened to my rebuke. I shall visit each household, and none shall be spared of my judgment, save those who have made the Lord their God. There shall be a great weeping and wailing unlike any that has been heard in all the earth. I will loosen your defenses, and my judgment shall not be stayed. No one shall be able to close the door upon my judgment," declares the Lord.

Repent, oh America! REPENT! For the Lord shall strip you of your wealth and in poverty and desperation of heart shall you cry out unto him; and your cries shall be unheard. Seek the Lord while he may yet be found. For in the day of His judgment, the Lord's ears will be closed to your pleas. The Lord has declared that once his angel of judgment is released, there shall be no resisting or turning him back; it will come swiftly and without warning. There will be massive loss of life, unparalleled by any natural disaster seen in generations. Our financial systems shall crumble and America will experience economic depression, which has not been seen since the days of the Great Depression. For the anger of the Lord is kindled upon America.

The Lord has declared that we have squandered wealth unto ourselves and have become fat with the pleasures of the flesh. We have forsaken the poor and are yet driven by the love of money (the root of ALL evil). People, please hear the word of the Lord and repent.

In this prophetic warning, the Lord likened his impending judgment to a Second Passover. Sadly, there were few who were spared because they failed to hear the rebuke of the Lord through the voice of his prophets, and many others procrastinated. In the hour of their judgment, they cried for mercy, and their cries were unheard. They foolishly rebuked "in the name of Jesus," the angel of the Lord who executed their torment. Their rebuke was clearly to no avail because God himself instructed it. Psalms 33:10 reminds us that the Lord would make the devices of the people of no effect. And the angel of the Lord's judgment would visit us without warning, save the prophetic words the Lord spoke beforehand.

There is no doubt that the United States of America has been and still is, by various measures, the greatest nation in the world. But are we losing the status of our greatness at the hands of our own pursuits? We are a nation that purports the ideals of freedom of (and from) religion as well as liberty and justice for all. The pursuit of happiness and the 'American dream' has guided our personal agendas and endeavors, often with great monetary rewards. However, in the process of our pursuit of an otherwise laudable goal, I am afraid we might have lost our soul – individually and as a nation. The Bible asks the question, *"For what shall it profit a man if he shall gain the whole world, and lose his own soul?"* (Mark 8:36).

The slogan, "America First," while catchy and contagious in its motive, may actually herald the decline of America. Jesus, in the 8th chapter of the gospel of Mark, advises us that if we are to follow him, we must deny ourselves. He further elaborates that whoever tries to save his life shall lose it, but whoever shall lose his life for Christ's sake and for the sake of the gospel shall save his life. This dichotomy intrigues me and is somehow lost in the pursuit of some to "Make America Great Again."

Selfishness is not measured by the paucity of your giving but by the smallness of your heart

---

We have become a nation of selfish people. I realize that we are still the most generous nation in the world in terms of charitable giving and humanitarian support, but selfishness is not measured by the paucity of your giving but by the smallness of your heart. Often, the motive for our giving is hidden in the benefit we can personally derive from the giving. We give for the benefit of tax write-offs and deductions. This is particularly important for the biggest givers in America. They employ the crafty intellect of accountants who advise them just how much to give to optimize (or minimize) their tax debt. Even as a nation, we give humanitarian support to countries around the world, not from the heart of benevolence, but rather in an effort to maintain national security and to secure the US dollar's position as the 'world's currency.' These are the wrong motives for giving.

Sadly, the motive of tax debt optimization also motivates the church which is supposed to be the most charitable organization of all. One of the reasons why many churches supported the candidacy and presidency of Donald Trump is because of his promise to restore 'religious liberty.' What that really means is that church leaders and pastors would like to have the ability to freely speak on or endorse political matters and candidates without compromising the all-important non-profit 501(c)(3) status that allows them to avoid paying taxes. From a fiscally responsible standpoint, I can understand it. But are the savings of taxes worthy of the cost of losing the soul of America? When churches and leaders compromise their values and their Christian witness in pursuit of financial or political benefit, the soul of America will soon be lost. Those who were supposed to be the salt of the earth have lost their savor. The Bible says we are then *"good for nothing, but to be cast out, and to be trodden under foot of men"* (Matt. 5:13). To maintain our value to the Kingdom of God, our focus must remain steadfast on edifying the Body of Christ, in every measure of human endeavor.

Feed The Sheep

After his resurrection, Jesus found Peter again fishing on a boat. Recall that this is what Peter was doing when he first encountered Jesus (Luke 5:4). Similar to the first encounter, Jesus told Peter to cast his nets out into the deep, and the nets again filled with fish (John 21:6). John, who was with Peter, recognized that it was Jesus and informed Peter who it was that instructed them to cast out. Peter, being the zealot he was, dove into the water and swam to meet Jesus. The scripture continues, *"Jesus said to them, 'Bring some of the fish that you have just caught.' So Simon Peter went aboard and hauled the net ashore, full of large fish, 153 of them. And although there were so many, the net was not torn. Jesus said to them, "Come and have breakfast"* (vs. 10-12). A very important dialogue occurs during the meal. However, before we discuss the details of their conversation a few key things are worth noting at this point.

Peter was one of Jesus' most passionate disciples. He also was one of the three that were closest to Jesus. Peter had witnessed innumerable miracles, signs, and wonders that Jesus performed during his time on earth. He sat under the tutelage of Jesus and learned of the plan of God. Of all the disciples, Peter was the one who had sufficient faith to step out of a boat during a storm and, at least for a moment, walk on water as he saw Jesus doing. This same Peter witnessed divine Jesus' transfiguration and communion with Moses and Elijah on the mountain (Matt. 17:2-4). If Peter was so close to Jesus and had such great faith, why then had he returned to doing the thing he did before he met Jesus? Why was he not still out instructing and edifying the church Jesus came to establish?

I submit that Peter was moved more by passion than by faith. Faith never fails! Both faith and passion have the ability to cause us to disregard logic and dive out into the deep. Passion, however, is a carnal force. Faith is spiritual. In passion, Peter attempted to assure Jesus that he would not allow him to be persecuted. Many people would consider this noble gesture by Peter to be honorable, knowing the potential threat it posed to his own life. They might assess that it was a faithful offer, but Jesus rebuked him, saying, *"Get behind me, Satan! You are a hindrance to me. For you are not setting your mind on the things of God, but on the things of man"* (Matt. 16:23).

Faith never contradicts the will of God. If a radical or seemingly courageous effort seems to be fueled by faith, examine it more closely to determine if it is more consistent with the things of God or the things of man. It cannot be both because the will of man or the flesh always opposes the mind of God and cannot be subject to the will of God (Rom. 8:7).

Knowing Peter's propensity to be moved by passion more than faith, Jesus warned Peter before he was crucified, saying, *"Simon, Simon, behold, Satan hath desired to have you, that he may sift you as wheat: But I have prayed for thee, that thy faith fail not: and when thou art converted, strengthen thy brethren"* (Luke 22:31-32, KJV). After that admonishment, Peter exclaimed that he would be with Jesus until the end. Jesus knew that passion was insufficient to sustain Peter, but Peter didn't. Jesus told Peter that before the break of dawn the very next morning, he would deny Jesus three times (vs. 34). This was inconceivable for Peter because he mistook passion for faith. Indeed, as Jesus predicted, Peter denied Jesus.

I can only imagine the agony of having realized that Peter had just done the very thing he vowed so emphatically that he would never do. This type of failure could reasonably cause one to disqualify himself from benefiting the one whom he had betrayed. Perhaps this is why Peter found himself back on the boat, doing what he did before his first encounter with Jesus.

Now, as Jesus, Peter, and the other disciples enjoyed a meal at the beach after this great catch Jesus inspired, Jesus questioned Peter's love for him. The Bible says, *"When they had finished breakfast, Jesus said to Simon Peter, 'Simon, son of John, do you love me more than these?' He said to him, 'Yes, Lord; you know that I love you.' He said to him, 'Feed my lambs'"* (vs. 15). It is unclear what "these" meant in this passage of scripture. We often conclude that it is a reference to the other disciples that are around. While this might be true, it seems irrational to me that Jesus would instigate competition amongst his disciples, who might squabble over who loves him the most. I am the first to admit that just because it doesn't comport with my sensibilities doesn't mean that it wasn't Jesus' intention. I will posit an alternate interpretation; the "these" that Jesus mentioned references the great catch he just had.

Recall, in their first interaction Peter's nets were filled with fish such that the nets broke and the boats began to sink. Having had this awe-inspiring encounter, Peter and others forsook all they had and committed to following Jesus (Luke 5:11). I believe Jesus was asking Peter this time, do you still have that same awe? Do you love me more than prosperity and the potential to attain wealth? If you do, forsake this again in favor of feeding my sheep. Jesus proceeded to ask Peter again, *"Do you love me?" Peter answered, "Yes." Again, Jesus said, "Feed my sheep." A third time, Jesus asked Peter if he loved him. By the third time, "Peter was hurt because Jesus had now asked him three times, 'Do you love me?' He said, 'Lord, you know all things; you know that I love you.' Jesus said, 'Feed my sheep'"* (John 21:17).

I imagine Peter grew frustrated by the third time Jesus questioned the sincerity of his love. It would seem reasonable that Peter began to wonder if his three-time denial of Jesus had something to do with Jesus' apparent distrust of his resoluteness. I don't believe Jesus doubted but instead wanted Peter to move beyond the failure of his past and commit to feeding the sheep. After all, before the denial and crucifixion, Jesus told Peter that he was praying that when he was "converted," he would go and strengthen his brothers (Luke 22:32) – that he would feed the sheep.

Jesus knew from the beginning that Peter's passion was insufficient to keep him and that, indeed, it would cause him to fail, resorting to things that seem right to the carnal mind. Jesus prayed that Peter would be converted, restored, and fully committed to faith. After that, he would then commit to disciplining the body of believers Jesus knew would desperately need sound teaching. Today, the same body of believers desperately needs earnest and faith-filled discipleship. Instead, much of what we get is passionate encouragements and endeavors from leaders who, like Peter, engage the sensibilities of man instead of adopting the mind of Christ.

It seems that certain pastors have forgotten the purpose of their calling – to feed the sheep. They presume that it is their responsibility to protect the sheep. Jesus never instructed Peter to protect the sheep. He said to feed them. The Good Shepherd will protect them. It seems logical that a shepherd would do what is necessary to defend the sheep, even putting himself in harm's way to protect them. But as logical as it seems, it was not the instruction Jesus or the Bible gave us. Ephesians 4 describes the purpose of what we would consider the five-fold ministry:

> *"And he gave some, apostles; and some, prophets; and some, evangelists; and some, pastors and teachers; For the perfecting of the saints, for the work of the ministry, for the edifying of the body of Christ: Till we all*

come in the unity of the faith, and of the knowledge of the Son of God, unto a perfect man, unto the measure of the stature of the fullness of Christ: That we henceforth be no more children, tossed to and fro, and carried about with every wind of doctrine, by the sleight of men, and cunning craftiness, whereby they lie in wait to deceive; But speaking the truth in love, may grow up into him in all things, which is the head, even Christ" (Eph. 4:11-15).

This passage does not mandate or authorize any member of the five-fold ministry to depart from the original charge of perfecting the saints for the ministry's work and helping us all come to the unity of faith and knowledge. Because these posts have been left vacant in pursuit of causes that mankind would deem laudable, young followers of Jesus have been left vulnerable to the cunning craftiness of deceit.

The Sermon Evangelical Pastors Forgot

I imagine there isn't a single pastor in America who hasn't at some point preached a sermon titled "As the Head Goes, So Goes the Body" or some version thereof. For generations, it has been long accepted in the church that Jesus is the head of the Christian church, and pastors are the "under-shepherds," so to speak. Leaders are crucial for setting the vision for the church and rallying disciples around that vision to accomplish the mission. Leadership courses and books have emphasized the importance of installing leaders of high integrity, character, and aptitude. "If the head is strong, the body will be strong" is the mantra that has been lauded. Another popular chant is "The anointing flows from the head to the body." In recent years, these seem to have been relegated only to religious ideology and not reality.

The climate in America is becoming increasingly hostile and intolerant. Political correctness, a term once used to describe tolerant decency in how we addressed each other in society, has now been villainized to be an ideal whose demise is venerated. The Trump presidential campaigns were marked by offensive rhetoric and gestures that seemed to rile the crowds into a bellicose disdain for civility. From the podium, Trump would mock the disabled, insult war heroes, and demean legislators for their nationality. There has been no shortage of discussion about how his rhetoric and lack of condemnation of racist speech has emboldened the resurgence of unabashed bigotry in America.

There remains a remnant of Americans that make at least a modest effort to resist base temptations to devolve into incivility. However, that remnant is ironically not the one that might be presumed. It would be a logical expectation that such behaviors would be repudiated by those who profess to be ambassadors of Jesus Christ on earth. Instead, these very leaders find themselves disregarding or defending if not actively participating in, these actions. Some ardently argue that President Trump cannot and should not be held accountable for his behaviors as long as he provides benefits of legislation and appointment of conservative judges and justices. They assert, "We didn't elect him to be our Pastor; we elected him to be the Commander in Chief."

I'm reminded of the teachings I've heard in every church I've attended – where the head leads, the body follows. I firmly agree that each individual is responsible for his/her words, thoughts, and actions. But I equally believe that when a person has been entrusted with great authority, influence follows. Influence induces the modeling of behavior, even in the absence of explicit instruction. As the head goes, so goes the body.

Undoubtedly, the President of the United States of America is able to influence national dialogue and sentiment. While his election might reflect the sentiment of those who elected him, his behavior and policies certainly guide the future of the country – not just economically, militarily, or judicially, but also morally. With each passing day, it becomes more evident that an unintimidated goal of the Trump presidential administration was/is the insidious waning of unity. The targets of disunity are various and foundationally include political party affiliation. I long for the resurgence of respect for every person, even if their political ideology is different from ours. Today, political opponents are villainized and marked as persons whose seats need to be irrevocably removed from the table. Both parties do it. The Republican party just seems to be more voracious in its execution. Moreover, it seems to be tolerant (or even rewarding) of those who employ divisive tactics. When the leader of a political party demonizes his opponent and constantly invokes vitriolic references and attitudes toward his opponents, we need to take heed of the downstream consequences. Other legislators, candidates, and supporters begin to do the same.

Disunity is insidiously invasive and extends its reach beyond its initial target. It begins to influence any number of issues, many of which may be completely unrelated to the initial one. At a time when there desperately needs to be a unifying voice, expectedly coming from our spiritual and elected leaders, there is only more divisive rhetoric. As a country, it seems that we seek more things on which we can be vehemently antagonistic and incorrigible instead of the things on which we can agree.

We retreat with unyielding fealty to our respective silos on matters concerning race, ethnicity, justice, vaccines, immigration, and even support for longstanding ally countries. These silos become echo chambers for the rhetoric that simply fuels our animus toward our enemies. There is no opportunity or desire for the discovery of common ground. We know, from the teaching of Jesus, that *"Every kingdom divided against itself is brought to desolation, and every city or house divided against itself will not stand"* (Matt. 12:25). America cannot sustain a prolonged continuation of these behaviors.

If there is any group of people that should know this teaching and swiftly encourage corrective action at the discovery of such destructive behavior, it should be the religious leaders of our society. However, the priorities of these so-called leaders have been distracted. Unity is no longer a desirable goal. Instead, the goal is to satisfy the demand of their political aspiration. As long as the economy is improving and conservative judges are appointed to the bench, White Evangelicals remain quietly permissive of the division.

Fully knowing his moral ineptitude, these Evangelicals elected Donald Trump to push forward their political agenda. In the process, they forgot the sermon they preached often from their pulpits about the importance of the head being just and upright. While no man (or woman) is perfect, and each candidate and past president has had moral failures, the mitigating trait is an awareness of the need to seek forgiveness from God and a willingness to do it. Blinded by their desperation to pass conservative legislation, White Evangelicals convinced themselves that somehow the self-aggrandizing Trump "found Jesus" and is now living a repentant life.

I don't fault those who believed that Trump might actually change if he surrounded himself with religious counsel, and he did just that. Unfortunately, those advisers appear to be just as confused about the mandates of God as Donald Trump is. Their presence and role in the administration appear to have been perfunctory. If not perfunctory, the influence that his spiritual advisors had on his behavior and speech was impotent. If there were any influence, it certainly isn't attested to by his displaying the fruits of the Spirit – love, joy, peace, forbearance, kindness, goodness, faithfulness, gentleness, and self-control (Gal. 5:22-23). Rather, Trump seems to have been emboldened because he has commandeered the strings of the marionette called Evangelicalism. He has gotten so bold as to seemingly profess, "I'm not Christian," during a 2024 campaign rally at The Believer's Summit – a gathering of conservative Christians who support his third candidacy for president.

Power has influence, and influence informs behavior

Now is the time for our evangelical brothers and sisters to repent, for the Kingdom of God is at hand. It is time that Evangelicals remember the importance of the head and recognize the dangers of delegating authority to one who so blatantly demonstrates a paucity of integrity that is required to faithfully wield power. Remember that power has influence, and influence informs behavior. Our Evangelical friends continue to underestimate the influence of the presidency, not just to shape policy but to shape attitudes. The Commander-in-Chief has the ability to call to arms, not just the military but also a host of people who trust and believe the words he speaks, even when they are patently false. There is an inherent danger when this power is left unchecked.

The crucifixion of Jesus provides an excellent example of the unchecked influence of leaders. When Jesus was brought before Pilate to be crucified, the accusations against him were made by the Chief Priests and other religious leaders. It appeared that the sinners had no quarrels with Jesus. In fact, the Bible says that neither Pilate nor Herod could find fault with him (Luke 23:14-15). Pilate, not wanting to crucify Jesus, brought him before the people.

"Now at the feast [of the Passover] the governor was in the habit of setting free any one prisoner whom the people chose. And at that time they were holding a notorious prisoner [guilty of insurrection and murder], called Barabbas. So when they had assembled [for this purpose], Pilate said to them, 'Whom do you want me to set free for you? Barabbas, or Jesus who is called Christ?' For Pilate knew that it was because of jealousy that the chief priests and elders had handed Jesus over to him. While he was seated on the judgment seat, his wife sent him a message, saying, 'Have nothing to do with that righteous and innocent Man; for last night I suffered greatly in a dream because of Him.' But the chief priests and the elders persuaded the crowds to ask for Barabbas and to put Jesus to death. The governor said to them, 'Which of the two do you wish me to set free for you?' And they said, 'Barabbas.' Pilate said to them, 'Then what shall I do with Jesus who is called Christ?' They all replied, 'Let Him be crucified!'" (Matt. 27:15-22).

The scripture says that the chief priests and elders handed Jesus over to Pilate because they were jealous. They knew the custom of the governor at the Feast of the Passover was to let one prisoner go. The governor offered Barabbas as a potential alternative to Jesus. Barabbas was guilty of sedition. He was a convicted insurrectionist and murderer. Surely, Pilate thought the people would not choose such a person over Jesus, in whom he personally could find no guilt. To his surprise, *"priests and the elders persuaded the crowds to ask for Barabbas and to put Jesus to death"* (vs. 20). The crowds, following the persuasion of their leaders, demanded that the insurrectionist and murderer be set free and the innocent one be crucified.

When leaders have significant influence over their followers, it can easily be exploited for unholy causes. This underscores the necessity that those who are endowed with great power also have great character. Otherwise, they might persuade their loyal followers to demand that insurrectionists be set free. Let's pause there for a moment, consider our own political landscape, and recognize the similarities.

At the time Jesus stood before Pilate, religious leaders were stirring the crowds to plead for the release of a murderous insurrectionist. Today, we have a former president of the United States and his followers, including religious leaders, advocating for the release of those convicted of insurrection. Donald Trump has made clear to his supporters what he expects from them if the election (or anything) doesn't go his way. He expects them to revolt! And, they have already. Despite the consequences the previous zealots suffered, he still has a cadre of loyalists who are standing back and standing by, waiting for his command to violently engage, should he deem it necessary. And Evangelical leaders placate the rhetoric, naively supposing that no harm would result. They convince themselves that no one takes Donald Trump literally. They've said, "Don't take him literally; take him seriously." When a self-serving leader who has been granted much power tells you of his intention, even if jokingly, by all means, take him seriously and literally

I agree that any leader, and especially a self-serving leader, to whom much power is given should be taken seriously. They should also be taken at their word. I believe Donald Trump should be taken both seriously and literally. Sadly, I think the unspoken part is that many Evangelicals want this type of action. They will not articulate that they want an authoritarian leader, but their actions speak for them. As long as a dictator executes the policies that they seek, Democracy is of little concern to them.

The problem with Democracy, in their minds, is that people who they consider sinful can have a say in the writing of laws. If Evangelicals could restrict the legislative influence of sinners, then all would be well in their world. Sinners should have no voice in making policies that center around moral issues, their actions suggest. The remedy, in their view, is to support even an amoral dictator as long as his promises are satisfactory. The problem with relinquishing power is that once it has been released, it is difficult and sometimes impossible to reclaim. This underscores the importance of choosing leaders with high moral character and whose actions are not intentionally incendiary.

I admonish my Evangelical friends, particularly the pastors who might still have influence over their parishioners, to preach to themselves that ever-faithful sermon that Character Matters. Prayerfully, that they might venerate integrity and morality as mandatory prerequisites before bestowing leadership authorities. *To whom much is given, much should be required* (Luke 12:48). The question then is, what do you require of a President? What do you require from a person who arguably has more power than any other single person on earth? Contemplate the potential consequence of unconstrained self-exultation and determine whether the promise of policy is worthy of its cost.

For Misplaced Affections

Throughout the Bible, there are many examples of how the people of God, whose intentions might have started honorably, became misguided over time. The people would often wander off into idol worship and self-gratification. It is not a new problem. It seems that it is an innate trait for mankind to seek his own will. Motivated by his eternal love for errant man, God would faithfully appoint a prophet or teacher to warn the people of their errors and plea for repentance. We find ourselves, as a nation and as a species, in that situation again. Religious leaders who enjoy celebrity and its attendant financial benefits have, like their parishioners, seemed to wander from the instruction of God. Unless the course is corrected, we too might face the wrath of God for having turned away from Him unto other strange gods.

The love of money is and always has been the root of all evil. The unfortunate but often disguised truth is that in our capitalistic society, success is measured in dollars. If the economy is doing well, we believe "America is on the right track." We must not be beguiled by the end result and overlook the process. The process is as important, if not more important, than the product.

The process is as important, if not more important, than the product

---

We all ascend to greatness on the shoulders of our predecessors. Shoulders are substantially strong to support the weight of our ascent without harming the one upon whose shoulders we stand. Hopefully, when we have attained whatever measure of greatness we sought, we gratefully acknowledge the persons on whose shoulders we stood. However, when our ascent is on the necks of our predecessors or contemporaries, we cripple those we leave behind in our pursuits. I'm afraid the latter has become the *modus operandi* of our recent efforts. We give the appearance of charitability, but a charitable heart is far from our fabric.

One of my favorite scriptures is Isaiah 58. In its first few verses, it describes the "acts" of sacrifice that are made as a show to hopefully make our voices heard by God. Knowing the heart and motive behind these outward displays of charity, God demands more:

> *"Is not this the fast that I have chosen? To loose the bands of wickedness, to undo the heavy burdens, and to let the oppressed go free, and that ye break every yoke? Is it not to deal thy bread to the hungry, and that thou bring the poor that are cast out to thy house? When thou seest the naked, that thou cover him; and that thou hide not thyself from thine own flesh? Then shall thy light break forth as the morning, and thine health shall spring forth speedily: and thy righteousness shall go before thee; the glory of the Lord shall be thy reward"* (Isa 58:6-8 KJV).

How much of this is our genuine pursuit? I fear that our motives poorly fulfill the mandate stated in this passage. The final prerequisite mentioned in this passage is that we hide not ourselves from ourselves but that we honestly assess our motives. When we do, we recognize that the impetus for our charity is nowhere near as magnanimous as we'd like to present it. God, who judges the heart, clearly knows the motive behind our endeavors, even when we shield it from ourselves.

Yes, our economy has done well. For longer than expected, we have been on a trajectory of strong economic growth. When consumer confidence and spending are up, the Church must remain resolute to not sell its soul for the promise of prosperity! It is in great jeopardy of doing so when many remain silently (or even vocally) supportive of the clearly divisive and unethical acts of a president or political leaders simply because they presume that candidate to be the one whose policies provide financial benefits for them. As a person who invests in commercial real estate, I have personally benefited from the tax breaks provided by some tax law changes. However, my allegiance cannot be purchased for any amount.

We cannot be ambassadors of God if our tactics insult him

We have been charged as a body of believers with the responsibility of regarding and caring for the poor, instead of using our political influence to exploit them and ensure that they will never rise from their state of poverty. Proverbs 14:31 says, *"Whoever oppresses a poor man insults his Maker, but he who is generous to the needy honors him."* We cannot be ambassadors of God if our tactics insult him. I hear the cervical spines of many Americans cracking with the certain end result of a division into two sects – the wealthy and the paraplegics whose necks were crushed by the weight of the wealthy's economic pursuits.

There is a natural inclination for man to be self-centered. In contrast, it requires intentional effort to ensure that we remain altruistic. In the absence of such effort, we default to self-gratification. When endorsed or advocated by respected outside influences, we will most certainly pursue a course of selfishness over altruism. Throughout recent years, Americans have done just that. Savvy politicians have capitalized on and benefited from the growing populist sentiment brewing in the country.

During his 2015 presidential campaign, Donald Trump promoted a policy platform that he called "America First." This isolationist and American nationalist campaign generally disregards global affairs in favor of focusing solely on domestic policy and promotion. There are numerous vulnerabilities in forsaking the sanctity of our relationships with international allies. However, this self-centered sentiment has remained popular, not so much because of its soundness for foreign relations policy, but rather because it resonated with a growing propensity for self-centeredness in American culture. Even when seemingly charitable acts are promoted, they are often motivated by the ability to derive a reciprocal benefit.

Luke 14:13-14 instructs us on how to execute genuine altruism. It reads, *"But when you give a banquet, invite the poor, the crippled, the lame, the blind, and you will be blessed. Although they cannot repay you, you will be repaid at the resurrection of the righteous."* Sadly, but predictably, the affluent in our society seem to be favored, even by those who profess to be followers of Jesus. Although we might be reluctant to admit it, it usually is because the prospect of reciprocation is a motivating force. A preoccupation with wealth and power for selfish gain causes many to ignore the employment of obviously corrupt and unscrupulous tactics. It seems that wealth immunizes an individual from societally imposed accountability. Not so with God! The Bible tells us to avoid such favorable protections for the wicked.

Psalm 82:2-4 reads, *"How long will you defend the unjust and show partiality to the wicked? Defend the weak and the fatherless; uphold the cause of the poor and the oppressed. Rescue the weak and the needy; deliver them from the hand of the wicked."* This mandate seems to have been readily forsaken. I have sadly watched an American president encourage law officers to 'rough up' their detainees. While some argued, "he didn't mean it literally; he was just joking," we must remember that our words have power and influence, especially when they come from the leader of the free world. The one who speaks these vulgarities knows the influence of his words and wields it craftily, expecting that his loyal supporters will again come to his defense. How long will you defend the unjust?

Police relations with communities of color have been strained since the inception of public policing. In recent years, the police have been heavily scrutinized for the mistreatment and disparate killing of African American men. It is extremely irresponsible for the president of the United States of America to even jokingly advocate for anything other than the fair and humane treatment of all detainees, even if they are criminals. Yet, those who have positioned themselves as the representatives of God on earth remain apologetically silent about this incorrigible behavior. Worse yet, many attempt to defend this unjust rhetoric.

The placation of offenses against the poor and underrepresented stands in contradiction to the command of Isaiah 58 and numerous other scriptures that discourage the mistreatment of the disenfranchised. God, through his prophet, warned Israel that because they had mistreated the poor, *"An enemy will overrun your land, pull down your strongholds and plunder your fortresses"* (Amos 3:11). It appears he has offered the same warning to America, as previously detailed.

On February 7, 2013, the Lord gave me another dream that specifically warned of our treatment of those whom society might deem dispensable. The contemporaneous recording of that dream follows.

> *My wife and I were with a group of people in a house. These were fairly shallow people, and I'm not sure what our connection to them was. Nonetheless, our association with them involved us in what follows. A stranger came to the group and essentially held the group hostage in this large home until his mob-type boss arrived with a whole gang of heavily armed men. We were certain that we would be killed but remained uncertain of the reason we were being held hostage or how to convince the man to spare our lives.*

After about a day or two of anticipating our inevitable demise, one by one, he had us each come from upstairs and pass a "simple" test to recite the chorus of a silly song. The lyrics were: "Simple, simple life is simple" or something similar to that. Most of us, extraordinarily nervous, could not remember this simple melody. When that happened, he sent us off for what we knew would be our last meal.

Several people who interfered, sometimes unknowingly and innocently, were instantly slaughtered because of this "evil" man's desire to seemingly torture us for reasons none of us could figure out. One thing was evident from this - our lives would soon end. Our final task was to place, in an envelope, items that were symbolic of those things that were most important to us. We could only put a picture of 1 or 2 people. Some people put keys to their homes, businesses, and cars. We also had to put a signed blank check in the envelope.

We gathered in a room that seemed to be our death chamber. Right before he prepared to execute us, he told us to open our envelopes and view them one final time. Everyone in the room was morbidly sobbing for fear, not just of losing our lives but being separated from the things that mattered most to us. While some in the room contained relatively shallow items of significance in their envelopes, they were still their most prized possessions. We mourned our pending separation from these things.

Then, to our surprise, the boss gave us an opportunity to spare our lives. The only way to preserve our own lives was to take the envelope that contained everything that was most important to us and give it to someone else who was unrelated to us without the expectation of gaining back anything else but our lives. Clearly, everyone in the room gladly took this opportunity.

We later learned the reason we were held captive in the first place. This group of prosperous but self-absorbed people apparently snubbed another young lady who wanted to join the group. Simply because she wasn't trendy, stylish, or popular, she was snubbed, ridiculed, and excluded. The young lady was, for some reason, devastated by this. Much to our shameful surprise, we learned that the mob boss was her relative who sought to avenge the offense perpetrated against this woman.

Of course, God is not a mob boss. However, he does allow unholy rulers to overtake and sometimes enslave or kill his people who have disobeyed his commandments. Such examples are plentiful in the scriptures. We now exist under a dispensation of grace, but Paul asks the poignant question, *"What shall we say then? Are we to continue in sin that grace may abound? By no means! How can we who died to sin still live in it?"* (Rom. 6:1-2). My question to our Evangelical brothers and sisters is, "Have you really died to sin?" The preeminent focus on the law frankly suggests that you haven't.

The Constitution of the United States requires the fair and equal treatment of all citizens. We understand that since its writing, America has never lived up to this ideal. In fact, in its original form, African American people were not considered persons but chattel. Throughout the centuries, we have indeed evolved, and with the passage of several amendments to the Constitution, we are attempting to treat all persons equally as citizens. We still have a long way to go.

The Fourteenth Amendment of the Constitution, though honorable, now places those Christians who embrace the ideal in a precarious position. This Amendment provided rights to people groups that promote behaviors that, according to our faith, would be considered sinful. In 2015, the Supreme Court of the United States ruled that the Equal Protection Clause of the 14th Amendment prevents states from excluding same-sex couples from civil marriage and that they should be recognized on the same terms and conditions as opposite-sex marriages. The Court noted that evolving societal norms inform the liberty rights of same-sex couples and reveal what it perceived to be an unjustified inequality with respect to traditional concepts of the institution of marriage.

This occurred under the administration of President Barack Obama, and many Evangelicals were infuriated. In one fell swoop, the Supreme Court overturned the proud legislative accomplishment that Evangelicals made wielding their political might. Less than 20 years prior, they were able to pass the Defense of Marriage Act (DOMA). DOMA declared that no state would be required to recognize a same-gender marriage performed in another state. It further defined marriage as only between a man and a woman for purposes of Federal law. Under the Obama administration, the 'liberal' Supreme Court overturned DOMA. This, in part, fueled the insatiable thirst of Evangelicals to win the 2016 presidential election and other legislative victories at any cost. In comes Donald J. Trump – the bulldog in the china shop who would be a warrior for their cause. As such, an unholy alliance was formed.

It is important to realize that fair and equal treatment can be afforded to all without the righteous condoning that which the Bible calls sin. A failure to acknowledge this forces some to continue to buck the system, fighting for more legislation. Such efforts can only be perceived by those who would be adversely impacted by successes as attempts to oppress or deny rights afforded them under the Constitution. It is then viewed as an act of hatred.

We must be cautious as Christians to not be perceived as haters of those who simply seek to exercise the same civil rights as we do. How, then, could we claim to love when all that is perceived is hate? We must be equally cautious, in our quest to provide equal rights and liberty to all, to not compromise our personal values and religious convictions. We should maintain the perspective that faith is a personal issue and conviction is formed in the heart. No law can be formed to mollify your heart's conviction. Only compromise can.

> ***When we are perceived as propagators of hate,
> our witness is irreparably compromised***

No law can instill conviction in one's heart. Consequently, attempts to resist what is the eventual will of the people under our laws and, as a matter of personal choice, serve only to undermine our witness of the Gospel. When we are perceived as propagators of hate, our witness is irreparably compromised. Though we might have personal objections to the ways of the world, we must remember that we are in the world but not of the world. Consequently, we should not conform to the world and its ideas, nor should we attempt to force into effect our or God's will by using the tactics of the world. We must always remain subjugated to the will and instruction of God. The Apostle Paul said it this way:

"I have been crucified with Christ. It is no longer I who live, but Christ who lives in me. And the life I now live in the flesh I live by faith in the Son of God, who loved me and gave himself for me. I do not nullify the grace of God, for if righteousness were through the law, then Christ died for no purpose" (Gal. 2:20-21).

As born-again believers, our lives are no longer our own. We do not pursue objectives because they comport with our sensibilities or suit our passions. We submit to the authority of God, including his mechanisms for doing things. In his profession, Paul acknowledges that a righteous pursuit of law nullifies the grace of God and suggests that Christ died for no purpose. Surely, we would never forthrightly articulate a nullification of God's grace. However, we do it every time we suppose that the passage of a law is a righteous cause.

Hear me, as I've said previously and will likely state many more times, we are permitted and encouraged under the laws of this land to exercise our civic duty and vote. But we must never misconstrue our political advocacy as a righteous endeavor. It is a carnal endeavor to its core because it was instituted and is implemented by mankind. If the laws that we endorse pass, praise the Lord. If they do not pass, we should not, in protest or defiance, find ways to subvert the justice and processes of this land to accomplish our preferences. We must not allow what is, on its surface, deemed to be a laudable pursuit to be polluted by a misguided tactic. Instead, we remain persuaded that the weapons of our warfare remain spiritual and full of might, regardless of how circumstances might appear to the natural eye.

For Love of Self

Our failure to prioritize God and his precepts has placed us on the path of God's inevitable judgment, as expressed in the prophetic warning shared in a preceding chapter. In light of recent events, I am stricken by the likening of the judgment to a Second Passover. Without overinterpreting this warning, I examine the potential of a pandemic (not necessarily COVID-19) to implement the stated judgment.

I wonder if our response to COVID-19 might have been a test or a forewarning. COVID-19 has had many profound impacts on our society and social interactions. Among the most significant is the impact on large public gatherings in enclosed spaces. Nothing drew more ire than the effect of the pandemic on church closures. While some churches readily prepared to help protect their members, others have full-throatily resisted mandates and recommendations to cancel gatherings. Some have even resisted expert recommendations for mask use and social distancing. I submit that the pandemic provided several opportunities for churches and The Church to be a beacon of light and hope for the world while engaging in innovation.

For about 20 years, I've encouraged pastors and church leaders to prepare their congregations for remote services. Admittedly, my urging did not anticipate a pandemic. Rather, it was predicated on the belief that one day, the physical church building would no longer be a sanctuary - a safe place. As leaders, we have an obligation to prepare fellow Believers to endure the persecution the Bible foretells will befall all those who profess the name of Christ. It was (and still is) my suspicion that the church building would become a target of terrorism. Whether through a suicide bomber or an active shooter, churches remain profoundly vulnerable to attacks. It is only by the grace of God that such atrocities have not occurred on a large scale to date. If or when they do, congregants will be reticent to gather in the sanctuary again. If the church has not been conditioned to gather remotely, we will be unprepared to handle when the persecution of The Church requires that we gather and meet secretly.

We have been given a blessing that, today, technology allows us to interact meaningfully with each other without leaving the safety of our own homes. Churches that did not have the foresight to prepare for this inevitability found themselves forced by the pandemic to make such changes or potentially close permanently. Some churches actually found that they operated more efficiently and fiscally sound with remote services. Many faithful Believers remained connected and continued to tithe in the face of these significant changes.

But the pandemic also exposed a deficiency of tenacious faith in people who have routinely attended Church as a social or religious tradition. Remote services, which are often not as soul- or flesh-stirring as in-person services, help to prove the resolve of our faith. Jesus told the woman at the well (in John 4) that the time will come when we will not worship God in the mountains or in Jerusalem. We can extrapolate that to reference churches, temples, or sanctuaries. Basically, he said there will be a time when you'll be unable to worship according to your usual traditions or preferences. But God is seeking true worshipers who worship him in spirit and in truth. COVID-19 identified those who are facile in worshiping in spirit and truth, distinguishing them from those who require carnal stimuli to direct their hearts and minds toward God.

One who is self-centered cannot move beyond his personal inconvenience even when it ministers life and health to others

---

The pandemic has keenly exposed a group of people who are also prone to self-service and rebellion. The scripture encourages us to esteem our brother more highly than ourselves. We often recite how the greatest love is exemplified in the act of laying down one's own life for a friend. However, we've seen many people who refused to simply wear a mask to help protect (even if in a menial way) their fellow man. They resorted to the tired excuse that mask-wearing might cause illness, a claim that was not supported by any science. Some people refused because they were unwilling to expose themselves to the messiness of mask-wearing, despite a plethora of data showing that this small inconvenience could produce tremendous benefits in protecting others. The one who is self-centered cannot move beyond his personal inconvenience even when it ministers life and health to others.

The blatant lack of altruism during the pandemic induced the writing of a series of mandates. Mandates became "necessary" only because people refused to exercise care in protecting their fellow citizens. Not surprisingly, mandates tested the resolve of many Christians to abide by the very scripture they quoted only a few years earlier. They exclaimed the writing of Paul in Romans 13:1-2, *"Let every person be subject to the governing authorities. For there is no authority except from God, and those that exist have been instituted by God. Therefore, whoever resists the authorities resists what God has appointed, and those who resist will incur judgment."*

Through the recitation of this scripture, they implored all to submit to the leadership of President Donald Trump. Yet, when those same authorities mandated mask use or advocated for employer-imposed vaccine mandates, rebellion ruled the day. Presumably, in their eyes, this circumstance offered an exception to that scripture. But really, it doesn't! They've fabricated the exception only in their own minds.

We saw that many justified their rebellion by wrongly claiming that the vaccine was the mark of the beast. IT ISN'T! Besides, the Bible places a clear distinction for those who would be condemned, stating that "they worshiped the beast" and received its mark. People get so distracted by the threat of "receiving the mark" that they miss the part that condemns (e.g., the worship of the beast). Those people, like me, who took the vaccine because they wanted to help protect others, by no means, can be considered to have worshiped the beast in that act. Scripture reminds us that the greatest form of love is demonstrated in giving oneself for the benefit of others (John 15:13). That's Christ's type of love. The antithesis to this would be self-gratification or self-preservation. COVID-19 tested the tenets of our faith - worship, love, and obedience. Unfortunately, many who profess to be Christians have failed this test miserably.

At the beginning of the pandemic, the government imposed a shutdown. Many professed Christians presumed its motive to be an exertion of control or flexing of its muscle over what it perceived to be its docile subjects. Others viewed it as a ploy by an elite cabal to attain even greater wealth by influencing government-imposed vaccination mandates, for which they owned stock. I believe, to the contrary, that the government recognized the potential for an enormous, unprecedented, and unquenchably massive loss of life – one similar to that mentioned in the prophetic warning the Lord gave me 15 years earlier. I choose to believe it was inspired by a more humanistic motive to preserve as many lives and to limit as much human suffering as possible.

A more cynical but potentially parallel impetus was to prevent the irreparable collapse of the economy that might be caused by COVID-19 ravaging society unhampered – another fate foretold in the prophetic warning. Like it or not, the initial shutdown bought time for us to learn more about the SARS-Cov2 virus, the disease it caused, and how to prevent the numerous deaths that were occurring from this contagious disease. Initially, COVID-19 was associated with a 3-4% case-fatality rate. If unremedied quickly, death rates this high, with the level of contagiousness the virus possessed, would have had a long-lasting and devastating impact on the U.S. and world economies.

Undoubtedly, the shutdown itself caused harm, and it's understandable why so many lamented and regretted having taken such a drastic proactive response. The backlash of a citizenry that values convenience, autonomy & individual rights over the lives of their fellow man (not necessarily over their own life) has all but assured that our governmental officials will never do that again, for any cause. They've almost all vowed such.

When the highly contagious but less deadly Omicron variant arose, more people were infected and subsequently immunized. In a matter of weeks, it became the dominant variant in this country and infected more than 800,000 people per day. If the death rate for Omicron remained at the initial death rate of 3-4%, that would have amounted to 32,000 deaths per day and nearly 1 million deaths in a month. That Omicron was less virulent is merely the grace of God. It certainly wasn't the consequence of some great humanitarian effort and was much less the advance of science that has created such fortune.

What if the Omicron variant was God giving us a second chance to get it right? Within a matter of a few weeks, tens of millions of people would get infected with Omicron. This less lethal variant helped develop herd immunity within the population, which helped further lessen the death rate from COVID-19. Most people simply self-isolated. Some were hospitalized, and relatively few (but still an undesirably high number) of people died from the Omicron variant. People who lost loved ones to the disease certainly grieved, but we all felt the sting of Omicron as the millions of people infected were unavailable to work for a period of time. The conveniences and luxuries we once took for granted were stifled. We grew increasingly frustrated by what we disparaged as bad service, vowing never to return to some establishments - even though the establishment had little control over its shortage of workers.

Effectively, we experienced another economic shutdown - not imposed by the government but by nature. The shortage of workers created a decrease in the supply of products, which made the cost of goods increase. People who already were suffering from lost income were doubly impacted by the rising cost of goods. Fortunately, while Omicron burned through the nation, it was short-lived. Favored by God's mercy, it left in its path a level of herd immunity such that the torment imposed by the initial strains of SARS-Cov2 was no longer experienced in this and most other industrialized countries.

My prayer, however, is that it, more importantly, leaves a valuable lesson. That is, WE NEED EACH OTHER. The employee you barely notice who stocks store shelves, the truck driver who traverses the highways at night and is rarely seen by the consumer, and each person along the supply chain for every good or service we consume all have worth and value.

May we learn to appreciate the value of each member of our society. May we esteem their lives and health more highly than our convenience and luxury. As suggested in the prophetic warning of 2005, there will most certainly be another communicable disease. It will be similar to a second Passover in that it will be more contagious and lethal than COVID-19 and all of its variants. Will we have learned the lesson of our interdependence, or will the grace of a less virulent Omicron variant have been wasted on stiff-necked, obstinate, and self-absorbed people?

May altruism mark the American spirit and obviate the need for mandates. Let our unselfish regard for our fellow citizens guide our behavior and motivate our willful sacrifice. It is this sentiment and act that would cause God's face to shine upon us and his hand to continue to shield, protect, and provide for us. But it requires first that we humble ourselves and repent of our selfish pursuits. The admonishment of Joel is very much appropriate for us at this moment:

> *"Gird yourselves, and lament, ye priests: howl, ye ministers of the altar: come, lie all night in sackcloth, ye ministers of my God: for the meat offering and drink offering is withholden from the house of your God. Sanctify ye a fast, call a solemn assembly, gather the elders and all the inhabitants of the land into the house of the Lord your God, and cry unto the Lord, Alas for the day! For the day of the Lord is at hand, and as a destruction from the Almighty shall it come"* (Joel 1:13-15 KJV).

CHAPTER 2

MODERN-DAY PHARISEES

The World That Hates

The foundational scripture of the Christian faith is John 3:16, *"For God so loved the world, that he gave his only Son, that whoever believes in him should not perish but have eternal life." Before that, John 1:9-12 tells us that Jesus, "The true light, which gives light to everyone, was coming into the world. He was in the world, and the world was made through him, yet the world did not know him. He came to his own, and his own people did not receive him. But to all who did receive him, who believed in his name, he gave the right to become children of God."* This Son, this true light, was Jesus – the Way, The Truth, and The Life (John 14:6).

The Apostle Paul offered a succinct summation of Jesus' mission: "The saying is trustworthy and deserving of full acceptance, that Christ Jesus came into the world to save sinners, of whom I am the foremost. But I received mercy for this reason, that in me, as the foremost, Jesus Christ might display his perfect patience as an example to those who were to believe in him for eternal life" (I Tim. 1:15-16).

There are numerous other scriptures that affirm the purpose of Jesus coming to earth and being crucified, which was to bring salvation to the lost. Many scriptures also speak of the great love God has for his people despite their repeated failures. In the Old Testament, there are many examples of how the wrath of God on His people might easily be misconstrued as hatred for His people. Anyone remotely learned in the scripture might offer a fierce rebuttal to that notion. In contrast, it was His great love that inspired his sending the gift of Jesus.

When we consider the life of Jesus, it becomes much more difficult to comprehend why one who was without blemish or fault and who was motivated only by love would be so hated by the world he sought to save. Clearly, the hatred was not subtle or hidden in any way. It was plainly made evident to him. It also was evident that their hatred for him was so fierce that it would be directed also toward those who loved and followed Jesus. In John 15:18-19, Jesus advises us, "If the world hates you, know that it has hated me before it hated you. If you were of the world, the world would love you as its own; but because you are not of the world, but I chose you out of the world, therefore the world hates you."

Let us first understand the context of the biblical references to the word 'world.' Throughout the New Testament scriptures, 'world' is used in different contexts. The first definition we'll consider is oikouménē, which simply refers to land or the globe. It is a geographical reference, such as the one in Matthew 24:14, "And this gospel of the kingdom shall be preached in all the world for a witness unto all nations; and then shall the end come." Another term, gē, has a similar meaning to 'land.'

A third definition or context is aiōn. Properly, the word means "age," and by extension, it means "perpetuity," including the past. This is demonstrated in Jesus' parable of the sower, "He also that received seed among the thorns is he that heareth the word; and the care of this world, and the deceitfulness of riches, choke the word, and he becometh unfruitful" (Matt. 13:22). He's saying the cares of this age, as well as the deceitfulness of riches, choke the word from us. This word is also referenced in many New Testament scriptures that reference the end of times or the perpetuity of God and His sovereignty.

Finally, the most commonly used word for 'world' in the Greek lexicon and the New Testament is kosmos, which means an orderly arrangement, a government, an order, or a constitution. It can also collectively refer to the inhabitants thereof. However, I think we have done a disservice to our understanding of Jesus' time on earth and the Gospel in general when we have reflexively made 'the world' synonymous with an ungodly host we collectively refer to as sinners. In doing so, we give cover to those who disguise themselves as godly men and women but who operate under and exploit the systems (or orderly arrangement/governments) of this world to execute their own wills.

In the common vernacular of Christianity, we refer to the world as "sinners" and presume that these must be the ones who hated Jesus and, therefore, will hate us. It has caused us to anticipate that these people will invariably resist any attempt to advance godly endeavors. With anticipation and preparation for a battle, we have, in my opinion, created a self-fulfilling mandate that we will be the enemies of sinners. But I remain confounded by the paucity, really non-existence, of Biblical examples of where any sinner hated Jesus. I am left to conclude that perhaps we have identified the wrong enemy.

If the sinners of this world (age) actually hate Christians, as many of my fellow Believers have been warned they would, perhaps it is not the fulfillment of prophecy but rather the response to our poor execution of Christ's commission. Jesus said, "The Spirit of the Lord is upon me, because he has anointed me to proclaim good news to the poor. He has sent me to proclaim liberty to the captives and recovering of sight to the blind, to set at liberty those who are oppressed" (Luke 4:18). Why should one resist liberation and good news? Moreover, why would one hate me because I offer such?

I've often been perplexed as to why sinners would hate me for offering them freedom and liberty. It just didn't seem to make sense to me. And two things occurred to me. Either the method of my offer was ineffective and didn't mirror Jesus', or it couldn't have been the sinners whom Jesus identified that hated him and would hate me. I think both may be true.

Briefly, I'll share the most influential instruction or encounter I've had with sharing the truth. During my first year of medical school, we had a class on human sexuality. The goal was to teach us how to deliver medical care with what they called unconditional positive regard. That meant that for physicians to deliver the best possible care, we could not allow our personal biases to influence our diagnosis and delivery of compassionate care. It didn't matter what the bias was. For some, there were gender biases. For others, there were cultural, racial, ethnic, or religious barriers. This was especially important in the early 1990s when the Acquired Immune Deficiency Syndrome (AIDS) was prevalent and threatened the life of well-intended healthcare professionals who might become infected through their interactions with an infected individual. At the time, AIDS was most prevalent in the homosexual population. Consequently, homosexuals were a prime target for judgment and castigation, especially from Christians, many of whom felt AIDS was a punishment from God for their lascivious behaviors.

To expose us to various aspects of sexuality, in the hope that we would not experience a culture shock of sorts when we first encountered the situation with patients, various groups of people were brought in to have panel discussions in a large room of total strangers. In these discussions, people would share very intimate experiences about sexuality. They brought in elderly panelists and persons with disabilities because they didn't want us to wrongly presume that these populations were asexual. They also brought in homosexuals to discuss their experiences. When the homosexuals presented, the students were provided explicit instructions that the discussion was not to become a moral debate. Our charge was to listen and ask questions without moral judgment. It seemed to be an easy enough task, even for a zealous Christian like me.

After a broader discussion in the lecture hall, we broke into small groups. With each group, a gay male and a lesbian spoke with the students. The gay man proceeded to tell his story and experience with sexuality and healthcare. He gave what I thought was a compelling presentation. The lesbian then proceeded. Early into her presentation, she said, "I just think it is unfair that society won't allow me to exercise my God-given orientation." "Wait a minute," I thought in my mind. "That just crossed the line into a moral discussion." Surely, as a devout Christian, I couldn't let that go unaddressed. But as soon as I had the thought, I felt the Holy Spirit commandeer my lips because the words that flowed out afterward were not typical of my nature, either in tone or choice.

I explained that I don't have a problem with her choice of lifestyle, but I do have a problem with describing her choice as a God-given trait or attraction. I proceeded to request that, like I shouldn't force a perspective on her, she should not force one on me. We are each persuaded by our own convictions (Rom. 14:5). I explained how I don't view her sin of homosexuality as any better or worse than mine if I looked at a woman and lusted. I will not justify my lust as a God-given urge, nor should I absolve her sin as such. Let us start with a basic understanding that we all fall short of the glory of God and are in need of forgiveness.

As I continued, one of the students, writhing in her seat, became intolerably uncomfortable with the directness of the conversation and screamed, "I can't take this. We need to change the conversation." It was unclear which side of the discussion she agreed with, but that was irrelevant. After the small group concluded, the gay man approached me and gave me what I have characterized ever since as one of the best compliments I've ever received. He said, "I don't know why she got so uncomfortable. No one has ever said the things that you have said and not offended me."

Those complimentary words reverberate in my mind and spirit even now, more than thirty years later. They inform and direct my approach to addressing sin in my own life, as well as in the lives of others who allow me to speak about their situations. In a later chapter, we will explore how to very practically administer such a compassionate declaration of liberating truth. But for now, we will refocus our attention on which 'world' hated Jesus and will hate us. Hopefully, we can concede that if the scripture referenced sinners in this regard, it would most likely be the consequence of the inept delivery of the truth on our part and not the message itself. Clearly, Jesus never had this problem. So, an alternate definition of the word might provide more clarity as to why the world would hate Jesus and us.

Throughout most of his time of ministry, Jesus was resisted and hated by a singular group of people. It was not a subtle thing. The religious leaders of his time, the Pharisees and Sadducees, despised Jesus. To a lesser extent, at least as elucidated in the scriptures, some member(s) of the Roman Empire hated him as well. However, those loathsome encounters were not as prominently portrayed. In fact, from the moment of his birth, a death warrant was placed on Jesus.

> *"Now after Jesus was born in Bethlehem of Judea in the days of Herod the king, behold, wise men from the east came to Jerusalem, saying, 'Where is he who has been born king of the Jews? For we saw his star when it rose and have come to worship him.' When Herod the king heard this, he was troubled, and all Jerusalem with him; and assembling all the chief priests and scribes of the people, he inquired of them where the Christ was to be born. They told him, 'In Bethlehem of Judea'"* (Matt. 2:1-5).

King Herod, being already a master deceiver, secretly summoned wise men to locate Jesus under the guise that he, too, would like to worship the newborn Messiah, the king of the Jews. Herod was currently King of Judea and had already killed others who threatened his rule. The prophetic arrival of Jesus certainly threatened to disrupt his power. After the wise men found the infant, they were warned in a dream to not return to Herod. King Herod, frustrated with the prospect of losing his authority to this new Messiah, issued a decree to kill all male children under the age of two years (vs. 16). But Jesus' parents, Mary and Joseph, had already been warned by an angel to escape to Egypt, until Herod the Great died.

Jesus grew up in obscurity and intended to keep himself of no reputation until the appointed time. He understood that his mere presence threatened the sociopolitical stability of the time. He knew that the world (kosmos) -- the governments, the established order and systems – would oppose the establishment of his Kingdom. Most of his confrontations occurred not with the sinner but with the Pharisees and Sadducees, who, at the time, exerted control over the Jewish people. The control they exerted pertained to legalistic, religious oppression. As long as they kept the Jewish people in order, there was no need for the Tetrarch appointed over the land, Herod Antipas, to intervene.

As Jesus grew in popularity and more people followed him, the religious leaders sought to kill and crucify him. Among those who sought to spare his life were those whom we, in religious circles, might reflexively, and out of context, call 'the world.' Sinners, like Pilate and even Herod Antipas, said they found no fault in Jesus. But it was the religious leaders who sought to kill Jesus and eventually succeeded in crucifying him, fulfilling the scripture.

I submit to you that the world Jesus said hated him and would similarly hate us is the religious and governmental order that seeks to exercise control of the followers of Christ. They are unbelievers because they refuse to submit to the authority, mechanisms, and practices of Jesus Christ. This world would like nothing more than to falsely accuse sinners of such, creating a convenient decoy. Under such cover, they can effectively execute their wills and hide the hands of their oppressive perpetrations. Such people remain under the influence of the god of this world and not the Almighty God, as they allege.

"The god of this world has blinded the minds of the unbelievers, to keep them from seeing the light of the gospel of the glory of Christ, who is the image of God" (2 Cor. 4:4). In this passage, the world referenced is aiōn. Thus, the god of this age or time has blinded the minds of unbelievers. That means the blinders will be on only for a season. Thanks be to God that the season wherein the "little god" -- the deceiver effectively hides the light of the Gospel, the Truth, from God's people is now over. The Truth has come and is now being revealed in this writing and those of others who prophetically admonish the unbeliever. He that has an ear to hear, let him hear what the Spirit of God is saying.

The Nexus of Evangelicalism

One might question what all of the aforementioned have to do with Evangelicalism and what's the poisoned fruit. I beg patience as we explore more deeply the relationship between the two. As mentioned previously, White Evangelicals have systematically infiltrated the political systems. While politics or political ideologies inherently have no direct impact on an individual's salvation, either positively or negatively, the deification of political pursuits does threaten one's salvation.

No clear-thinking evangelical will ever verbalize their worship of a legislative agenda, but actions reveal the idolatry that the mouth tries to conceal. The adage that actions speak louder than words proves to be veracious. Jesus said of the Pharisees, *"This people honors me with their lips, but their heart is far from me; in vain do they worship me, teaching as doctrines the commandments of men"* (Matt. 15:8-9). The spirit that drove the Pharisees then is alive and active today in the hearts of evangelicals who seek to conflate their legislative aspirations with divine mandates.

Actions reveal the idolatry that the mouth tries to conceal

The term Evangelical or Evangelicalism is often recited in public discourse today, especially within the political sphere. However, many Americans are likely unaware of what it actually means. Is Evangelicalism a political advocacy group, or are they the national representatives of Christianity? How have they garnered the public influence they now enjoy and wield as the moral authority in the country? Let us first consider the very basic definition and the origins of the term Evangelicalism.

Evangelicalism is defined as "a worldwide trans-denominational movement within Protestant Christianity that maintains the belief that the essence of the Gospel consists of the doctrine of salvation by grace alone, solely through faith in Jesus' atonement."[1] Essentially, an Evangelical is any individual who subscribes to Protestant Christianity, regardless of denomination. By this definition, most Christians might consider themselves an Evangelical. Merely believing that salvation is attained by grace and faith in Jesus Christ qualifies one as such, according to this definition.[2] However, I urge you to not so readily associate yourself with the sect of Americans, and likely citizens of other countries, who consider themselves to be Evangelicals. There's more to the affiliation than is suggested by the aforementioned definition.

Evangelicalism emerged as a distinct religious affiliation out of a series of religious revivals that began in Britain and New England in the 1730s. The movement was marked by and fueled by the belief that conversion through faith in Jesus alone was sufficient to endow ordinary men and women with the confidence and authority to share the gospel and convert others outside of the control of established churches. What an amazing concept! Individuals could actually spread the word of God through their own testimonies and sharing of the gospel? This seems to be the very definition of Evangelism. However, Evangelicalism has evolved and uniquely distinguished itself from Evangelism over time.

Historian David Bebbington notes four distinctive aspects of evangelical faith, three of which are consistent with the precepts of Evangelism.[3] The four dictums are conversionism, biblicism, crucicentrism, and activism. Conversionism is the belief that salvation through Jesus Christ causes a conversion from the old man of sin to a new creation who is no longer under the bondage of sin. Biblicism is a strong adherence to the truth, inerrancy, and infallibility of scripture; the Bible is the inspired word of God. Crucicentrism is the belief

---

[1] Wikipedia Contributors, "Evangelicalism," Wikipedia (Wikimedia Foundation, November 13, 2019), https://en.wikipedia.org/wiki/Evangelicalism.

[2] Mark A. Noll, *The Rise of Evangelicalism: The Age of Edwards, Whitefield, and the Wesleys* (Downers Grove, Ill.: InterVarsity Press, 2003).

[3] D W Bebbington, *Evangelicalism in Modern Britain: A History from the 1730'S to the 1980'S* (London: Routledge, 1996).

in substitutionary atonement – that Jesus, who was without sin, was crucified to atone for our sins.

The fourth central tenet of Evangelicalism seems to have become the dominant one in recent generations: activism. Activism refers to the active expression and sharing of the gospel in diverse ways. This not only includes preaching the gospel, as Evangelism requires, but it also separately involves social action—often in the form of political and social activism.

Although Evangelicalism has roots in a genuine desire to spread the Gospel of Jesus Christ, with time and intention, it uniquely distinguished itself from the precepts of Evangelism (the Biblical correlate). With strategic precision, it has grown substantially in power and influence in many countries. In 2016, there were approximately 619 million evangelicals in the world. That represents approximately 25% of all Christians worldwide. American Evangelicals comprise the majority of Evangelicals worldwide and are the single largest religious group in the nation, making up 25% of the United States population.[4], [5] Their influence has become palpable and can no longer be ignored. And Evangelicals know it!

It was not a coincidence, nor was it a sovereign act of God. It resulted from the strategic infiltration by those who subscribed to their ideology into the political systems of America. The Netflix mini-series *The Family* documents the clandestine ploy of evangelicals to infiltrate and influence American politics. Journalist Jeff Sharlet, who broke the story and produced the series, plainly reveals their belief that there are select individuals who are chosen by God to execute his legislative agendas. Evangelism – the proselytization of the lost – no longer is the priority of Evangelicals. Political and legislative influence is. The ultimate goal is to alleviate man's voluntary submission to the will of

---

[4] "How Many Evangelicals Are There? | Wheaton," web.archive.org, January 30, 2016, https://web.archive.org/web/20160130062242/http://www.wheaton.edu/ISAE/Defining-Evangelicalism/How-Many-Are-There.

[5] David Masci and Gregory A. Smith, "5 Facts about U.S. Evangelical Protestants," Pew Research Center, March 1, 2018, https://www.pewresearch.org/short-reads/2018/03/01/5-facts-about-u-s-evangelical-protestants/.

God and institute laws that would reflect and impose the laws of God on most, if not all, citizens.

On the surface, this seems to be a laudable goal of those who consider themselves to be Christian. Why would a God-fearing Christian not want to have godly men and women in positions of power within America's legislative, executive, and judicial branches of government? They quote the Bible saying, *"When the righteous are in authority, the people rejoice: But when the wicked beareth rule, the people mourn"* (Prov. 29:2 KJV). Pertinent to the writing of this book, they've ignored the first verse of the same chapter, which states, *"He who is often reproved, yet stiffens his neck, will suddenly be broken beyond healing"* (vs. 1).

Yes, it is desirable for people of good moral character and even of Christian faith to be in positions of power unless you subscribe to a different faith or none at all. One of the most prized benefits of U.S. citizenship is the First Amendment of the Constitution, which affords us freedom from any government-imposed religion. If this were a predominantly Muslim, Buddhist, or even Jewish country, most Christians would greatly defend that freedom. But, because Christianity is the predominant religion in this country, many feel empowered or even ordained by God to enact laws that reflect their Christian beliefs. Moreover, they will do whatever is necessary to accomplish this perceived mandate.

If we are to submit to the authority and principles of God's kingdom, our evangelistic pursuits should not be empowered through the mechanisms of government. Rather, it must be done the way that God has ordained in his word – through the sharing of the Good News, not the imposition of moral mandates. Otherwise, our government would no longer be a democracy (or a republic, depending on your political persuasion); it would essentially become a theocracy, which cannot happen under the Constitution.

Not many evangelicals will publicly admit their desire to eliminate democracy in favor of theocracy, but when one advocates for U.S. laws to reflect God's laws, especially using unethical tactics, their intention is exposed. To effectively implement their goal in an unobtrusive manner, they consolidated their message and representation. The end product is Evangelicalism.

In America, "Evangelical" is most notably and almost exclusively used in relation to politics. We usually hear most about Evangelicals when presidential elections loom in the near future. We don't often hear the term used in reference to organized efforts to evangelize the lost or to provide humanitarian aid. We don't hear of Evangelical efforts to serve the poor or stamp out poverty. We don't even hear Evangelicals pursuing justice or mercy. How can it be that the reference to this religious group is exclusively in relation to legislative and political agendas?

I submit that it is intentional and reflects the overarching goal of its collective organization. That goal is not the spreading of the Gospel of Jesus Christ, as Evangelism would require. Instead, it is the attainment of political and legislative power. Its ultimate objective is control, a form of witchcraft.

In election polling, Evangelicals refer to an even narrower group of people. It does not universally apply to all persons who identify as born-again Christians or to people who subscribe to the concepts of biblicism, conversionism, and crucicentrism. Rather, it references those people who are exclusively included in their particular group of activism. Most people don't realize that when the media or Pew Research Center references Evangelicals, they refer to a group of people who meet only two criteria: 1) they self-identify as evangelical, and 2) they are White (Caucasian). Indeed, the political polls do not include African Americans, Latinos, Asians, or any other race of people who also practice Christianity – only White People.

Concerningly, there is no other test given to establish their rite as an Evangelical apart from race and a simple, unauthenticated self-identification. They do not attest in any way that they are born-again, actively practicing, obedient to, or filled with the Spirit of God. They simply assert that they are White and identify as Evangelical. These are the people who are referred to in the media, but they do not represent all evangelicals and certainly not all persons of Christian faith. About a quarter of Americans (26%) are self-identified evangelicals. Of them, two-thirds are white (64%), while 19% are black, 10% are Hispanic, and the remaining 6% are Asian, mixed race, or other ethnicities.[6] The opinions of at least 36% of evangelicals on political matters are not considered or represented in the presentations by the media.

Why would a whole third of American evangelicals be ignored when presenting the sentiments or beliefs of evangelicals? I propose that it is because the inclusion of other races, who often have diverse activist goals, will dilute the message of White Evangelicalism and consequently diminish their political influence and power. As long as their ideals can be presented publicly and they present themselves as the ambassadors of God on earth, they can implement their strategy to obtain legislative and social dominance unimpeded by other Christians who disagree with their legislative pursuits. It is not a novel pursuit. This initiative has persisted since before the time Jesus walked the earth.

Because White Evangelicals are highly motivated by their unquenchable thirst for legislation, I consider them to be modern-day Pharisees. Recall that biblical Pharisees were not only students of the law, but they were lovers of the law. The law of God was their highest priority. They called themselves Haberim, which, in the language of the Mishna, means one who is associated with the law and observes it strictly. Not only did they allegedly keep all the written and oral laws, but they even added 1,500 new laws to the ones directly ordained by God and sought to enforce them among the people. They believed righteousness was imparted unto them through following the law. They reasoned that if following the few laws that God specifically gave made them righteous, then the creation of additional laws that expanded upon God's law would make them more likely to achieve righteousness and closeness to or approval from God.

The Pharisees were known as separatists and took the position of the teachers of the law (an assignment God gave to the Levites). They did not

---

[6] Sarah Eekhoff Zylstra, "1 in 3 American Evangelicals Is a Person of Color," News & Reporting, September 6, 2017, https://www.christianitytoday.com/news/2017/september/1-in-3-american-evangelicals-person-of-color-prri-atlas.html.

associate with people who they believed were not God's chosen ones and certainly not with those who didn't subscribe to their laws. The highest law for them was the Sabbath.

Above all, the people were expected to keep the Sabbath. One who failed to do so would be castigated as a sinner. Because of their high esteem for the law and especially the Sabbath, it should be no surprise that they were incensed when Jesus replied to their inquiries about which law was the greatest. Jesus said to him, *"You shall love the Lord your God with all your heart, with all your soul, and with all your mind.' This is the first and great commandment. And the second is like it: 'You shall love your neighbor as yourself.' On these two commandments hang all the Law and the Prophets"* (Matt. 22:37-40). Jesus' assertion that loving God and each other were preeminent over keeping the Sabbath infuriated the Pharisees. They subsequently sought to entrap Jesus mostly on issues related to the Sabbath.

Because the Pharisees also possessed political clout, the more favor Jesus gained among the people, the more their governmental authority was challenged. To prevent this, they conspired to eliminate Jesus and his increasingly popular doctrine. They were so committed to this goal that they found themselves favoring a convicted criminal, Barabbas, over Jesus to protect their political prowess and agendas.

Now, consider Evangelicals. Like the Pharisees, their highest passion appears to be the law. Although they would never verbalize this position, their behaviors and priorities suggest that they believe that morality and righteousness can be achieved through the law. At the very least, they believe that the law should be an instrumental part of achieving righteousness. Their actions reflect a strong belief that things considered unlawful or sinful by God should be illegal under American law. While few, if any, will admit to having this mindset, their actions prove the focus of their attention. Their efforts are concerted and directed most ardently at enacting legislation. Those efforts overshadow any collective effort to win people to Christ using the methods and strategies that Jesus instructed.

The Pharisees perseverated on what they perceived as Jesus' violation of laws concerning the Sabbath and communing with Gentiles. To Jesus, this exposed where their hearts were. While today's Evangelicals are less concerned about the Sabbath and with whom one shares a meal, they have clearly identified their top legislative priorities. Preeminent among them is the abolishment of abortion. Like my former pastor, many Evangelicals cannot fathom how one can be Christian and not support anti-abortion legislation. Their fanatical allegiance to Pro-life agendas is so emphatic that they are willing to favor even the most unethical of political candidates if he or she vows to uphold this most highly esteemed legislative agenda of Evangelicals.

It was widely reported that Donald Trump was elected to the presidency in large part because 80% of those individuals who identify as White Evangelicals voted for him. Similarly, Judge Roy Moore's candidacy for the U.S. Senate seat in Alabama was met with the strong support of White Evangelicals. Their unyielding support persisted despite Trump's unapologetic announcement that he has never asked God for forgiveness and despite Judge Moore's alleged illegal sexual contact with minors. Desperate for someone who would support their political agenda, Evangelicals clung to the feckless denials of the would-be senator and completely disregarded Trump's apostatic proclamations.

Much like the separatist Pharisees, White Evangelicals (at least those in the power positions) are careful to preserve their racially exclusive influence. The opinions, agendas, and votes of Evangelicals of color are never mentioned in the media or in reference to political power. It always references only the agenda of White Evangelicals. They will accept the avid support of Evangelicals of color when the optics are improved by it. But make no mistake about it: their political agenda is well-fortified by the influence of their White counterparts.

Among the Pharisees, some secretly supported the message of Jesus. Likewise, there are some White Evangelicals who will secretly acknowledge the folly of their ethical compromise. However, very few will admit it publicly for fear of being ostracized by their fringe majority. Jesus warned his disciples to beware of the leaven of the Pharisees (Matthew 16:6) because even a little destroys the whole lump. We, the church of God, must remain vigilant to beware of legalistic doctrine and an inordinate commitment to legislative goals that require us to compromise our requirement that legislators have some impunity of character. Like leaven (e.g., yeast), only a small amount of compromise is needed to impact the entire group.

To those earnest Christians who believe in the substitutionary atonement of Jesus' sacrifice, I say beware of the leaven of the Evangelicals. The path that seems to be right can easily lead to destruction because of the Evangelicals' leaven. An argument that is well-articulated by a popular and charismatic Evangelical can easily be made to sound rational according to societal norms and religious tradition when, in fact, it has no Biblical validity or support. If we are not vigilant to scrutinize these assertions against the word of God, we will be easily misled by the laudable passions of those whom we admire or follow.

The Leaven of Evangelicals

I read an article by a prominent evangelical pastor. I'll not mention the name of the pastor. I'd like to think that the Holy Spirit by now has convicted him of his proclamation, but sadly, he is unlikely to have heeded such rebuke. The identity of the individual is much less important than the ideals that he espoused. In the article, he explains why he has supported and continues to support former president Donald J. Trump. His rationale was not significantly different from that of many other White Evangelicals with whom I have relationships and have had conversations concerning this matter.

This pastor claims that Trump has demonstrated "extraordinary leadership in the face of incredible adversity—a different kind of moral fiber..." In making this claim, the author redefined what morality is and how it is demonstrated. He clearly outlined what the evangelical construct for morals is, regardless of how far the new definition strays from the well-established and understood definition.

So, let's start with what most of us know to be true. Morals are standards of behavior or beliefs concerning what is and is not acceptable for a person or group of persons. Morals are not the actions but rather the compulsions behind the actions. One can perform an honorable act with an immoral motive. In so doing, the individual is not justified by the act. He remains as corrupt after completing the act as he was before.

Those who benefit from a good deed might be persuaded by the benefit to overlook the glaring moral deficiencies of the benefactor. Consequently, they might erroneously consider the individual to have good moral character because they performed a desirable act. For such persons, it is more conciliatory to focus on a 'different kind of moral fiber' as the author of the article did. Moral fiber is the capacity to do what is right regardless of the circumstance. In this case, we must consider what the 'right thing' is from the perspective of Evangelicals. Fortunately, the author gratuitously provides clarity in this regard.

The author asserts that Christians should "stand with the leader who stands for the very things you would hope a president would stand for—the sanctity of life, religious freedom for private citizens and business owners, conservative federal judges, standing with the nation of Israel, and a better tomorrow for those living in poverty, especially in our largest cities." These are the values and policies for which we should pray, he suggested.

I don't disagree that we should pray for these things, but a central tenet in Christian teaching is that what a person does is less important than who a person is. In Matthew 7:21-23, Jesus warns us that there will be many who will claim that they did many great works in His name. They cast out demons, prophesied, and healed the sick – all in His name. In this vein, I might extrapolate that they have passed conservative laws, protected religious freedoms, and appointed conservative judges and justices in Jesus' name. However, they were all considered to be works of iniquity because the ones who performed these 'good deeds' had no relationship with Jesus.

Who we or our elected leaders are is far more important than the good things the individual does for you personally or even for the nation. The fallacy of Evangelicalism is that work justifies the individual and the process. It doesn't! Man is not justified by works but by faith in Jesus Christ (Gal. 2:16).

The author goes on to convey sentiments echoed by many White Evangelicals that from 2008 through 2016, Christianity has been incessantly attacked. Religious freedoms of individuals, businesses, and even churches were allegedly being assailed. Government funds were being used to pay for abortions. Not stated in his article, but alleged by many evangelicals, homosexuality was being normalized, and our children were being inundated with images that promote this sin. The viability of Christian faith and values was becoming progressively bleaker. He asserted then that 2016 was, and 2020 would be, a time when "Christians all across this nation are stepping out of the shadows and onto the stage, off the sidelines and into the game in record numbers."

Such a proclamation suggests that prior to, and apart from, finding their political voice, Christians were all but weak and defenseless against a liberal government that sought to annihilate their faith and standards. This implies that our prayers offered in closets and sanctuaries render our voice of little renown in the political marketplace and feckless to effect change in the world. It further suggests that because we had little governmental authority and power, we remained oppressed by a liberal legislative regime.

This is a good time to remind all Christians first that the weapons of our warfare are not carnal but are mighty through God to the pulling down of strongholds (2 Corinthians 10:4). I suspect the author had forgotten this as he appeared to disparage the effectiveness of these weapons. He actually put into his writing a statement that blatantly contradicts our faith. He wrote, *"We prayed, we guarded our churches and our families, and we waited for our chance to speak out at the ballot box."*

Is he suggesting that prayer is somehow subordinate or inferior to the power of the ballot box? Apparently, in his mind, absent of assistance from carnal mechanisms, our spiritual armamentarium is anemic. Such inadequacy apparently renders Christians vulnerable to perpetual victimization, according to his argument. The unbelievable audacity and misguided conviction of one who is charged with the responsibility of instructing parishioners or congregants on the unyielding power of prayer is astounding. It could be characterized as pastoral malfeasance or imprudence, at best. For the believer, there is no greater power we have than that of prayer and supplication. This is how we make our requests known to God (Philippians 4:6-7). And with earnest expectation, we patiently await God's intervention - not ours.

I am sympathetic to the impatience and growing uncertainty amongst many Evangelicals that God might not intervene until the state of the world has seemingly gotten too far out of control. I understand the urge to intervene when the promise seems to tarry. Like Abraham, who received the promise of an eternal seed, when it seems delayed or forgotten, we tend to seek alternative solutions. While they satiate our desire to nudge God along in the fulfillment of his promise, they subvert the plan of God.

Abraham had two sons - one born as the fulfillment of the promise; the other was born out of impatient carnality. In Galatians 4:24, Paul reveals that these things are an allegory. They refer to two covenants - one based on law, which imparts bondage, and the other based on faith, which imparts freedom. When we grow impatient in waiting for God's spiritual intervention, we devise strategies (often legal in nature) to accomplish the goal. We then attempt to justify it as a Godly action. In actuality, the scripture warns us that this imparts bondage.

The reality is that evangelicals felt that they were at war. And, as the author states in his opinion piece, they were looking for "a fighter—someone who saw the challenge for what it was, the fight of our lifetime." What they failed to consider, and to reconcile even today, is how this fighter fights and for whom he really fights. This, too, will only lead to bondage. The better way would be to continue in faith, exercising spiritual warfare, which is the only way to bring about lasting 'religious freedom.'

Any reasonable Christian would understandably desire to see the lives of unborn babies spared and homosexuality established as the sin we believe that the Bible asserts it is. The faith-filled Christian, however, is considerate of how these things are accomplished and how God is represented in the process. As Christians, we know that only the transformation of heart and mind will produce true righteousness. The law could never accomplish this.

In Galatians 3, Paul calls the Galatians stupid or foolish for believing that they could somehow produce righteousness through the law. I urge those who are so committed to accomplishing these goals through legislation and who conclude that the method matters less to read the book of Galatians. It will reveal the profound limitations of the law. Moreover, we should heed the admonishment that Paul provides therein. In Galatians 3:21, he reminds us that though the law is not against faith, the law cannot provide life - only faith can.

Confoundingly, evangelicals have prioritized legislation over prayer and faith. As ambassadors of Christ, we should always consider how our allegiance to an individual and silence about the misbehavior of our endorsed candidates impacts our witness of faith. The world observes hypocrisy between those who profess Christ but remain silent about and supportive of brazen bigotry, adultery, fornication, uncleanness, lasciviousness, idolatry, witchcraft (manipulation), hatred, variance, emulations, wrath, strife, seditions, heresies, envyings, revellings, and other such works of the flesh (Galatians 5:19-21) - all fully operational in some of their chosen candidates. It becomes apparent to those who are 'lost' – the ones we hope to evangelize – that evangelicals would rather align themselves with one who displays no fruits of the spirit to win legislative victories than to remain true to their Christian values and seemingly lose.

Never abandon your eternal perspective,
pursuing a mortal objective

Like the Pharisees who cried out in favor of the convicted criminal, Barabbas, over Jesus, those who compromise their witness have indeed lost faith. It is evidence that they esteem the attainment and preservation of political power over principle. Proof that they've lost faith in the plan and perhaps the power of God is found in their acceptance of solutions that are contrary to the foundations of their professed faith. The calculation made by White Evangelicals is that the end will justify the means. What is the end? Enactment of spiritually feckless laws at the expense of a witness that has eternal spiritual consequence. I caution my evangelical friends and all Believers to never abandon your eternal perspective, pursuing a mortal objective.

What other choice do they have, the author of the article asks? How about you continue to pray and guard your congregations? Let us exercise our civic duty and vote for whomever we choose, but realize that the laws enacted will not produce an ounce of righteousness, nor will they bring the spiritual life that God esteems and offers. Above all, preserve your own souls and your witness by letting your light shine in a manner that would compel people to willingly glorify God instead of forcing submission through the enactment of laws.

Pursuit of political power sharply distinguishes Evangelicalism from Evangelism

Stand for truth, character, and integrity. Do not compromise our demands for such virtues in exchange for political prowess. As Christians, we must demand truthfulness and scrupulousness, even if it comes at the expense of the policies and values that matter most to us. Anything short of this suggests that we have placed our political agendas above our quest for truth. The unyielding pursuit of political power sharply distinguishes Evangelicalism from Evangelism.

Evangelicals will emphatically defend their conviction that Christians should seek political power. To this, I reply with the words of Paul: *"Share in suffering as a good soldier of Christ Jesus. No soldier gets entangled in civilian pursuits, since his aim is to please the one who enlisted him"* (2 Tim. 2:3-4). Again, I am not suggesting that we should not get involved in political matters and try to influence them. But we must never attempt to use sly tactics or compromise our values to achieve influence through these or other carnal means. Moreover, we should not be entangled in these civilian pursuits. That means we should not be interweaved, entwined, or twisted inseparably in these activities. They should not become part of our fabric or characterization, even while we exercise our civic duties. Our influence should be enacted through evangelistic endeavors – preaching the Gospel – not through political tricks.

It is understandable why Christians would easily revert to carnal tactics instead of relying on spiritual devices, which at times can seem to have slow or no effect if we view the results from a carnal perspective. Jesus spent much of his time on earth trying to get his followers to see through an eternal or kingdom perspective. It is doubtless that Jesus, at times, became frustrated with this. Shortly before he was to be crucified, Jesus contended with his disciples to not be troubled by the things around him. They sought to see and to know God, but Jesus reminded them, *"If you had known me, you would have known my Father also. From now on you do know him and have seen him"* (John 14:7). His frustration became evident in the words that followed:

> *"Have I been with you so long, and you still do not know me, Philip? Whoever has seen me has seen the Father. How can you say, 'Show us the Father'? Do you not believe that I am in the Father and the Father is in me? The words that I say to you I do not speak on my own authority, but the Father who dwells in me does his works. Believe me that I am in the Father and the Father is in me, or else believe on account of the works themselves"* (vs. 9-11).

Jesus is contending with his disciples, trying to teach them to see beyond the natural. Yet, it seems to have been ineffective even until the point when he came to Jerusalem to be crucified.

The Bible tells us that as Jesus entered Jerusalem on what we commonly refer to as Palm Sunday, he requested the colt of a donkey (Matthew 21). By all human standards, Jesus riding on the young offspring of a donkey does not convey an air of victory or authority. However, it was prophesied to the children of Israel in Zechariah 9:9, *"Rejoice greatly, O daughter of Zion! Shout aloud, O daughter of Jerusalem! Behold, your king is coming to you; righteous and having salvation is he, humble and mounted on a donkey, on a colt, the foal of a donkey."* Many of the people in the crowd were likely familiar with this prophecy, as they expected Jesus to be their liberator.

As Jesus entered the city, *"most of the crowd spread their cloaks on the road, and others cut branches from the trees and spread them on the road. And the crowds that went before him and that followed him were shouting, 'Hosanna to the Son of David! Blessed is he who comes in the name of the Lord! Hosanna in the highest!'"* (Matt. 21:8-9). Hosanna, in this context, is a passionate plea to save or rescue. The people rightly recognized Jesus as the liberator he was, but their expectation of the method was carnal. They wrongly expected that in that moment or in the ensuing days, he would overthrow the Roman Empire using carnal force.

Much like they did previously after Simon liberated the Jewish people, the people laid their clothes out before Jesus and waved palm branches as he entered Jerusalem. These were gestures to show their allegiance to and exultation of Jesus as their triumphant king. Palm branches were engraved on Jewish coins when the Jewish nation was free. They, therefore, represented the financial freedom and wealth of the nation. Additionally, palm branches carried religious significance. I Kings 6:29 tells us that palm trees were engraved on the walls of the temple. As part of the celebration during the Feast of Tabernacles, the people would rejoice, waving palm branches (Lev. 23:40).

The Feast of Tabernacles and the waving of palm branches therein was significant because it was a time when the children of Israel gathered in Jerusalem to remember God's provision in the Wilderness. They would remember how God delivered them in the past, but they would also look ahead to a promised Messianic age when all nations would come to Jerusalem to worship the Lord. *"And it shall come to pass that everyone who is left of all the nations which came against Jerusalem shall go up from year to year to worship the King, the Lord of hosts, and to keep the Feast of Tabernacles"* (Zech. 14:16).

The Feast of Tabernacles reminded the Jewish people that all of the nations that once aligned themselves against the Israelites would one day submit to the sovereignty of their God. Taken together, the symbolism of palm trees represented a return to Jewish nationalism, wealth, and religious freedom. Such was the expectation of the crowds who gathered as Jesus entered Jerusalem.

When the crowd spread their clothes on the road before Jesus as he entered Jerusalem, it was a gesture of submission to the authority of kingship. The only other biblical occurrence of such was when Jehu was anointed King of Israel by the prophet. 2 Kings 9:13 says, *"They quickly took their cloaks and spread them under him on the bare steps. Then they blew the trumpet and shouted, 'Jehu is king!'"* At the time, Joram was the King of Israel, and Jehu was an officer in his army. Even though Jehu and all the other officers with him were servants of Joram, after the prophet anointed Jehu, the officers quickly spread their clothes under him as a sign of their allegiance and submission to his new authority. At that moment, authority had shifted in the minds and hearts of the people around Jehu. They now were submitted to his instruction, and the first order of business was to violently overthrow Joram and the House of Ahab, the royal bloodline that had done evil in the sight of the Lord. Recall that Ahab was married to Jezebel, who worshiped Baal and ordered the murder of God's prophets.

When the young prophet poured the oil on Jehu's head to anoint him king, he said:

> *"This is what the Lord, the God of Israel, says: 'I anoint you king over the Lord's people Israel. You are to destroy the house of Ahab your master, and I will avenge the blood of my servants the prophets and the blood of all the Lord's servants shed by Jezebel. The whole house of Ahab will perish. I will cut off from Ahab every last male in Israel—slave or free. I will make the house of Ahab like the house of Jeroboam son of Nebat and like the house of Baasha son of Ahijah. As for Jezebel, dogs will devour her on the plot of ground at Jezreel, and no one will bury her.'"* (2 Kings 9:6-10)

The Jewish officers were more than ready to join Jehu in the fight to regain their religious freedom. The overthrowing of Joram and his brother Ahaziah, King of Judah, would be a brutal bloodbath. But this was not a deterrent for those who were desperate to regain their religious freedom.

As Jesus entered Jerusalem, the crowds undoubtedly were likewise prepared for whatever means would be necessary to overthrow the Roman government, as their promised Messiah had arrived. Just as Jehu bought their liberty with the price of blood, they supposed that Jesus would do the same. Indeed, he would. However, it would not be through the method they had expected.

At the Last Supper, the disciples anticipated the rise of Jesus's kingdom and squabbled about who would be the greatest among them. It was evident to Jesus that they still processed his kingdom through their carnal perspective. He challenged their paradigm by paradoxically stating that the greatest in his kingdom would be the servant of all. He contrasted his kingdom with that of the world's system, stating, *"The kings of the Gentiles exercise lordship over them, and those in authority over them are called benefactors. But not so with you"* (Luke 22:25-26).

Then Jesus seemingly indulged their carnal perspective, telling them, *"You are those who have stayed with me in my trials, and I assign to you, as my Father assigned to me, a kingdom, that you may eat and drink at my table in my kingdom and sit on thrones judging the twelve tribes of Israel"* (vs. 28-30). Surely, by the time Jesus tells them that if they have no sword, go buy one (vs. 36), they had a full expectation that the battle would likely be one of violence.

Fully ready to engage, Peter would later cut off the ear of a Roman soldier when they came to apprehend Jesus. Rather than resist and fight, as they had expected, Jesus surrendered himself to the Roman soldiers. Clearly disillusioned by what seemed to be Jesus' failure to ascend to the throne, Peter followed at a distance as the chief priests escorted Jesus to the courtyard to be falsely accused (Matt. 26:59). After confirming that Jesus' fate would most likely be crucifixion as opposed to the victorious overtaking he expected, Peter then dissociated himself from Jesus, denying him three times – just as Jesus warned he would do.

After Pilate and Herod could find no fault in Jesus and after their failed attempts to persuade the religious leaders of the time to let Jesus go free, Pilate had one last ploy to release Jesus without inciting a riot. He determined, as was his usual custom, to let one prisoner go free. Surely, the crowd would choose to pardon Jesus, who had done no wrong but instead healed the sick and freed people from demonic possession. In contrast, Barabbas was a murderer and insurrectionist. The decision was an obvious choice in the mind of Pilate. *"But they all cried out together, 'Away with this man, and release to us Barabbas'"* (Luke 23:18).

It defies logic that the multitudes who only days earlier heralded Jesus as their liberating king would now call for his crucifixion and choose to free a murderer instead. I submit to you that the crowd didn't choose Barabbas, the person, over Jesus. Rather, I believe they chose Barabbas' way over Jesus' way at the urging and stirring of the religious leaders of that time.

When desperation prevails, compromise follows

The Bible tells us that *"the chief priests and elders persuaded the multitudes that they should ask for Barabbas and destroy Jesus"* (Matt. 27:20). Jesus' way was spiritual, but it appeared weak according to natural standards. Barabbas' way was that of insurrection. Though he failed to accomplish a violent government takeover, at least he demonstrated that he was a 'fighter,' which was much more than they had witnessed of Jesus.

Like the crowds who were stirred by the religious leaders to demand the release of Barabbas, we are most vulnerable to compromise when it seems that we are losing the battle. We tend to resort to carnal tactics when our spiritual weaponry seems to be delayed or ineffective. Growing weary of prayer and longsuffering, like the prominent Evangelical pastor and author, we acquiesce to manipulating the levers of democracy to accomplish that which we conceded faith would not do in a timely fashion.

I am sympathetic to their cries for relief and vindication. King David often lamented in his psalms with a similar sentiment. He cried:

> *"Rise up, O Judge of the earth; Render punishment to the proud. Lord, how long will the wicked, How long will the wicked triumph? They utter speech, and speak insolent things; All the workers of iniquity boast in themselves. They break in pieces Your people, O Lord, And afflict Your heritage. They slay the widow and the stranger, And murder the fatherless. Yet they say, 'The Lord does not see, Nor does the God of Jacob understand'" (Psalm 94:2-7 KJV).*

Like David, our refrain after such lamentation must be one of faith that God will comfort his people until the day that he avenges them. When we have fasted and prayed but still have not seen the manifestation of God's promise, we must not become disheartened. When desperation prevails, compromise follows.

I'm reminded of when Jesus was tempted by the devil after fasting for forty days. The devil presumed that Jesus was at his weakest point and that he would be most vulnerable to compromise. The devil first tempted Jesus by appealing to his mortality, suggesting that he turn the stones into bread so he (or his cause) would not die. Jesus denied him, understanding that the cause of Christ would not die even if his mortal body did because the word of God, which is eternal, sustains the cause.

Power is demonstrated through our praise, not our protest

The second time, Jesus was tempted by a challenge to his identity. The devil provoked Jesus to prove that he was indeed the Son of God. Jesus, being confident in who he was and the authority given to him by God, was not swayed to tempt God. Jesus, thereby, withstood this second temptation.

Finally, the devil tempted Jesus with power, offering him all the kingdoms of this world if he would only bow and worship Satan. Knowing that all power already belonged to God and, more importantly, not desiring to ascend to such a position, Jesus replied that we should worship only God. In this passage, we see that the devil tempted Jesus with threats or promises to his viability, identity, and authority/power. Jesus resisted each.

Jesus provided the perfect example for us as those who follow him. Despite our growing fatigue with seemingly being pushed to the margins by a society that is growing increasingly decadent, we must remain steadfast in the proclamation of who we are, whose we are, and what we stand for. We recognize that they can never erase the identity of who we are in the world's standing, no matter how much they try to silence us. Our power is demonstrated through our praise, not our protest.

Finally, and above all, capitulation to the devil or those who perpetuate his works is never justified by a promise of power or political influence. All power already belongs to our God. He has allocated it to us to use for his glory in the earth. For God to be glorified in our exercise of such power, it must be used according to his prescription and not according to man's machinations.

CHAPTER 3

THE UNSEEN CHURCH

Christian But Not The Church

In the book of Romans, Paul masterfully and definitively outlines God's plan for salvation and the foundational beliefs of His Church. In the first eight verses of the eighth chapter, Paul makes clear the necessity of Jesus' sacrifice. He explains how the law of the Spirit has accomplished the salvation that the law of sin and death could not accomplish because the written law was *"weakened by the flesh"* (vs. 3). He goes further to assert:

> *"Those who live according to the flesh set their minds on the things of the flesh, but those who live according to the Spirit set their minds on the things of the Spirit. For to set the mind on the flesh is death, but to set the mind on the Spirit is life and peace. For the mind that is set on the flesh is hostile to God, for it does not submit to God's law; indeed, it cannot"* (vs. 5-7).

At the time Paul wrote his letter in Romans 8, Rome was a very powerful city. It was an important center for trade and consequently possessed much wealth and military might. The Roman army controlled all the countries that surrounded the Mediterranean Sea. The city of Rome employed many people in addition to having many slaves.

Unlike most other cities to which Paul wrote letters, the Church in Rome was not established by Paul. At the time of his letter, many in Rome were already followers of Jesus. They had accepted the doctrine of Christ and consequently were not new to this walk of faith. Nonetheless, Paul felt compelled to remind them that their salvation was brought about and maintained through their continual living in the Spirit and not the flesh.

Paul wrote these letters to the Romans for several reasons. First, and perhaps most importantly, he wanted to give a clear explanation of the Gospel – what it takes to gain salvation. Most of the entire book of Romans, in some way, deals with the need for and the plan of salvation. In his writing, Paul also sought to give practical advice about how Christians should behave towards each other (chapters 14-15) and towards their rulers (Romans 13:1-7).

In this passage of scripture, Paul is giving hope to those members of the Church in Rome. He assures them initially that for those who are in Christ, there is no condemnation. This is quite a reassurance because there are many who follow Christ but have differing beliefs about what is truly the heart of God. At times, it becomes difficult to distinguish the heart of God from our own passion. When we presume our passion to be a Godly cause, some will perceive a failure to endorse the idea or activity as a disingenuous allegiance to Christianity.

Sadly, in the public sphere, I have frequently heard some Christians emphatically state, *"You can't be Christian and vote for a Democrat."* I've heard similar assertions from other Christians that you can't be Christian and vote for Donald Trump. Such proclamations from respected and prominent religious leaders can bring condemnation to those who voted differently. I will remind the hearer and the speaker of these idolatrous proclamations that *"there is no condemnation for those who are in Christ Jesus"* (Rom. 8:1). That freedom from condemnation hinges on one very important condition – that is that they must be in Christ. It begs the question, what does it mean to be in Christ?

The United States today has many similarities to Rome during the time of Paul's letter. We are the wealthiest nation in the world and for centuries have, whether rightfully or not, touted ourselves as the leader of the free world. We have certainly enjoyed many blessings from God for reasons God, in His sovereignty, deemed sufficient. But somewhere along the way, we seem to have begun to rely less on God and depend more on our own financial and military might. We have become so independent of God and strayed so far from his will that we even depend more on our own moral code rather than use the Bible as our guide for moral conduct. One thing that is certain is that money and power have the potential to corrupt people who are entrusted with them. It appears to have done so for our governmental officials, our religious leaders, and our country as a whole.

I Timothy 6:10-11 reminds us that *"the love of money is a root of all kinds of evils. It is through this craving that some have wandered away from the faith and pierced themselves with many pangs."* Even our religious leaders have been so eager for money, fame, wealth, and large mega-churches that they have compromised their faith. Soon, as the Bible predicts, they will be pierced with many griefs. We have wandered so far from faith that now it is often difficult to distinguish the church from the world. We try to perpetrate as if we are the Church by using the language of the church and supporting the supposed causes of the Church, but we are far from the Godly representation of the True Church.

The Bible says that all of creation travails in great pain, longing for God to finally reveal who his children really are (Rom. 8:19). Creation is groaning because instead of being salted by the true Church, the impostors make much noise, proclaiming to be such while denying the power thereof (2 Tim. 3:5). Paul warns us to avoid such people. They profess to be Christian, but their values and behaviors demonstrate that they are not the Godly representation of The Church. They might be Christian, but they are not The Church!

> *"Cry aloud, spare not, lift up thy voice like a trumpet, and show my people their transgression, and the house of Jacob their sins. For day after day they seek me out; they seem eager to know my ways, as if they were a nation that does what is right and has not forsaken the commands of its God. They ask me for just decisions and seem eager for God to come near them. 'Why have we fasted,' they say, 'and you*

have not seen it? Why have we humbled ourselves, and you have not noticed?' Yet on the day of your fasting you do as you please and exploit all your workers. Your fasting ends in quarreling and strife, and in striking each other with wicked fists. You cannot fast as you do today and expect your voice to be heard on high" (Isa. 58:1-4).

See, the people thought it would be sufficient to perform all the acts and say the words of the church without being The Church. This is absolutely not acceptable. The prophet goes further to show what The Church would do instead. Such is the fast that God calls for, *"to loose the chains of injustice and untie the cords of the yoke, to set the oppressed free and break every yoke... to share your food with the hungry and to provide the poor wanderer with shelter – when you see the naked, to clothe them, and not to turn away from your own flesh and blood"* (vs. 6-7). When The Church becomes this, the Bible says, our light will break forth, healing will come, and God will answer our prayers (vs. 8-9).

The Church is not identified by its actions but by its nature

---

Yet, creation continues to groan and travail for the manifestation of the sons of God because our light has not yet broken forth. The book of Romans tells us that all of creation groans. If we were to interpret the Bible, we would agree that creation includes animals, fish, vegetation, and climate. These all suffer because Christians continue to not be The Church. A remnant of them has been content being boisterous impostors, proclaiming to the world, "We are the ambassadors of God – the arbiters of morality in the earth."

The impostors say, "We are the Church because we support legislation that seeks to prevent gay marriage. We are surely the church because we appointed conservative federal judges and Supreme Court justices. We are the church because our efforts, no matter how unscrupulous, were successful in overturning Roe vs Wade. And now, the most innocent of lives will be spared. We must be the church because we have elected a man to office who is going to restore religious freedom when we elect him a second time. Then, the church will no longer be persecuted by ungodly and immoral people." No, these are not the representation of The Church! At least not Jesus' Church.

The impostors are identified when the goals and victories they tout contradict the written word of God. The scripture tells us that the law is weak and that it cannot produce righteousness. The law cannot be fulfilled in legislation but only in those who live, not after the flesh but after the spirit. Paul admonished the church in Rome that God had set them free from the law. Yet, they continued to defend and pursue more feckless laws. If God's written law was insufficient, they arrogantly presume that they should make their own that somehow will be more effective than God's. It will only be effective in appeasing their thirst for power and control. It will have no righteous or eternal benefit, according to scripture.

These impostors remain anxious about the threat of persecution. Again, they seek legislation to protect them from the persecution God foretold they would experience. Religious liberty is a fabrication of man. Throughout its existence, persons who followed Christ have been persecuted. Jesus warned us that it would continue. Yet, there is not a single scripture that instructs us on mechanisms to put an end to it and usher in this so-called religious liberty.

The impostors are so fearful of persecution that they would place their faith in a man who, by his own admission, has never had to ask God for forgiveness. To justify it, they will convince themselves that he has found or will find God while in the position of power they bestowed upon him. This merely illuminates the extent of their fear and the fervor of their quest for power.

By contrast, The Church is not identified by its actions but by its nature. The Church is not identified by the end result but by the method used to accomplish the end. It could be argued that the things the impostors support are laudable causes, but if the method is not Godly, the work is done in vain. God doesn't effect change through the law; He affects change through the heart. Rather than ministering to the hearts of man by very practical and meaningful methods as outlined in Isaiah 58, the impostors would rather return again to the weak and ineffective Law to bring righteousness. They continue to do the exact opposite of what was required for God to hear their cries.

God doesn't effect change through the law;
He affects change through the heart

Rather than loose the chains of injustice, they minimize and dismiss it as non-existent. Some are so bold to claim that it never happened or that it was actually beneficial in some obscure way. Rather than set the oppressed free, they seek to maintain or expand the oppression. Rather than sharing food with the hungry, they seek to remove every charitable governmental act (e.g., welfare and health insurance). They allege that while the government should involve itself in some moral matters, others should be left to individuals and charitable organizations like churches. Rather than provide the foreigners with shelter, they seek to build a wall to prevent them from wandering into our land. Should a migrant enter our land, they prefer to criminalize the individual and inflict harsh, inhumane punishments on him.

Fueled by religious conservatism and determined impostors, America, and other democratic nations have become selfish people moved not by compassion but by greed and a quest for power. They have forsaken the foreigners and the disenfranchised in favor of political and economic clout. Still, in all these things, the impostors purport to be ambassadors of Jesus Christ. That façade ends with the manifestation of the real people of God – The Church.

The Church knows that they will endure persecution for the sake of Christ, and no man, least of all one who claims he has no need for forgiveness, is able to protect them from eventual persecution. The Church believes I Corinthians 4:12, which says, *"We work hard with our own hands. When we are cursed, we bless, when we are persecuted, we endure it."* They believe Matthew 5:10-12: *"Blessed are those who are persecuted because of righteousness, for theirs is the kingdom of heaven. Blessed are you when people insult you, persecute you, and falsely say all kinds of evil against you because of me. Rejoice and be glad, because great is your reward in heaven, for in the same way they persecuted the prophets who were before you."*

The Church is not relegated to silence by threats to remove tax breaks or 501(c)(3) status for speaking God's truth. They recognize that this is not persecution. They also understand that the prohibition of praying in public schools is not persecution. It's the way of the world. The Church knows that efforts to prevent you from discriminating against someone because their religious beliefs are different from yours are not persecution. We haven't begun to see persecution yet, but The Church is preparing for it.

The Church are those Christ followers who, like God, love justice. Those who believe an injustice anywhere is an injustice everywhere. They fight for the restoration of justice. They work hard to loose the bands of oppression. They live to feed the hungry and are compassionate to the foreigner in their land. When they see the naked, they clothe them, even if it costs them greatly. The Church is those who have a true relationship with Christ and are not just doers of good. The Church recognizes that in the absence of a relationship with Jesus Christ, even the good that we do are considered works of iniquity (Matthew 7:21-23).

The Church is led by the Spirit of God (Romans 8:14) and distinguishes itself from the impostors because it no longer alienates itself from Christ by seeking the law (Galatians 5). In Matthew 16, Jesus warned his disciples to beware of the impostors – the Pharisees and Sadducees. The Church does not worship God only with their mouths, as the impostors do. But their hearts are subjugated to the will of God. They have the appearance of godliness and also embrace the power thereof.

The Church never denigrates the effectiveness of God's redemptive power by preferring carnal mechanisms to accomplish its goals. They understand that though the world seems to have the unfettered ability to teach heresy, the God of The Church is greater than the god of this world. But the impostors, like some of the people Paul admonished in Rome, have forgotten or simply ignored this truth. God, therefore, has ordained a prophet to lift up his voice like a trumpet and show the impostors their transgressions.

Process Preempts Product

As previously mentioned, God is more concerned with the means than the end result. In the early 1990s, I had a series of impactful and God-inspired dreams. On three different occasions over a period of about 6 months, I had a recurring dream about a miraculous resurrection from the dead that would take place in the midst of a worship service. In the first dream, God revealed that he desires to do such miracles. In the second, God confirmed that he would do these miracles and desired to use me in doing so if I had sufficient faith. The third dream was the most impactful and most relevant for this discussion.

As with the previous two dreams, we found ourselves at a funeral. This was no ordinary funeral because it did not reflect the grief that is usually experienced during the funeral of a loved one. While the dead body was present for viewing, the funeral attendees paid little attention to it. Instead, they focused on worshiping God just for who he is. There was no request attached to the motive for our worship, and the worship was not inspired by an intensely emotional experience. Such unadulterated worship was apparently pleasing to God. Consequently, he performed a miracle, raising the body from death in the midst of our earnest praise.

In the absence of redemption, the performance of a reparative act is useless

---

Upon witnessing this miracle, everyone in the church fell to their knees and worshipped God all the more. Everyone did this except one person. It seemed that I was the only one who noticed or cared that the one person who didn't worship God was the one who was himself raised from the dead. God drew my attention again to the man and quietly whispered to me that all the people in the church were deceived. He said, "The man doesn't worship me because he can't. He can't worship me because I am not his god, and I did not raise him from the dead."

In this dream, the Lord cautioned me not to be so impressed by the product that I fail to discern the process. The process is important! The more subtle but equally important message was that many Christians, at different stages of growth in their faith, would easily be deceived by focusing on the miracle. By doing so, they would ignore how their infatuation would impact their allegiance to the miracle worker.

"For there shall arise false Christs, and false prophets, and shall show great signs and wonders; insomuch that, if it were possible, they shall deceive the very elect" (Matthew 24:24 KJV). God reminded me that wherever there is the genuine, there will also be the counterfeit. In the seventh & eighth chapters of Exodus, we learn that for each miracle Moses and Aaron performed, Pharaoh's sorcerers duplicated. It wasn't until the miracles had been spiritually interrogated that there was a discernment that the God of Moses was the true living God.

I am deeply troubled when I hear devout Christians say things like, "I don't care about the character or lies of my elected representative as long as he is implementing policies I support." I'm equally concerned when I hear people excuse the racist or misogynistic behaviors of other legislators because of their past good deeds or potential future promises to help the communities or individuals they've marginalized. Understand me, I believe in the power of redemption, as was Saul impacted in his conversion to Paul. However, without true repentance and genuine contrition, redemption is not possible. In the absence of redemption, the performance of a reparative act is useless. The heart of the man (or woman) remains dark. Consequently, his or her works remain dark.

More concerning to me is that many Christians have obviated the power of and need for redemption through the blood of Jesus - so long as good deeds or 'godly policies' are implemented. As long as the individual is producing a product they can endorse, the process is irrelevant. This sentiment is destructive to the souls of man. If Jesus viewed such a person's seemingly good works as works of iniquity (Matthew 7:22-23), we should. These are inarguably good deeds, and some might contend that the kingdom of God was nonetheless advanced by the actions of these fallible men and women. But Jesus makes clear that the product or outcome is not his priority.

Like Pharaoh's sorcerers duplicated the wonders that Moses and Aaron performed, and like the man in my dream who was resurrected, signs, wonders, miracles, and policies can and will be accomplished by the ungodly. These are the same people whom Jesus will rebuke because they never had a true relationship with him. The works of their efforts, though lauded by man, are deemed iniquity by the eternal God.

Zealous to gain legislative favor for political agendas that they deem to be godly, many have endorsed and advocated for the unredeemed. In the process, they have forsaken or subverted a godly process. The scripture serves notice that we will give an account for such actions. *"For we [believers will be called to account and] must all appear before the judgment seat of Christ, so that each one may be repaid for what has been done in the body, whether good or bad [that is, each will be held responsible for his actions, purposes, goals, motives--the use or misuse of his time, opportunities and abilities]"* (2 Cor. 5:10 AMP).

The process is important because the world is watching how Christians comport themselves. When they see the 'by any means necessary' approach of the impostors to achieve legislative gains, they rightly cry out, "Hypocrisy!" They decry that those in the church provide no better example of righteousness than those whom they call sinners. Jesus gave the following charge to his disciples, saying,

> *"You are the salt of the earth, but if salt has lost its taste, how shall its saltiness be restored? It is no longer good for anything except to be thrown out and trampled under people's feet. You are the light of the world. A city set on a hill cannot be hidden. Nor do people light a lamp and put it under a basket, but on a stand, and it gives light to all in the house. In the same way, let your light shine before others, so that they may see your good works and give glory to your Father who is in heaven"* (Matt. 5:13-16).

When our methods mirror the methods of the world, our witness is of no value. Sadly, in some cases, the methods employed by the impostors are even worse than those employed by the world. Then, their witness is good for nothing but to be thrown out and trampled under people's feet, Jesus said.

As ambassadors for Christ on earth, our methods and tactics should be unimpeachable. A light that is set upon a hill should not be hidden. If we have to perform our deeds under a shroud of secrecy, it cannot be the light that compels others to glorify God. If it is done with unabashed boldness but does not exemplify God's method and virtue, then it is dimly lit and still of no value to onlookers.

Christians need to stop at once, trying to have one foot in the world and its systems and the other foot in the Kingdom of God. The angel of the Lord said to the Church of Laodicea, *"I know your works: you are neither cold nor hot. Would that you were either cold or hot! So, because you are lukewarm, and neither hot nor cold, I will spit you out of my mouth"* (Rev. 3:15-16). This behavior by Evangelicals will be met with the same rebuff. You cannot love, and certainly cannot exploit, the world's system and claim to love God also. Attempts to do so are repulsive and nauseating to God.

The hypocrisy of Evangelicals has been unashamedly on full display over the past few years. Apart from an unequivocal endorsement and defense of Donald Trump, we see that they endorse underhanded political gesturing – anything necessary to accomplish their legislative goal.

In 2016, after the death of Justice Antonin Scalia, President Obama was charged with the authority to appoint another Supreme Court Justice. In March 2016, he nominated Merrick Garland. Rather than succumb to precedent, Republicans in the Senate prevented the appointment, asserting a new claim that it would be unethical to appoint a justice during the last year of a presidency so close to the election. They argued that it should be deferred until after the election, some eight months later. At the time, they claimed that if the situation were reversed and the President were a Republican, they would uphold the same position. Obama was denied his right to appoint Merrick

Garland to the Supreme Court. Later that year, Trump won the presidency and successfully appointed Neil Gorsuch in April 2017.

On September 18, 2020, Justice Ruth Bader Ginsburg died of metastatic pancreatic cancer less than two months before the presidential election. Eight days later, Amy Coney Barrett was nominated by President Trump, and less than four weeks before the presidential election, she was confirmed to the seat. There was no greater display of hypocrisy of Senate Republicans than this, and Evangelicals celebrated while the world watched.

I will not belabor the point by enumerating the many other instances, including gerrymandering, where Evangelicals have compromised their witness by supporting or endorsing unethical tactics to achieve legislative and judicial victories. My greater concern is for those who would come to Jesus, but because of the example set before them, they are repelled. Jesus said to his disciples, *"It is impossible but that offences will come: but woe unto him, through whom they come! It were better for him that a millstone were hanged about his neck, and he cast into the sea, than that he should offend one of these little ones"* (Luke 17:1-2 KJV). In this context, Jesus uses the word offense to mean placing an obstacle to prevent one of the lost from coming to him.

To those who would argue that the good of the result overshadows the negative short-term press about the methods, remember the scriptures require that those who are stronger in faith and who exercise the liberty provided through Christ Jesus defer to those who are weak in faith so that they would not be a stumbling block (Romans 14). We should be careful to not cause the good that we do to be evil spoken of. In so doing, our service is acceptable to Christ if we instead pursue that which makes for peace and mutual upbuilding (vs. 16-19).

Jesus, The Liberal

One of the reasons conservatives and White Evangelicals have become so desperate for legislative victories and compromised their values and their witness is their immense fear that liberalism is taking over. Somehow, liberalism is going to taint their children and draw them into a life of depravity and sin, they believe. They've underestimated the power of God, when appropriately employed, relative to the power of the world to influence. The term liberal itself has consequently been villainized and now is used synonymously in some Christian circles with heathens. A historical and biblical exploration of the dreaded concept of liberalism is in order.

The conservative versus liberal animus is not a modern invention. It has a longstanding history extending back to the time when Jesus walked the earth. Conservatism, in its purest sense, can be defined as a commitment to traditional values and ideas with opposition to change or innovation. In this politically charged environment and in recent decades, it has been used to reference the holding of political views that favor free enterprise, private ownership, and socially conservative ideas. The commitment to socially conservative ideals has particularly garnered the unyielding fealty of Evangelicals, who consequently have become a formidable political force. It could be argued that in so doing, Evangelicals, who craftily wield their political might, have abandoned the utility and effectiveness of their most venerable weaponry - faith and prayer. Sadly, many condemn those who choose to abstain from conservative political activism as part of the problem. They label such people as accomplices to the 'liberal takeover' of this country.

Before moving forward, we must also define liberalism. In a rush to misjudgment, the term liberal is interpreted by many conservatives to mean pro-abortion, pro-homosexuality, or socialist. These references often evoke a hostility that clouds the rational interpretation of liberalism as promoting liberty, its root word.

For centuries, "liberal" had pre-political meanings, such as generous, tolerant, or suitable to one of noble or superior status. It promoted ideas of freedom, equality, and justice. It wasn't until 1777, when William Robertson published a book, The History of the Reign of the Emperor Charles V, that the word liberal began to be commonly used in a political way.[7] Its political definition seems to predominate and yet remains poorly defined as a political ideal, apart from simply being the opposite of conservatism. Prior to Robertson's publication, the concept of liberalism or liberty was not new.

Liberalism is broadly referenced in New Testament teachings. From the acts of the new church in bringing all their possessions to the church so they are equally shared among all to the repeated references to the fecklessness of Mosaic law and its fulfillment or subsummation by the law of Christ, New Testament endorsements of liberalism are abundant. Central tenets of liberalism extend past the expulsion of rigid traditional teachings to more ethereal concepts such as equality, fairness, and justice. Liberalism especially focuses on the protection of the poor from the machinations of the rich and powerful. Examples of these are also abundantly evident throughout the New Testament.

Liberalism is also referenced repeatedly in the Old Testament. In Deuteronomy 14 and 15, God instructs his people to give liberally to the Levites, strangers, widows, the poor, and even the slaves. He demands that at the end of every seven years, debts be forgiven to encourage Israelites to remember when they were once bondservants in Egypt. Such welfare and generosity today are viewed by many as socialism. It ignores the assertion of Proverbs 11:25 that the liberal soul shall be enriched.

Isaiah 32:8 (KJV) uses liberal synonymously with noble, *"But the liberal deviseth liberal things; and by liberal things shall he stand."* In the preceding verses, he distinctly references how the poor are mistreated by those who are less liberal, referred to therein as vile people. It is ironic how the scripture references those who are not liberal as vile, but modern Christians do the

---

[7] Robertson, William. *The History of the Reign of the Emperor Charles V.* A new ed. Dublin: W. Whitestone, 1777.

opposite. It is not happenstance that such irony exists. This very scripture references the irony, stating that when righteousness rules, the person who was wrongly called vile will be rightly called noble (or liberal), and the one who was once called bountiful will be rightly called churlish [mean-spirited and impolite] (vs. 5). The religious systems of this world have confounded the definitions, but the Lord will set these perversities right.

Sadly, a perusal of social media posts exposes social and political conservatives as among the most churlish of advocates. The atrocities shouted at people who are considering making what is perceived by many as abominable choices at the abortion clinics seem contradictory to the passion Jesus had for the lost. The concept of hate the sin but love the sinner has all but been abandoned or forgotten in exchange for a more aggressive political takeover by conservatives and evangelicals.

At political conservative political rallies and on conservative television shows, hateful rhetoric abounds. More concerningly, the bellicose rantings of their revered political leaders are cheered with great enthusiasm. There is no public or private repudiation of such base behavior. Instead, it appears to be contagious and extends beyond the boundaries of political gatherings, infiltrating daily casual conversations.

Those who also consume conservative news media are inundated with vitriolic and insulting language by people who are supposed to be delivering news in an objective form. And strangely, or perhaps tellingly, the vile, hateful language is in no way repulsive to them. I personally get embarrassed simply listening to it, especially since it comes from the people who most vociferously claim that they are the righteousness of God on earth. Ironically, tolerance, mercy, and forgiveness seem to be the message of those who are villainized by conservatives for being liberal.

While the Old and New Testaments indeed repeatedly instruct charitable liberalism, we can see that Jesus' teachings often challenged those who were unyieldingly wed to traditional values and ideas - the Pharisees, Sadducees, and

Scribes. These were Jesus' contemporary conservatives. They strictly adhered to and demanded that all people of Jewish descent adhere to Mosaic law.

Under Roman leadership, Sadducees possessed most of the political and economic power in Jewish culture. They assimilated into Greek culture (e.g., Hellenization) and would use any means necessary to maintain the status quo of their positions and peace amongst the Romans. While the Pharisees completely resisted Hellenization, they remained strictly adherent to the written and oral Torah. In fact, they even expounded on it, making their own rules in an effort to seem even holier in man's eyes.

For example, Jewish Law required one day of fasting per year on the Day of Atonement. However, by the time of Jesus' arrival, that frequency had become as often as twice weekly. They believed that if they more fervently exercised their religious or conservative traditions, God would come and deliver them from the evil Romans. Hence, when they recognized that Jesus and his disciples didn't fast, they challenged him on it (Mark 2:18).

Conservatives today have similarly inappropriately extrapolated God's laws to create a litmus test for Christianity. They say, "How can anyone consider himself a Christian and yet support those who promote abortion?" Some go even further to suggest that if one supports choice, they de facto support abortion. For these adamant conservatives, there is no spiritual, political, ethical, or legal rationale for how one can be against abortion and still be for a woman's right to choose.

Of course, the Bible instructs us to not kill and states that hands that spill innocent blood are an abomination to God. We can all rightly and logically conclude that God is against abortion. Certainly, He would, at a minimum, be against elective abortions of convenience. However, political advocacy for pro-life policies or any man-made policies is never advocated in scripture. It certainly is not established as a mandate for the devoted follower of Christ. Yet, it has become the defining position for one who considers himself a conservative.

Much of Jesus' conflicts on earth were instigated by the conservatism (e.g., strict adherence to tradition) of the Pharisees, Sadducees, and Scribes. Whether it was cutting down wheat, healing the sick on the Sabbath, or having the audacity to forgive a man sick of palsy, these conservatives would seek to impugn Jesus for his liberalism. In a practical sense, it is easy to understand why they would do so.

Religious tradition had persisted for hundreds of years before Jesus came on the scene. These traditions led the Jewish people through centuries of oppression. Then, under the governance of the Roman Empire, the Jewish people were economically exploited and subjected to many Pagan views and practices. This made them subject to various religious impositions. The Pharisees seemed well justified in their skepticism.

I imagine the Pharisees felt much like conservatives do today - that their customs and religious traditions are threatened with extinction by the inculcation of liberal thought and practices in their society. The notion that people should be allowed to determine for themselves and their families whether they would serve God or violate his commandments seems to be absurd. Moreover, it has become wholly unacceptable to shun or condemn one who chooses an ungodly lifestyle. If one dared have the audacity to label a behavior such as homosexuality as a sin, it would result in swift indictment by the 'political correctness police.' Certainly, the liberals have gone too far! This sentiment was shared by the Pharisees when they saw Jesus eating and consorting with publicans and sinners (Mark 2:15-17).

In Jewish culture, having a meal together was more than a time to feed for nourishment. It was an important opportunity for intimate fellowship and exchange. This particularly became a sacred event, especially after the Temple was destroyed and the family table essentially became the temple. It was utterly sacrilegious for a Jew to break bread, which historically had been used to symbolize or commemorate a covenant, with sinners. Moreover, Jesus' disciples would do it even without washing their hands. Who would dare enter the temple and perform such sacred acts without washing first? In their conservative minds, the Pharisees were well justified in their disdain for this behavior.

Along comes Jesus with his liberal views, practices, and teachings. He's working on the Sabbath, participating in sacred activities with sinners. In the process, he upset the religious status quo. Not only that, but he's also threatening their political clout. He dared to have the audacity to stand in the synagogue and profess his liberal manifesto, *"The Spirit of the Lord is upon me, because he hath anointed me to preach the gospel to the poor; he hath sent me to heal the brokenhearted, to preach deliverance to the captives, and recovering of sight to the blind, to set at liberty them that are bruised"* (Luke 4:18 KJV). As could be expected, the conservatives were infuriated at this saying and threw him out of the city (vs. 29).

The liberal teachings of Jesus not only involved topics of religious importance, but he also espoused liberal economic beliefs. One such example is found in Luke 14, *"But when you give a feast, invite the poor, the crippled, the lame, the blind, and you will be blessed, because they cannot repay you. For you will be repaid at the resurrection of the just."* (vs. 13-14). Some would even consider his economic leanings socialist when he instructed the rich man who desired to enter the kingdom of God to sell all that he had and give it to the poor (Luke 18:18-23).

Eventually, Jesus' liberal teachings, which were viewed as contrary to the traditional law, caused him to be delivered to Pilate for crucifixion at the demand of the conservative Pharisees and Sadducees. However, his precepts were carried out and shared by his apostles and disciples, who, in various scriptures, introduced teachings that seemed contrary to the traditional law. Instead, they represented the spirit of the law.

Paul, in 2 Corinthians 3:17, sums it up nicely by saying, *"Now the Lord is that Spirit: and where the Spirit of the Lord is, there is liberty."* A dispensation of grace is afforded to all who believe in the redemptive power of Christ. We are no longer slaves to the law but are set free by the spirit of the law, in Christ Jesus. The transformation that occurs when a soul is submitted to God occurs individually at the level of the heart, not at the ballot box or within a legislative body. This is the liberalism that Jesus died for and desires to see enacted in his body until he returns.

The liberalism that Jesus espouses will always be opposed by conservatives who consider them to have derived from inimical sources. The laws and traditions of conservatism arose from a need for the carnal man to recognize or become conscious of sin (Romans 5:13, Romans 4:15). But, after Jesus himself fulfilled the law, our charge became the fulfillment of the spirit of the law. In so doing, we walk in the liberty, nobility, equality, and justice - the liberalism that Jesus came to bring.

> *"There is therefore now no condemnation to them which are in Christ Jesus, who walk not after the flesh, but after the Spirit. For the law of the Spirit of life in Christ Jesus hath made me free from the law of sin and death. For what the law could not do, in that it was weak through the flesh, God sending his own Son in the likeness of sinful flesh, and for sin, condemned sin in the flesh: That the righteousness of the law might be fulfilled in us, who walk not after the flesh, but after the Spirit. For they that are after the flesh do mind the things of the flesh; but they that are after the Spirit the things of the Spirit. For to be carnally minded is death; but to be spiritually minded is life and peace. Because the carnal mind is enmity against God: for it is not subject to the law of God, neither indeed can be. So then they that are in the flesh cannot please God"* (Romans 8:1-8).

CHAPTER 4

THE WAY THAT SEEMS RIGHT

Ours is the Kingdom

The ultimate goal of Evangelicalism is not the spreading of the Gospel of Jesus Christ. Rather, it is the attainment of political authority and rule. Many Evangelicals share the belief that we have a God-given authority and mandate to subject the kingdoms of this world to the kingdom of our God. Consequently, they feel emboldened to use the levers of Democracy to accomplish this goal, even if accomplished through ill-gotten means. Worse yet, they will wrongly apply scripture to legitimize their objective.

They confuse the dominion that God declared in Genesis to mean domination over the world and all of its systems. "And God said, Let us make man in our image, after our likeness: and let them have dominion over the fish of the sea, and over the fowl of the air, and over the cattle, and over all the earth, and over every creeping thing that creepeth upon the earth" (Gen. 1:26 KJV). For clarity, the scripture names animals, insects, and vermin (e.g., creeping things). It does not give us dominion over other humans and world systems, as many Evangelicals would purport.

Dominion can be defined as sovereignty or control. It is also used to refer to the territory or government under the control of one who has dominion. Taken together, this supports the conclusion of many Evangelicals who believe we are to have sovereign control of the governments and territories of this world. They allege that though we lost dominion with the sins of Adam and Eve, Jesus reclaimed it on our behalf with his sacrifice.

The rationale for such belief is Jesus' post-resurrection proclamation, "All authority in heaven and on earth has been given to me" (Matt. 28:18). He then commissioned his disciples to "Go therefore and make disciples of all nations, baptizing them in the name of the Father and of the Son and of the Holy Spirit, teaching them to observe all that I have commanded you. And behold, I am with you always, to the end of the age" (vs. 19-20).

That commission is interpreted by many to be an endowment of his followers to be his ambassadors. It logically follows, for many, that this ambassadorship is equipped with the delegated power and authority of Jesus. Thus, if Jesus has all authority, his ambassadors also have all delegated authority. Besides, the scripture already tells us that Jesus had already given us the keys to the kingdom of heaven and authorized us to bind and loose things on earth and heaven (Matt. 16:19). Such interpretations, I believe, are misguided. Indulge me while I explain the basis for my belief.

In Matthew 16, the religious leaders of the time, the Pharisees and Sadducees, sought multiple ways to ensnare Jesus because he threatened to disrupt their current political order and power. They asked Jesus to prove that he was the Messiah. They requested a sign despite having previously witnessed him heal the sick and cast out demons. Instead of allowing these miracles to be sufficient proof, they alleged that Jesus performed these miracles through the power of Satan (Matt. 12:24). In so doing, they began laying the foundation for their ploy to eradicate Jesus and his influence.

Jesus recognized that his message and presence threatened the oppressive establishment of the Pharisees and Sadducees if people would actually embrace and embody his teaching. But he also recognized that no sign or wonder would persuade them from their pursuits to maintain their power. He responded, informing them that "no sign will be given to it except the sign of Jonah" (Matt. 16:4).

Jonah, after three days of being in a metaphorical grave (e.g., the belly's whale), rose and preached a message of redemption to the people of Nineveh. The people then repented and were saved. Jesus was signifying that the only sign Pharisees would receive would be the redemptive power of his crucifixion and resurrection. In a sense, he was announcing that his message would prevail despite their attempts to thwart it and maintain their oppressive regime. Moreover, he wouldn't have to physically overthrow their kingdom to establish his own.

After the encounter, Jesus warned his disciples, "Watch and beware of the leaven of the Pharisees and Sadducees" (vs. 6). They were confounded initially by what he was saying, but Jesus, at this moment was telling them to beware of religious traditions that seek to maintain hierarchical socioeconomic and political power through the oppression of others. While the disciples might or might not have been aware of the ultimate goal of the Pharisees and Sadducees, Jesus was. He admonished them to not adopt their ways.

It must not be overlooked that this discourse and the profound interaction that occurred thereafter happened along the road to Caesarea Philippi. Caesarea Philippi was a rock-faced city where a pagan temple was built to honor the Greek god, Pan. Pan was said to be the god of victory in battle, hunting, herding, music, and related activities. Before the Greek gods arrived on the scene, Baal was reported to have been worshipped there. Archaeologists have identified 14 pagan temples that have occupied this site.[8]

As Jesus and his disciples entered the district, it must not have been lost on his disciples that this was a region fraught with pagan worship. Jesus then asks the question of his disciples, "Who do people say that the Son of Man is?" And they said, "Some say John the Baptist, others say Elijah, and others Jeremiah or

---

[8] Andrea M. Berlin, "The Archaeology of Ritual: The Sanctuary of Pan at Banias/Caesarea Philippi," *Bulletin of the American Schools of Oriental Research* 315 (August 1999): 27–45, https://doi.org/10.2307/1357531.

one of the prophets" (vs. 13-14). Jesus then asked his disciples, "'But who do you say that I am?' Simon Peter replied, 'You are the Christ, the Son of the living God.' And Jesus answered him, 'Blessed are you, Simon Bar-Jonah! For flesh and blood has not revealed this to you, but my Father who is in heaven. And I tell you, you are Peter, and on this rock I will build my church, and the gates of hell shall not prevail against it'" (vs. 15-18).

This scripture is among the most frequently quoted in all of Christianity. It assures the Believer that no force or effort of the world will ever prevail against the Church that Jesus declared he would establish. However, a few key findings must be further elucidated in this exchange.

First, when Peter had his profound revelation, Jesus responded and acknowledged that Peter knew who Jesus was and Jesus knew who Peter was. Jesus was saying that he would establish his Church on a relationship with the Truth – Jesus, the way, the truth, and the life (John 14:6). The Pharisees had only the letter of the law. They never sought to establish a relationship with the Truth. Consequently, their kingdom, or rule, would be temporary and potentially overthrown. The kingdom established on a relationship with The Truth would be indestructible.

Jesus was very intentional about what he said, to whom he said it, how he said it, and when he said it. Standing in a district that represented centuries of ongoing pagan worship, Jesus made the declaration that 'upon this rock' he would build his church. Theologians have posited that Jesus chose the word rock because Peter's name is interpreted as such, and that might be the case, at least in part. However, it should not be ignored that the entire district of pagan worship was etched within the walls of what many of the locals considered to be a glorious rock city.

It was a place in which the systems of the time were well-established and accepted. While the religions that were practiced upon that rock were numerous in times past, Jesus was likely communicating that upon that rock, or in the midst of worldly and pagan worship and surrounded by ungodly systems and oppressive forces, he would build his Church. And nothing will be able to stop it.

The Church that Jesus intended to build did not have to be surrounded by accouterments of righteousness. There was no need for Jesus to overthrow the existing governments to establish his kingdom. He would confoundingly establish his spiritual rule right in the middle of worldly chaos. And to all those who would submit to his kingdom, he said, "I'm going to give you the keys of the kingdom of heaven." But remember, he first gave the admonition, "Watch and beware of the leaven of the Pharisees and Sadducees."

The power Jesus bestowed upon his disciples then, and you and me today, was a spiritual power. Regardless of misguided perceptions and goals influenced by the leaven of Evangelicals, Jesus intends for us to execute his theocratic rule using the spiritual weapons he provided us, not the carnal weapons of this world.

The evangelical mind presumes that because we have been afforded certain authority and rights under the constitutions of our nations, we have the divine responsibility and charge to institute the kingdom of God through exercising and manipulating the levers of Democracy. If they can recruit sufficient numbers in key areas of influence, even though they might not represent the majority, they can impose their will upon the necks of unwilling people. Jesus rebuked this strategy of the Pharisees. He warned, "They tie up heavy burdens, hard to bear, and lay them on people's shoulders, but they themselves are not willing to move them with their finger.... But woe to you, scribes and Pharisees, hypocrites! For you shut the kingdom of heaven in people's faces. For you neither enter yourselves nor allow those who would enter to go in" (Matt. 23:4, 13).

Few heeded Jesus's admonishment. I am not so foolish as to presume that my words would be any more persuasive. Nonetheless, my charge is to identify the strategy or the leaven of the Pharisees and Sadducees.

That Jesus' warning to his disciples had a political meaning is evidenced by Mark's accounting of the warning. Mark writes, "Watch out! Beware of the leaven of the Pharisees, and the leaven of Herod" (Mark 8:15). Mark specifically mentions Herod. He doesn't specify whether it was Herod the Great or his sons, Herod Antipas, Herod Archelaus, or Herod Philip. Even though Herod Antipas was the tetrarch of Galilee after Herod the Great died, it is possible that Jesus was referring to the whole Herodian line of rulership. As such, Jesus was warning his disciples to be leery of those who aspire to rule this world (kosmos). His admonishment was to not adopt their ways and aspirations.

Under the dictatorship of Julius Caesar, Herod's father, Antipater the Idumaean, was charged with oversight of public affairs in Judea. Through nepotistic relationships and the favor his father enjoyed with Caesar, Herod rose to power.[9] Around 47 BCE, Herod was appointed provincial governor of Galilee. In that role, Herod enjoyed many successes. He also cultivated a good relationship with the acting Roman governor of Syria, Sextus Caesar. Sextus Caesar appointed Herod as general of Coelesyria and Samaria, greatly expanding his realm of influence. He enjoyed the favor of the Roman empire while being despised by the Jewish Sanhedrin for his acts of brutality.

Five or six years later, Herod was promoted again. This time, he was appointed as a Tetrarch to support Hyrcanus II, who was named King of the Jews. When Hyrcanus II lost his rule to his cousin, Antigonus, Herod rushed to Rome to advocate for the reinstitution of Hyrcanus II as king. In an unexpected turn of events, Herod was instead named by the Roman Senate to assume the kingship. He returned and defeated Antigonus, who had stolen the throne from his cousin. In an attempt to secure his claim to the throne and gain Jewish favor, a clearly political move, Herod married the granddaughter of Hyrcanus II, Mariamne. To further solidify his position of influence, he banished his previous wife and son. Thus began the Herodian Dynasty.

Whether Herod was Jewish or not is a matter of scholarly debate. Many believe that he professed to be Jewish, but his behaviors never mirrored those espoused by Jewish faith. Apart from banishing his first wife and young son, he later executed Mariamne, his second wife. It appears that Herod was willing to do whatever it took to maintain his position of power and sociopolitical authority.

---

[9] Wikipedia Contributors, "Herod the Great," Wikipedia (Wikimedia Foundation, August 11, 2024), https://en.wikipedia.org/wiki/Herod_the_Great#CITEREFThe_Jewish_War.

Prior to Herod's reign, Judea had been under the rulership of the Jewish people, the Hasmonean kings, from 140 to 63 BCE. Even after being brought under Roman subjection, the Hasmonean kings kept their titles until Herod overthrew Antigonus. Anyone or anything that threatened his maintenance of power was met with brutal and lethal opposition.

Herod's Jewish mother-in-law, Alexandra (Mariamne's mother), sought to secretly restore Hasmonean leadership back to the people of Judea by requesting that the leader of Rome appoint a Hasmonean Jew, Aristobulus, as High Priest. Fearful of how this might challenge his rulership, Herod ordered Aristobulus to be assassinated when he learned of the plan.

It has been suggested that Herod used secret police to spy on the general population to report to him how the populace felt toward him. He prohibited protests and had opponents removed by force, if necessary. It was clear that Herod had no intention of ever relinquishing power. As long as he could curry favor with the Roman Empire and feign allegiance to the Jewish population, he would maintain his position. Anything that threatened to challenge Herod's authority would be extinguished quickly. This is presumably why he issued the decree to kill all the male children born in Judea when it was prophesied that Jesus would be born. He knew the Jewish tradition heralded the Messiah as the delivering king of the Jews. He wanted to ensure that his reign would not be threatened by it.

Herod was a cunning king. He understood that to be most effective, he needed to appease the Roman Empire and enlist the support of Jewish religious leaders that might hopefully quiet the people of the land of Judea. His appeasement, or bribe, to the Jewish inhabitants, was to build the second Jewish Temple. Surely, there would be many who so desperately longed for the rebuilding of their temple that they would overlook his other, more atrocious behavior. The Jewish people knew, prima facie, that Herod's profession of Judaism was perfunctory. However, several embraced him because of his gratuitous offerings. These were the so-called Herodians. However, his constant concern for his reputation and purchase of expensive gifts, which emptied the kingdom's coffers, upset most of his Jewish subjects.

Both major sects of Jewish leadership, Pharisees and Sadducees, despised Herod. And his sons were not much better tolerated. But when they had a common enemy, Jesus, the Bible says the Pharisees and the Herodians conspired together to kill him (Mark 3:6). There's a saying that the enemy of my enemy is my friend. No truer words ring true within the sphere of politics. You can have diametrically opposed views, but when you have a common enemy, one who has the potential and influence to remove you both from power, you can unite in an attempt to preserve your personal fight for another day.

The two gospels use different references. One disciple interpreted the warning to be of Sadducees' leaven, and the other disciple heard the warning to beware of Herod's leaven. Could it be that Jesus referenced the Sadducees and Herod synonymously? It is possible. It is also possible that Jesus was denouncing manipulative, secretive, and often unscrupulous tactics employed by Herod to acquire and maintain political power. Honestly, I think it is both.

It was clear that the goal of the Pharisees, Sadducees, and Herod was to keep the people of Judea under subjection. Their tactics were simply different. The Pharisees and Sadducees used the condemning influence of religion. Herod, on the other hand, cared less about how you thought of him as a religious leader. And many Jews could care less whether Herod was a religious leader as long as he promised to fulfill their most passionate wish. To this end, he utilized the coffers of politics in two ways: by exploiting the passions of his subjects or by threatening to extinguish all those who opposed him. Beware of the leaven of the Evangelicals.

The Vulnerability of Passion

Evangelicalism was birthed from the earnest desire of people to share the redemptive message of Jesus Christ. However, through the centuries, it has adopted the core belief that the teaching of conversion must also be accompanied by activism. This adoption propelled Evangelicalism into the heart of the marketplace and political discourse. Evangelicalism has solidified its position as a political force, not to be ignored or minimized, through the systematic recruitment of political candidates. More importantly, these candidates have the vociferous backing of an entire religious institution, organized and aligned by a singular passion for a unified political goal.

Passions can be defined as strong and barely controllable emotions (Oxford Languages Dictionary). The very mention of a thing for which a person is passionate elicits strong emotions that help form firmly held beliefs or opinions called convictions. Convictions compel behavior. Thus, if one seeks to instruct a particular behavior in an individual or group of individuals, an effective strategy is to ignite the passion of that individual or group. When passion is continuously fed by reinforcing information (whether truthful or not), conviction inevitably follows.

Conviction can still occur without the influence of passion. In such cases, it relies more heavily on information that is deemed credible and obtained from a credible source. But when passions are coupled with what one considers credible information, a desired behavior can be more readily prescribed and replicated.

Consider this example: If you or a loved one has ever been brutalized by a police officer, there is a good probability that your next encounter with a police officer, regardless of his demeanor, race, tone, or size, will likely evoke a strong emotional response. You will likely have some trepidation about the ensuing encounter and will likely modify your behavior as a result. The part that's not readily acknowledged is the strongly held belief or opinion (e.g., conviction) that instructs the behavior. In this case, your behavior has been directly instructed by your conviction, which itself was influenced by a strong emotion or passion.

Now consider another circumstance wherein you have the same passion and conviction about police brutality. A friend recalls to you an encounter with a police officer. During the altercation, the friend was uncooperative with the police and resisted arrest. Most of your friend group, who don't have the same passion as you about police brutality, conceivably would have an easier time identifying the wrong of your friend than you. In fact, you might be the only one among your friends who finds it difficult to agree that the officer acted in good faith. If your passion is too strong and has been repeatedly reinforced by numerous accounts that mirror yours, seeing the body camera footage, which clearly shows the rightful action of the police officer, will be insufficient to persuade you. In this case, your passion has blinded you to objective reasoning and made you susceptible to manipulation and loyal recruitment into efforts of radical police reform.

If you're like me, you have encountered people or are friends with people who have some pretty incredulous beliefs. No amount of persuasion or presentation of facts can even marginally dissuade their conviction. Religion often demands that we not be persuaded from our conviction, as the consequences are too great. Your trusted spiritual leaders, week after week, advise you that there's a world or a group of people out there that seek to destroy you. If, even for a moment, you let your guard down, you too may be swept away in their whirlwind of sin.

Faith, which I intentionally distinguish from religion (particularly organized religion), requires that you believe something that confounds wisdom and defies logic. Otherwise, it isn't faith. Please understand me, I am not disparaging religion and certainly not faith because I practice both. I am, however, trying to illustrate how even an honorable passion can be exploited to produce dishonorable behavior.

Religion is such a powerful weapon because it ties our passions, convictions, and behaviors to an eternal consequence or benefit executed by a sovereign God. To not be influenced by that, you'd have to entirely dismiss the concepts of deity and eternity. While many in our society have done just that, there is a large contingency of the population who haven't. In fact, the more other people do to dismiss it, the more radical those who haven't disregarded it become. Consequently, the exploitation of passions has become a powerful tool for recruitment and radicalization, and Evangelicalism has mastered the art of inculcation and manipulation.

Lack of emotional sobriety distract us from the work of evangelism

While Evangelicals' passions are various, to be politically influential, their goal must be singular and clearly identified. The recruitment of a devout militia must be strategic and emotively compelling to produce unyielding fealty. Consequently, they exploit the various passions of committed Christians. Pro-life policies, religious freedom, defense of heterosexual marriage, eradication of child sex trafficking, and a host of other very emotive issues are fertile ground for recruitment. If they can identify people who have strong personal and emotional ties to any of these issues, they can reinforce their convictions by incessantly evoking the imagery of these atrocities. The end result is the assurance of an ardent allegiance.

In 2 Timothy 4:3-5, Paul encourages the disciples to remain sober-minded, to endure suffering, and to continue the work of an evangelist. He offered this admonition because he realized that passion and lack of emotional sobriety distract us from the work of evangelism and draw us into the work of social and political activism. In Matthew 13, Jesus outlines a series of atrocious events that will herald the end times. Tribulations will abound, and unthinkable acts will take place. But Jesus admonished his disciples to not be alarmed. In no part of the scripture did Jesus persuade them to intervene and attempt to stop the barbarity. But when passions prevail over sobriety, they inspire desperate attempts to quail the suffering.

The systematic exploitation of laudable passions is a formidable instrument for recruiting individuals to a political cause. When presented as a divine mandate, the potency of the tactic is exponentially increased. An added boost of fearmongering and a deluge of hyperbolic or false statements solidifies an unyielding fealty to a political candidate who can successfully intertwine the ingredients.

Take a moment and explore how passionately Evangelicals repudiate the actions of sinners. The public display of their lasciviousness is offensive and intolerable. A mutual disdain for an unabashed engagement in unholy acts bonds otherwise unacquainted Evangelicals in a unified allegiance to abolish any laws that permit these abominations. But isn't it interesting that no matter where Jesus was, he didn't seem to be too bothered by the sin that surrounded him? It wasn't that he endorsed or justified the sin, but instead, he knew that the sinner was his assignment. It was the Pharisees and Sadducees who scoffed at even the prospect of being in the company of sinners.

> *"And when the Pharisees saw this, they said to his disciples, 'Why does your teacher eat with tax collectors and sinners?' But when he heard it, he said, 'Those who are well have no need of a physician, but those who are sick. Go and learn what this means: "I desire mercy, and not sacrifice." For I came not to call the righteous, but sinners'"* (Matt. 9:11-13).

Like Jesus, we should not be too disturbed when the world around us seems overtaken by sin. This is merely a field ripe for harvesting if we utilize the tactics of evangelism rather than evangelicalism. Instead of being repelled in passionate distress when we witness the magnitude and breadth of their sin, we must be moved with compassion toward those who are lost in sin, like Jesus was.

It is impossible to love sinners the way that Jesus loved them and it be perceived as hatred

---

As he moved about casting out demons and healing the sick, the Bible says that Jesus was *"moved with compassion"* (Mark 1:41). He had compassion on the crowd that had been with him for three days and had nothing to eat (Matt.

15:32). Moved by that compassion, he performed the miracle, feeding more than 5,000 people with two fish and five loaves of bread.

Every time Jesus was moved with compassion, he was moved into action to help the people who were hurting or who were in need. His compassion was inspired by love, and he always had the goal of alleviating suffering. Those whom he sought to help never perceived his actions to be oppression. Rather, his teaching and ministry were attractive. They drew the attention of followers who sought to be wherever Jesus was.

If we mimicked Jesus' method and compassion, I believe that we would experience a similar response from the sinner. Instead, we too often repel the sinner, which suggests that there is something erroneous about our method. It is impossible to love sinners the way that Jesus loved them and it be perceived as hatred. If what we believe is motivated by compassion is perceived as anything other than love, we have not appropriately modeled Jesus in that circumstance. I submit that we err when we allow our emotions to get too far out of control.

Few scriptures reference Jesus exhibiting strong emotion or passion. Even when he did, it didn't inform his actions. Those moments when Jesus exhibited the strongest emotions it was often because those who had been around him still hadn't learned to have. Despite having witnessed repeated miracles, the disciples and other followers resorted back to faithless reveling when faced with a challenge.

In another passage, Jesus wept when he arrived at the tomb of Lazarus, who had recently died (John 11:35). It is unclear why Jesus wept. The passage states only that when he saw Mary and the people around her weeping, he was deeply moved in his spirit and troubled greatly. Some people took his weeping to reflect his love for Lazarus. We can be certain that though Jesus exhibited the emotion, he was not moved by his own emotion. The scripture states that he was moved before he wept. Moreover, Jesus would certainly not fret over the death of Lazarus as the people around him did. He knew that he could and would raise Lazarus from the dead. Having confidence in the power and plan of God, Jesus did not need to fear an undesirable or dreaded outcome. Before he wept, he assured Martha that her brother would live again (vs. 23).

Other circumstances wherein Jesus displayed what we would presume to be a strong emotion seem to center around the bondage of legalism. Mark 3 describes a situation where Jesus encountered a disabled man whose care was deemed less important than the observance of a religious tradition. When Jesus entered the synagogue,

> *"a man was there with a withered hand. And they watched Jesus to see whether he would heal him on the Sabbath so that they might accuse him. And he said to the man with the withered hand, 'Come here.' And he said to them, 'Is it lawful on the Sabbath to do good or to do harm, to save life or to kill?' But they were silent. And he looked around at them with anger, grieved at their hardness of heart, and said to the man, 'Stretch out your hand.' He stretched it out, and his hand was restored"* (vs. 1-5).

Here, we see that Jesus was angry at the religious people because of their hard hearts. This emotion was not directed at the sinner. He had compassion for the sinner, even when it meant violating the most sacred rules esteemed by the religious sect.

Another time it appears that Jesus exhibited a strong emotion was when he entered the temple to find merchants selling goods in the house of God. The scripture does not specifically identify that Jesus had an emotional response. Even if he did, as most of us surmise, his ire was not sparked by how he was treated or even how another human was treated, but rather how the sacred place of God's dwelling was treated.

That which angered Jesus distinctly contradicts that which usually upsets us. We are often moved by emotion when the action adversely affects us or some person we love. Rarely do we get emotionally moved by the disrespect or disregard for God, his sacred dwelling place, or the misrepresentation of his precepts. I submit that this is because we prioritize mortal life and fair treatment of ourselves and loved ones over obedience to God. Our passions are misplaced, and consequently, our convictions and behaviors will similarly be misguided.

Perhaps the most informative example of how Jesus managed emotion is how he prayed in the Garden of Gethsemane. He confided in his disciples, *"My soul is very sorrowful, even to death" (Matt. 26:38). For the first time, it appeared that Jesus was emotional about what might happen to himself. Although he prayed for there to be another way for salvation to be wrought, he concluded, "Nevertheless, not as I will, but as you will"* (vs. 39). Jesus demonstrates herein that it is wholly okay for us to desire a different outcome than the one we dread. However, our final conclusion must be, as his was, "Nevertheless, not my will but your will be done, God."

If passions do not advance the fulfillment of scripture, they are misguided

---

If there were a biblical example of a disciple moved by passion more than compassion, it would be Peter. Peter's zeal and strong passion made him a prime target for manipulation by the devil. When in the district of Caesarea Philippi, as mentioned previously, Peter had a great revelation from God. But shortly thereafter, he succumbed to the carnality of his passion. When Jesus tried to warn his disciples that he would be apprehended and killed, Peter, steeped in his emotion, rebuked Jesus. Peter vowed that he would never let such an injustice occur. Jesus said to Peter, *"Get behind me, Satan! You are a hindrance to me. For you are not setting your mind on the things of God, but on the things of man"* (Matt 16:23). That which would have been deemed a chivalrous and selfless act by man was deemed a manipulation by Satan. That is because the seeming valiant gesture was contrary to the fulfillment of the word of God.

On another occasion, when Jesus was about to be apprehended by the Roman soldiers, Peter, moved with passion, cut off the ear of one of the soldiers in an effort to protect Jesus from certain harm. This was a harm that was predicted by the Bible and for which Jesus came to endure. But Peter's humanity could not suffer him to witness such an injustice. Again, Jesus rebuked Peter, saying, *"Put your sword back into its place. For all who take the sword will perish by the sword. Do you think that I cannot appeal to my Father, and he will at once send me more than twelve legions of angels? But how then should the Scriptures be fulfilled, that it must be so?"* (Matt. 26:52-53). Here, Jesus demonstrates that what is most important is the fulfillment of the word of God. If our passions for a cause do not advance the fulfillment of scripture, they are misguided and reflect the manipulation of Satan. No matter how humanly noble the cause might appear, it will eventually result in a work of futility.

Many Evangelicals are exploited because of their righteous concern that the ways of the world are inching out and replacing the Christian principles that have historically predominated in our society. I might argue that the true precepts of Christ have never been fully embraced by those with an evangelical mindset, but for the sake of argument, let's presume they did.

The enactment of legislation that promotes homosexuality as a natural alternative to the biblical representation of marriage infuriates many. Social mandates to incorporate homosexual representation in television shows, award shows, movies, commercials, and even elementary school textbooks are incendiary. Adding to the fury is the ready access to abortion, whether elective or medical. The prospect of losing political influence in a country that was once dominated by White men with Judeo-Christian values is fear-evoking for others. Together, the witnessing of societal denigration into moral depravity, with people engaging in any activity they deem productive for self-gratification, makes the field of recruitment to Evangelicalism grow all the more fertile.

To be clear, I am not suggesting that Christians should be spiritual ostriches, burying our heads in the sand to remain oblivious to all the sin that abounds around us. Of course, Christians should be active in their communities and should advocate for admirable and even godly ideals such as mercy, righteousness, and justice. After all, God loves righteousness and justice (Psalm

33:5), and faith without works is dead (James 2:26). But remember, our penultimate fate is to suffer persecution.

If we think we can subvert an inevitable unjust persecution through the enactment of laws that we think will insulate us, we think with a carnal mind. Peter was rebuked for this effort, and we certainly should be as well. Jesus' focus was the fulfillment of every aspect of the prophesied word of God. As painful as it might be to witness and endure, we must, through faith and with a sober mind, hold firm to the profession of Jesus Christ.

Like David, we might cry out, *"How long will the wicked triumph?"* (Psalm 94:3). But ours is the charge to endure. Rather than being armed with the fury or fear evoked by the strength of our passions, we should look upon the sinner with compassion, always ready to bring health and healing to those whom Jesus considered unwell.

How, then, can such an endeavor be misled? Why would I dare attempt to disparage these efforts to employ our passions to advocate for legislation that resembles godly precepts? Simply put, these endeavors, while honorable, are all carnal in that they relate to the human condition. I do not minimize the importance of ameliorating the condition of human suffering. In fact, I strongly advocate that we do precisely that. The method whereby we do this, however, is key.

The scripture tells us that *"no soldier gets entangled in civilian pursuits, since his aim is to please the one who enlisted him"* (2 Tim. 2:4). Am I suggesting that Christians shouldn't be involved in politics or shouldn't vote? Absolutely not! However, in our engagements, we should always remember that weapons of our warfare are spiritual (2 Cor. 10:4). They are not civilian or carnal. When we place too high an emphasis on using a carnal tool to accomplish a spiritual good, we err and fall victim to the manipulation and influence of Satan.

The Ministry of Compassion

I recognize that my writing up to this point may have been challenging because it seems to harshly criticize efforts that, on their face, appear to be perfectly Christian in nature. I am in no way condemning a just cause, only a perverted motive or method. Most of us accept that we should have pure motives in everything we do. However, the motive can be unveiled by examining the method of the action.

For the believer, the notion that the ends justify the means should not be part of our lexicon. God is more concerned with the means than the end. As the Apostle Paul writes, *"For the weapons of our warfare are not carnal, but mighty through God to the pulling down of strongholds"* (2 Cor. 10:4 KJV). We must spiritually discern the root. Instead, we mistakenly focus primarily on eradicating the fruit. In doing so, we attempt to eliminate the consequence of sin without addressing the sin itself. If you address the cause, the consequence would be non-existent. If you pluck a tree up by the root, it will never produce the evil fruit we seek to eliminate. If the means of our efforts are not executed according to God's instruction, the result will be of no effect anyway. As Jesus taught: *"Every plant which My heavenly Father has not planted will be uprooted"* (Matt. 15:13 NKJV).

Motive can be unveiled by examining the method of the action

Unlike the Pharisees, Jesus was not intimidated by a person's sin. He knew how to get to the heart of the matter – literally and figuratively. As it is written in Hebrews, *"For the word of God is living and powerful, and sharper than any two-edged sword, piercing even to the division of soul and spirit, and of joints and marrow, and is a discerner of the thoughts and intents of the heart"* (Heb. 4:12 NKJV).

In John 4, Jesus encounters a Samaritan woman at the well. Before He approached her, He already knew all the sins that characterized her existence. Yet her sin was not His focus. When He asked her to bring Him some water, her first response was one of shock. As the scripture notes, *"For Jews have no dealings with Samaritans"* (John 4:9 NKJV). The mere fact that He would engage her was atypical and contrary to what another religious observer would expect or condone.

Jesus, on the other hand, was not concerned about what the religious elites might have thought about His consorting with such a person. He knew the woman was not only a Samaritan but that she was considered a prostitute in her own culture. Still, He knew she had value. Jesus was more concerned about her eternal salvation than what others might think or say about His interactions with her. As He later taught, *"For the Son of Man has come to seek and to save that which was lost"* (Luke 19:10 NKJV).

He knew that her salvation could never be achieved by simply telling her to stop fornicating. Even the act of stopping that sin was insufficient to produce salvation. Obviously, the law was insufficient at that time to keep her from sinning. His focus was eternal. Consequently, He could not be distracted by the carnal. Enforcement of the law or religious traditions, He understood, would not prove to have any eternal benefit for her. This aligns with Paul's later teaching: *"Therefore by the deeds of the law no flesh will be justified in His sight, for by the law is the knowledge of sin"* (Rom. 3:20 NKJV).

Seeing past the woman's sin and circumstance, Jesus discerned that this woman was thirsty for something she had never received – something more eternal and valuable. While the Bible doesn't explicitly state her deficiency, its existence was evidenced by the fact she found herself coming back to the same place repeatedly and apparently making the same mistakes over and over.

Jesus could easily have condemned the woman for her sin. He could immediately have told her that it was unethical to sleep with various men. Instead, He offered her water that would quench her thirst forever, saying, *"Whoever drinks of this water will thirst again, but whoever drinks of the water that I shall give him will never thirst. But the water that I shall give him will become in him a fountain of water springing up into everlasting life"* (John 4:13-14 NKJV).

In offering to alleviate her deeper deficiency (i.e., the root) before He acknowledged or addressed her sin (i.e., the fruit), Jesus provided an example of how we should interact with sinners to bring about lasting conversion.

Before we acknowledge a person's sin, we must acknowledge the person and the underlying hurt that produces the sin. The nidus of all sin is separation from God. The Bible says the woman was thirsty, and there are multiple biblical references that connect thirst to the state of being apart from God.

Jesus teaches in the Beatitudes, *"Blessed are those who hunger and thirst for righteousness, for they shall be filled"* (Matt. 5:6 NKJV). Later, He proclaims, *"If anyone thirsts, let him come to Me and drink. He who believes in Me, as the Scripture has said, out of his heart will flow rivers of living water"* (John 7:37-38 NKJV). Jesus Himself, when He was on the cross, cried out only once about His current state of suffering. He didn't moan about the stripes that tore the flesh off His back. He did not complain about the crown of thorns placed on His head or the weight of the cross He dragged up the hill of Golgotha. Not once did He cry out from the agony of stakes being driven through His hands and feet.

In the moment when all the sins of the world were placed upon Him, His eternal Father turned away from Him. For the first time in eternity, Jesus was separated from God by the stain of sin, and He cried out, *"I thirst"* (John 19:28 NKJV). While it is written that Jesus said this to fulfill the scripture in Psalm 69:21, He clearly thirsted. I submit that, unlike any other thirst, this one had spiritual meaning, indicating that He suffered in this new but temporary experience of being apart from God.

In His encounter with the Samaritan woman, Jesus offered her water so that she would never thirst again. He knew that the manifestation of her sin derived from an underlying separation from God. With this water (symbolizing a relationship with the Truth) that He could offer, He could forever eradicate the emptiness that tormented her.

Her acceptance of His offer opened the door for Him to subsequently acknowledge her sin. Even in His acknowledgment of her sin, He was non-judgmental. He didn't condemn her for her sins but simply asked her to go get her husband, offering her the opportunity to openly confess her own sin. As John records, *"Jesus said to her, 'Go, call your husband, and come here.' The woman answered and said, 'I have no husband.' Jesus said to her, 'You have well said, "I have no husband," for you have had five husbands, and the one whom you now have is not your husband; in that you spoke truly'"* (John 4:16-18 NKJV).

Proving her fidelity to her desire for transformation, she confessed that she had no husband despite her ongoing cohabitation with a man. Jesus further revealed that she was living in sin with this man and that she had four others before him. Again, He did this without condemning her. He pointed this out for her benefit and not her judgment. His motive was evidently pure and provided an avenue for the woman's advancement to her next stage of transformation.

Perceiving that Jesus was a prophet, the woman asked the question that was most important to her: How should we worship God? Jesus explained a basic truth to her: She must first know Him and then worship Him in spirit and truth. As He said, *"God is Spirit, and those who worship Him must worship in spirit and truth"* (John 4:24 NKJV).

Let's analyze the progression of events in this encounter:

1. Jesus was willing to engage and affiliate with the unclean and unholy. He knew her sin but prioritized her needs.

2. Jesus offered help to alleviate her suffering or deficiency.

3. The Samaritan woman accepted Jesus' offer.

4. The woman acknowledged her sin before Jesus did.

5. Jesus revealed to her the missing component in her life that would quench her eternal thirst – her separation from God – and introduced her to the way to God.

Note that the first four events occurred before Jesus even acknowledged her sin. If we really want to help people out of sin, we must stop focusing on the sin and its consequences and rather see the underlying suffering or deficiency that produces the sin. Sin is merely the manifestation of an underlying problem – usually a separation from and lack of a genuine relationship with God.

There's a saying that people don't care how much you know until they know how much you care. Through His engagement with the Samaritan woman, Jesus established a rapport of trust. If we are to minister to sinners as Jesus did, we must first demonstrate our genuine desire to be of benefit to that person, wanting nothing in return but their freedom. After we've achieved a certain level of trust and the individual has invited us to speak into their lives, we can engage in discussions about their sin.

Religious pursuits must never be inspired by the pursuit of control or domination

---

Interestingly, the conversation about the woman's sin was initiated by her. Knowing she was not married but was living with a man, Jesus chose not to broach the topic with accusations of guilt. Instead, He allowed her first to feel comfortable sharing aspects of her sin when she was ready to share them. It is foolhardy to expect someone who did not give you permission or with whom you don't have a relationship to receive your critique of their sin 'just because the Bible says so.' They have no idea of your motive or intention and will likely perceive it as condemnation. This Samaritan woman appears not to have felt condemned by Jesus' acknowledgment of her sin. I submit that it was because she felt His genuine concern for her well-being. The door was then opened for repentance, growth, and further evangelism.

When our method is questionable and unartfully executed, one must question the motive for the act. In Jesus' warning that we beware of the leaven of the Pharisees and Sadducees, He was sounding the alarm for us to ensure that religious pursuits must never be inspired by the pursuit of control or domination. If the motive is indeed not to exert control over an individual, then our method should be modified such that it cannot be construed as such.

In Romans 14:16, Paul encourages us to *"not let your good be spoken of as evil."* Some will argue that the context of this was related to eating meat or celebrating a holiday, but the underlying message remains true. He adjures us not to allow any matter of carnal relevance, which has no eternal benefit or consequence to the individual, to be a cause for stumbling for those who are weak in faith. In winning souls for the Kingdom of God, we must be moved by compassion according to the example of Jesus to be most effective.

CHAPTER 5

THE ISSUES OF LIFE

The Sanctity of Life

The Evangelical approach to matters of sin, particularly with hot-button items such as abortion and homosexuality, in no way mirrors Jesus' approach with the Samaritan woman at the well. It seems that their top priority is alleviating the consequence of the sin and not so much the cause. The focus is on making sure that "the baby isn't killed." I submit to you that death is always the consequence of sin. It is written, *"For the wages of sin is death, but the free gift of God is eternal life in Christ Jesus our Lord"* (Rom. 6:23). Yes, it matters that we, whenever possible, try to prevent the consequence, but we should address it from the root.

I realize this statement might challenge some with strong Evangelical convictions, but when a woman contemplates abortion, there are matters weightier than the death of the fetus. These should be of at least similar concern, if not more. Yes, the sparing of the fetus' life should be a priority. However, if we believed the Bible, we would concur with and be assured by the assertion of Ecclesiastes 4:2-3: *"Therefore I praised the dead who were already dead, more than the living who are still alive. Yet, better than both is he who has never existed, who has not seen the evil work that is done under the sun"* (NKJV).

117

I know to many, this sounds sacrilegious. If it offends you that the scripture states this, and I recite it in relationship to abortion, it merely confirms that you esteem mortal life more highly than God does. I am merely a messenger, quoting the Bible.

Now, my heart aches for an aborted fetus, just like any well-intentioned Evangelical. But if we believe the Bible, that baby who is aborted is better off than one who lives and experiences the injustice of this world. Am I justifying abortion? Of course not! I am simply trying to refocus the misplaced affection of my evangelical friends. The woman who aborts the fetus, however, remains alive on earth and in the least favored category, according to the stated scripture. She will likely continue to suffer and possibly suffer more when she tries to reconcile the act of aborting her pregnancy.

If we claim to be pro-life, let's be more emphatically pro-eternal life. By that, I mean let us place a much higher priority on eternal life than we do on mortal life. After all, this is the priority of Jesus and of scripture. As Jesus said, *"For what profit is it to a man if he gains the whole world, and loses his own soul? Or what will a man give in exchange for his soul?"* (Matt. 16:26 NKJV).

The woman who has completed or is considering abortion does not need you or me to immediately shout "Sin!" or "Sinner!" She needs you to, as Jesus did, offer her a drink that will cause her never to thirst again. She needs love, guidance, and help that will cause her never to find herself in the situation of an unwanted pregnancy again. But the Evangelical spirit is so legalistic that it can see nothing as more important than following the law, *"You shall not murder"* (Exod. 20:13 NKJV). I keep repeating because I know the extreme sensitivity of this issue: that abortion is absolutely wrong. But the eternal is much more important than the mortal.

When Jesus healed a man on the Sabbath, it was likely just as egregious to the Pharisees as a woman who commits an abortion is to Evangelicals. However, Jesus could not allow upholding the law to usurp the ministry of life to the man who needed it. While Jesus intended to heal the man, it is evident that He had another goal of demonstrating to the Pharisees that their focus on the law impeded their ability to see and minister to human suffering. As He asked them, *"Is it lawful on the Sabbath to do good or to do evil, to save life or to kill?"* (Mark 3:4 NKJV).

Dogmatic positions on sin impede effective ministry

Many Evangelicals have become so committed to anti-abortion legislation that it prevents them from being able to see the suffering of the women who have abortions. Some find it extremely difficult, if not impossible, to forgive such a woman, let alone continue to engage them on an eternally beneficial level. This is inconsistent with their professions of biblicism and crucicentrism and exemplifies how the leaven of Evangelicalism has poisoned the individual lump. Jesus bore the sin of abortion when He hung on the cross. The woman does not need to bear it again.

A foundational principle that drives the anti-abortion stance of many evangelicals is the concept of the Sanctity of Life. Curiously, it seems that the designation of sanctity is often ascribed only to the lives of fetuses, infants, and children. If it applied to all lives, there would not be a forsaking of the poor and rejection of the foreigner. However, for the purpose of this writing, we will focus on the life of the unborn.

Like my former pastor, many evangelicals cannot endure the atrocity of abortion under any circumstance. I submit that one who has such a perspective will be of no ministerial benefit to a woman who is contemplating abortion. Dogmatic and unyielding positions on sin impede effective ministry to those who desperately need it. To overcome the great obstacle of abortion, Evangelicals must understand why abortion exists. Many presume that abortion is the fruit of selfishness, lasciviousness, and carelessness. Indeed, this might be true, especially in today's society. But more importantly, death (including abortion) is and always has been the consequence of sin. More than anything, God hates sin. God dislikes sin so much that He instituted death as the consequence. Sin is simply disobedience to the word or command of God. Therefore, the consequence of disobedience to God is death.

Upon creation of man, God told Adam and Eve that if they disobeyed Him and ate the fruit of a certain tree in the garden, they would surely die. While some people will argue that God was referring to a spiritual death, I believe differently. Throughout scripture, God offers His people the option to choose life over death. As it is written, *"I call heaven and earth as witnesses today against you, that I have set before you life and death, blessing and cursing; therefore choose life, that both you and your descendants may live"* (Deut. 30:19 NKJV). Having given them an option, God clearly intended the choice to rest in the hands of mankind. If they chose poorly, God would not hesitate to terminate life. This makes clear that there are principles that God values more highly than mortal life. God esteems obedience, integrity, and honesty more highly than human life. How do I know? Because God terminated human life for violations of either of these. Sometimes, that life was that of a so-called 'innocent' child.

The Biblical examples of where God ordered, performed, or permitted the killing of infants and fetuses are numerous. I will present several of them, not as an effort to condone abortion by any means, but rather to demonstrate that God doesn't sanctify mortal life the way we humans do. Moreover, He understands that death and even abortion, in some circumstances, is necessary. I will concede that in these examples, the determination of the appropriateness of the death was made by God and not man.

> ### *God esteems obedience, integrity, and honesty more highly than human life*

According to 1 Samuel 15, God intended to punish the Amalekites for their sin, using death. Through His prophet, God told Saul, *"Now go and attack Amalek, and utterly destroy all that they have, and do not spare them. But kill both man and woman, infant and nursing child, ox and sheep, camel and donkey"* (1 Sam. 15:3 NKJV). Pregnant women were undoubtedly included in this nation of people at the time the commandment was given. An omniscient God clearly knew this. Acknowledging this and other circumstances is incredibly inconvenient to the Evangelical argument and conviction. Here, God is telling His chosen leader to kill pregnant women and the fetuses within them. This truth is unconscionable in the minds of Evangelicals. But it happened at the commandment of God.

To convince Pharaoh to release the people of Israel from captivity in Egypt, God personally sent His angel to kill all the firstborn males of Egypt (Exodus 12). Surely, some of these were neonates. Evangelicals would be astonished at the suggestion that God killed these infants, as it seems to be worse than even late-term abortion. But there's more.

God sovereignly processes righteousness through the perspective of eternity

---

King David sinned by sleeping with Uriah's wife, Bathsheba. She became pregnant with David's child. To cover up this sin, David had Uriah sent to the front line of battle, where he knew Uriah would certainly be killed. God was so displeased with the sins of David that God pronounced that the child that he bore with Bathsheba would die because of the sin. The scripture says, *"Then Nathan departed to his house. And the Lord struck the child that Uriah's wife bore to David, and it became ill"* (2 Sam. 12:15 NKJV). Seven days later, the child died because of the affliction God placed on the child. This was the consequence of David's promiscuity and conniving to cover up the sin.

Perhaps the most disturbing and demonstrative of all examples is the pronouncement by the prophet Elisha to Hazael. In 2 Kings 8, the reputation of Elisha, the prophet, had grown because of his works, including raising a Shunammite woman's son from the dead. King Ben-Hadad, who was sick, heard that Elisha had come to Damascus. The king instructed his servant, Hazael, to take a gift to Elisha and inquire whether the king's sickness was fatal.

Hazael did as he was instructed by the king. *"And Elisha said to him, 'Go, say to him, "You shall certainly recover." However the Lord has shown me that he will really die'"* (2 Kings 8:10 NKJV).

Let's pause for a moment to examine this exchange. We see here that the prophet of God just instructed Hazael to go lie to the king, telling him he would live when the word of the Lord was that the king would certainly die. This is worth noting because it emphasizes how things that seem inconsistent with righteousness in our eyes, God yet commands. Most Christians would agree that an instruction for Hazael to lie to the king is wrong, and not many of us would endorse it as righteous obedience. That is because we process righteousness through our finite understanding. God sovereignly processes righteousness through the perspective of eternity. Remember, sin is simply disobedience to God's command. If God instructs the prophet to tell a lie to the king and the prophet refuses, the prophet sins in his refusal, not in telling the lie.

Elisha does as he is led by God and tells the servant to lie to the king. The scripture says the man of God then began to weep. When Hazael asks why Elisha wept, he replies, *"Because I know the evil that you will do to the children of Israel: Their strongholds you will set on fire, and their young men you will kill with the sword; and you will dash their children, and rip open their women with child"* (2 Kings 8:12 NKJV). Elisha went further and prophesied, *"The Lord has shown me that you will become king over Syria"* (2 Kings 8:13 NKJV).

It strains credulity in the mind of pro-life advocates that God would ever ordain one who aborted tens of thousands of fetuses with such treachery to become king. There is no way to explain this gruesome depiction and foreshadowing by God through His prophet if we insist on using the lens of our understanding or our righteousness. This is, without exception, mass abortion. It would seem untenable that one who commits such an atrocity would be spared his own life, let alone elevated to the position of king. And the kicker is that God knew it would occur! Moreover, He commanded His servant to prophesy it and to do nothing to prevent it.

This undoubtedly perplexes the minds of Evangelicals who believe that at all costs, abortion should be prevented. I suspect that if Elisha were an Evangelical or had the mindset of modern evangelicals, he would not have prophesied the words God instructed. In that case, his disobedience would have been a sin. I am sympathetic to the anguish that such obedience would cause. Presumably, that's why Elisha wept. But he understood the necessity of submission and obedience to God's sovereign instruction.

I am not suggesting that God loves or endorses abortion or any death. But I am saying that in certain circumstances, sovereignly determined by God, He tolerates abortion. I will go further to insist that in His infinite and eternal wisdom, He knows that there are times when abortion is necessary. If we insist that abortion is never necessary, we elevate the influence of our dogma over the sovereign wisdom of God. Our stubborn arrogance and evangelical indoctrination forbid us from acknowledging that, unlike God, we just don't know all the answers, and we don't know the future.

A deed done with good intentions is an offense to God if it is done in disobedience

---

That same argument is used to justify pro-life activism – we don't know what the future would have produced for that aborted fetus. But God does! That future could have been promising for great philanthropic feats or humanitarian accomplishments, or it could have been the nexus to unspeakable evil. Am I attempting to justify abortions of convenience? Absolutely not! What I am saying is that only God truly knows the impetus for one's decision to have an abortion. It is not our authority as ambassadors of Christ to halt all abortions through the enactment of laws that prevent it. Doing such, as previously stated, represents an effort to alleviate the consequence of sin without addressing the root of the sin.

Our focus, as those who seek to evangelize the lost, must be the alleviation of the underlying sin so that the consequence is non-existent. This admonishment will inevitably fall on deaf ears, despite the indelible support of scripture, because the leaven of the Evangelical has closed the ears of many of its followers to the scriptures. Like the Pharisees saw no circumstance under which God would allow violation of the Sabbath, many staunch Evangelicals simply cannot envision a circumstance under which God allowed, let alone ordered, abortions as a consequence of sin. Consequently, they will blithely disregard the scripture's rebuff of their position and persist headstrong in their own conviction. Worse yet, they will misrepresent their own disobedient, self-righteous conviction as a mandate from God. *"Woe to you, scribes and Pharisees, hypocrites!" Jesus would say. "For you are like whitewashed tombs which indeed appear beautiful outwardly, but inside are full of dead men's bones and all uncleanness"* (Matt. 23:27 NKJV).

While God values human life, He also recognizes that it is but a vapor in comparison to eternity. As James writes, *"For what is your life? It is even a vapor that appears for a little time and then vanishes away"* (James 4:14 NKJV). It is here today and gone tomorrow. God always maintains an eternal perspective; He will never esteem mortal life over obedience. We do. We see several examples in the scripture where human life was snuffed out by God because the person(s) was disobedient to God. Even a deed done with good intentions is an offense to God if it is done in disobedience.

When David was transporting the ark of the Lord into the city, it began to shake as they crossed the threshing floor. To prevent the ark from falling, Uzzah reached out to catch it, *"and the anger of the Lord was kindled against Uzzah, and God struck him down there because of his error, and he died there beside the ark of God"* (2 Sam. 6:7 ESV). God killed Ananias and his wife, Sapphira, for lying about bringing all the profits earned from the sale of their land when, in actuality, they held some back for themselves (Acts 5:1-11). Because they both separately lied to God, they were instantly struck dead.

According to today's standards, we would consider these relatively minor infractions. We lie and/or imperfectly follow God's instructions all the time. But God views disobedience and bearing false witness as abominable. It is only by the grace of God that we are not consumed by His wrath when we commit them. It underscores the notion that God esteems obedience more highly than mortal life. Jesus further elucidated the futility of trying to sanctify life. He said, *"For whoever desires to save his life will lose it, but whoever loses his life for My sake will find it"* (Matt. 16:25 NKJV).

By contrast, the leaven of the Evangelicals demands that life, specifically of the unborn, be preserved at all costs or nearly all costs. They exploit relatively few scriptures to support their emphatic position. In doing so, they ignore the context and even the immediately adjacent scriptures to justify their assertion.

The Shedding of Innocent Blood

A favorite reference of Evangelicals concerning abortion is Proverbs 6:16-19, which states:

> *"These six things the Lord hates, Yes, seven are an abomination to Him: A proud look, A lying tongue, Hands that shed innocent blood, A heart that devises wicked plans, Feet that are swift in running to evil, A false witness who speaks lies, And one who sows discord among brethren" (NKJV).*

Our Evangelical friends hone in on the part that describes the shedding of innocent blood as an abomination to God. Indeed, it is. For this reason, I will never refute that it is abhorrent to God. There are a few things that must be mentioned in this regard, however. It is disingenuous to emphasize this one abomination as a justification for endorsing, without limitation, and defending a president who embodies the other six abominations. It seems right to them to ignore the sowing of discord, the feet that swiftly run to evil, the haughtiness, the lying tongue, and false witness of Donald Trump because he promised to appoint judges to the bench that will reverse what is perceived to be the indiscriminate shedding of innocent blood. There is a way that seems right to man, whose end thereof leads to destruction (Prov. 14:12).

Though it can be inferred, this scripture doesn't say that the taking of life itself is abominable. Indeed, the sixth commandment says, *"You shall not murder"* (Exod. 20:13 NKJV). Worthy of note, this commandment chronologically is positioned before (and presumably in higher priority than) the commission of adultery, theft, lying to your neighbor, and coveting your neighbor's wife. But there are five other commandments that precede it. We can infer, based on their stated position, that the first five commandments are of higher priority to God than the latter five. Among the top five are idolatry, making images and bowing unto them, use of God's name in vain, and failing to keep the Sabbath. These all deal with the preservation of our relationship with God and not being deterred or drawn away by any other priority.

> ***When commitment to a cause requires the sacrifice of values, the cause becomes a god unto itself***

Jesus confirms this when He states, *"'You shall love the Lord your God with all your heart, with all your soul, and with all your mind.' This is the first and great commandment. And the second is like it: 'You shall love your neighbor as yourself.' On these two commandments hang all the Law and the Prophets"* (Matt. 22:37-40 NKJV). We are charged to keep all the commandments and not just certain ones. Ideally, we wouldn't rank sins because the Bible tells us that *"whoever shall keep the whole law, and yet stumble in one point, he is guilty of all"* (James 2:10 NKJV). But, if we were to prioritize any commandments, it should be the ones Jesus did – loving God and loving our neighbors. Instead, evangelicalism prioritizes the sixth commandment and seemingly excuses the violation of the first five.

Pro-Lifeism itself has become a god to many evangelicals. The passion of my former pastor was laudable by human standards. However, when a person's commitment to a cause requires the sacrifice and compromise of values, the cause becomes a god unto itself. Increasingly, it demands rigid loyalty and defense, even when offering such requires the abandonment of principles that were previously held in the highest regard. *"You shall have no other gods before Me,"* says the Lord (Exod. 20:3 NKJV) – not even Pro-Lifeism.

The specification of innocent blood suggests that not all deaths are abominable. Ecclesiastes 3 tells us that there is a time for everything – *"A time to be born, And a time to die; ... A time of war, And a time of peace"* (Eccl. 3:2, 8 NKJV). If murder under every circumstance were abominable in the sight of God, one would have to conclude that God is abominable to Himself. Because God made death the consequence of sin, death by necessity will occur. God sovereignly determines which deaths are abominable, not man. In the passage, it appears that the shedding of innocent blood is abominable. However, we must contextually understand what the shedding of innocent blood is and what it refers to.

Various scriptures throughout the Bible specifically reference shedding innocent blood. Exodus 23:7 makes clear that we should *"Keep yourself far from a false matter; do not kill the innocent and righteous. For I will not justify the wicked"* (NKJV). God assures us here that He will not acquit the wicked. In this passage, the children of Israel are being instructed to avoid falsely charging and executing an individual. It emphasizes that we should not allow personal altercations we have against a foe or biases against the poor to impede the faithful application of justice. Without delving further into unnecessary discussion about this topic, we do know that many innocent persons have been executed through our justice system, often influenced by biases of race or social status. God promises to not let those who wickedly commit these atrocities escape His judgment.

Exodus 23:8 informs us that even one who takes a bribe to shed innocent blood will be cursed: *"And you shall take no bribe, for a bribe blinds the discerning and perverts the words of the righteous"* (NKJV). It confounds wisdom to purport that the taking of the bribe itself is the nidus of the curse.

It can be reasonably inferred that the actual shedding of the blood similarly invokes the curse. But in the context of the preceding scriptures, we must consider what else represents an abomination. Deuteronomy 27:15 says, *"Cursed is the one who makes a carved or molded image, an abomination to the Lord, the work of the hands of the craftsman, and sets it up in secret"* (NKJV). We see here that worship of or sacrifice to an idol is an abomination to God.

This is why we must consider more broadly the context of the abomination referenced in Proverbs 6:17. The mere shedding of innocent blood alone conceivably might not be the part that is abominable to God. To this end, God instructed Abraham to shed the innocent blood of his son, Isaac, as a sacrifice to Him (Gen. 22). Abraham took his son, wood for the burnt offering, and the knife and proceeded to build the altar in the place the Lord instructed. The Bible suggests that Abraham had every intention of using the knife to slay Isaac, his innocent son, in obedience to God. Abraham bound his son and laid him atop the altar, which had been prepared for the sacrifice, and reached out his hand to grab the knife. Moments before he would shed the innocent blood of his son, at the instruction of God, an angel stayed his hand and affirmed Abraham's fear of and obedience to the Lord.

If the mere act of shedding innocent blood, as we narrowly interpret it to mean, were abominable to God, why would He instruct Abraham to commit such an abominable act? That He did make such a demand of Abraham supports the notion that God esteems obedience much more highly than mortal life. In fact, it was Abraham's obedience that spared Isaac's life and secured generational blessings for Abraham and his offspring: *"In your seed all the nations of the earth shall be blessed, because you have obeyed My voice"* (Gen. 22:18 NKJV).

Psalm 106:37-38 might provide more understanding of the context of shedding innocent blood. It reads, *"They even sacrificed their sons And their daughters to demons, And shed innocent blood, The blood of their sons and daughters, Whom they sacrificed to the idols of Canaan; And the land was polluted with blood"* (NKJV). The first commandment makes clear that God is a jealous God and that He desires to have no other gods before Him. He commits the first five commandments to ensuring that His people remain faithful to Him and Him only. Above, we learned that the creation of idols and worship thereof is abominable to the Lord.

Considering how Jesus emphasizes that all the law hinges on our loving God and loving our neighbor, we can better interpret the abominations mentioned in Proverbs 6 to be those that deal treacherously with our neighbor (e.g., lying tongue, running to evil, a false witness, sowing of discord) and those that are personal offenses to God (e.g., pride and shedding of innocent blood). It can be reasonably concluded that based on the pagan practices of the time, the shedding of innocent blood might reference the offering of children to idols as sacrifices. Psalm 106:40 explains that God's anger was so badly kindled by this practice that *"the wrath of the Lord was kindled against His people, So that He abhorred His own inheritance"* (NKJV).

I do not purport that the shedding of innocent blood for reasons other than idol sacrifice is acceptable to God. Of course, it isn't. I'm simply positing that the abomination commonly referred to in evangelical thought as being evoked by abortion might not be as definitively accurate as it has been presented. While it offers a persuasive cursory argument in support of anti-abortion efforts, a more diligent study of the scripture, as presented here, potentially exposes such a misapplication as a tactic to advance the pro-life agenda. Logically, there might be no more persuasive argument than to use God's word in support of the cause.

I will offer, as a final example, the murder of Abel by his brother, Cain. Genesis 4 tells the story of how both Cain and Abel offered a sacrifice unto God. God favored Abel's offering over that of Cain's. The Bible doesn't tell us why God showed such favor; it simply states that He did and that it angered Cain. Cain consequently slays his brother. When the Lord discovered this and approached Cain about it, Cain initially feigned ignorance about it. God subsequently cursed Cain and the ground Cain would till because of the innocent murder. There perhaps was no more innocent blood, except for Jesus, ever shed than that of Abel's. Abel was slain by his brother simply because he offered an acceptable sacrifice to God. Yet, the Bible does not indicate that even this act was abominable. Was it punishable? Absolutely!

Because of his shedding of innocent blood, Cain was cast from the presence of God. Cain assessed this fate to be unbearable and a sure prescription for his own murder. But God still had mercy on Cain, saying, *"Therefore, whoever kills Cain, vengeance shall be taken on him sevenfold." And the Lord set a mark on Cain, lest anyone finding him should kill him. Then Cain went out from the presence of the Lord and dwelt in the land of Nod on the east of Eden"* (Gen. 4:15-16 NKJV). The Bible delineates an entire lineage of Cain that extended hundreds of years after the commission of his sins. What is clear is that there was not the abhorrence of Cain that we see the scripture describes for the people of Israel who sacrificed the blood of children to idols.

Taken together, it can be reasonably concluded that:

1. God punishes the shedding of innocent blood;

2. The offering of the blood of innocent children to idols is abominable to God.

God's eternal perspective challenges our mortal perceptions

Yes, God laments the shedding of innocent blood, regardless of whether it's that of an unborn child or a full-grown man who offers an excellent sacrifice to God. We must resist our natural inclination to aspire, intentionally or unintentionally, toward omnipotence and attempts to be gods ourselves. This would keep us from dogmatic endorsements of guilt or innocence, which only God can make.

We can only make presumptions of innocence. The fact of the matter is that because we don't have eternal foresight or insight, we cannot know the mind of God concerning who should die or how they should die. We can simply rely on the knowledge that God will avenge the innocent and will prosecute the guilty. Our admittedly imperfect justice system recognizes that it cannot proclaim an individual's innocence. At best, it can declare one 'not guilty.' Even that does not mean that the individual is innocent. Only God, who searches the heart and knows the end from the beginning, is capable of definitively declaring innocence.

Importantly, the criteria by which God declares innocence are vastly different from our presumptions of innocence. Our humanity presumes all the Amalekite children, the first-born children of Egypt, and certainly the unborn fetuses that were in the wombs of the Israelites to be innocent. Yet, God permitted or ordered their death. We can infer that God knew that these children did not need to be born and/or grow to adulthood for reasons that only He knows. As difficult as it is for us to accept it, God's eternal perspective challenges our mortal perceptions.

Let's be clear: I am not justifying abortion and certainly not asserting that the aborted fetuses and murdered children needed to die due to lack of innocence. What I am saying is God doesn't process situations through a mortal lens as we do. Isaiah writes, *"For My thoughts are not your thoughts, Nor are your ways My ways,' says the Lord. 'For as the heavens are higher than the earth, So are My ways higher than your ways, And My thoughts than your thoughts'"* (Isa. 55:8-9 NKJV).

God's supremacy will never diminish to conform to our ideals

When we try to comprehend His actions and His tolerance using our finite understanding, we denigrate His sovereignty. God's supremacy will never diminish to conform to our ideals. Our rightful position is to submit to His sovereign instruction, without question.

This perspective challenges us to approach complex moral issues with humility and caution. It reminds us that while we may have strong convictions about what is right and wrong, our understanding is limited compared to God's omniscience. This doesn't mean we shouldn't strive to make ethical decisions or stand up for what we believe is right. Rather, it calls us to do so with an awareness of our own limitations and a willingness to continually seek God's wisdom and guidance.

In the context of the abortion debate, this understanding might lead us to approach the issue with more compassion and less judgment. While we may still view abortion as morally wrong, we can recognize that the situations leading to it are often complex and that our most noble role should be to offer love, support, and God-inspired alternatives rather than condemnation.

Ultimately, this perspective calls us to a deeper trust in God's sovereignty and justice. It challenges us to balance our convictions with humility, recognizing that God's understanding far surpasses our own. As we engage with difficult ethical issues, we are called to do so with faith, wisdom, and a commitment to both truth and love.

The Beginning of Life

Another scripture that fuels the insatiable quest in Evangelicals for pro-life legislation is Jeremiah 1:5: *"Before I formed you in the womb I knew you"* (NKJV). For them, this proves that fetal life is indeed human life and consequently should be afforded every protection that a fully developed human life receives. Some people use this scripture to assert that from conception, the embryo should be considered a human life because it has the potential to develop into such. I won't argue that they are wrong for their beliefs. I respect that people are entitled to establish for themselves the limits of their morality.

One of the wonderful things about living in the United States of America is the ability for us to have freedom of and from expression, beliefs, and religion. I appreciate that the government does not force me to subscribe to values espoused by a religion different from the one I practice, or any, for that matter. Instead, I am freely allowed to choose what I believe is moral and amoral, what is righteous or what is evil. Appreciating that liberty, I would never seek to force someone, through legislation, to believe the way that I do.

Our senses of morality are often prescribed by cultural norms. The United States of America is a mosaic of various cultures, which I believe enhances the American experience. The dominant culture, however, should never force assimilation, even if assimilation is its strong preference. The various races and ethnicities, and consequently cultures, were created by God and should be tolerated, if not celebrated. The variation occurs even within a particular culture. In any culture, there remains a diversity of thought, and not all cultural norms are adopted by each member of that particular culture.

Christianity, the foundational culture for Evangelicalism, itself has a variety of expressions. We call them denominations. Some denominations believe that we should worship on Saturdays or refrain from eating pork. Others assert that women should not be ordained as preachers or pastors and should not wear pants or make-up. There are denominations of Christianity that believe you should not play musical instruments in church, while others embrace an elaborate, concert-like production as part of the worship service. The list of varying thoughts and convictions can go on and on, but it demonstrates the point that even within a single religious faith, there are variations in interpreting what God desires, intends, or expects. All of them, in my opinion, should be protected under the First Amendment of the Constitution.

When we think we know the mind of God with surety, we become vulnerable to self-deification.

The topic of when human life begins represents a volatile topic of such variation in opinion and interpretation. Despite a professed commitment and allegiance to the same God and the same Bible, not all Christians agree with such a designation. Some believe life begins at conception. Some believe that it starts at the time of a measurable heartbeat, while others assert that it begins at the age of viability. On the extreme end, some Christians might believe that human life doesn't start until the time of birth, and they might all have biblical support, depending on one's interpretation of scripture.

Perhaps the Bible is silent or at least is not explicit on certain matters because God never intended for us to contemplate these matters. Even if He desired for us to contemplate them, perhaps He never wanted us to know with absolute certainty. When we think we know the mind of God with surety, we become vulnerable to self-deification. An omniscient God must, by definition, know some things – actually, an infinite number of things – that His servants necessarily don't know. Our quest for knowledge that God never intended for us to know predisposes us to sin. Sometimes, it's best to simply say, "I don't know." If it bothers you too much, you can conclude it by saying, "But this is what I believe, and I invite you to believe the same."

Taking my own advice, I will readily admit that I do not know the perfect or complete permissive will of God. Consequently, I will not make any affirmative statements but hopefully will offer perspective both for those whose paradigms are rigidly fixed and for those whose opinions are fluid because they lack cogent articulation. That said, I also realize that for some with rigid paradigms, also referred to as dogma, the mere suggestion or offering of biblical support for what they consider abhorrent might be dismissed immediately as heresy. That such an individual would be completely reticent to even consider that a biblical interpretation vastly different from theirs might have validity is evidence of the infiltrative influence of evangelicalism. They are constrained by dogma.

Cambridge Dictionary defines dogma as "a fixed, especially religious, belief or set of beliefs that people are expected to accept without any doubts." I submit then that dogma is the product of indoctrination. One who has been indoctrinated to a particular belief, whether true/accurate or not, is dogmatic in their adherence to that belief. To them, it is inconceivable that their interpretation or what they've been taught might be incomplete or even inaccurate.

One valuable lesson I've learned over the past eight years of intentional engagement with people who think differently than I do is to respect the validity of their convictions. Although I might not concur with their perspective, it remains valid to them. More importantly, from the standpoint of being an effective witness, I've learned to identify and mollify the dogmatism of my own faith. It is a difficult skill to acquire, but with prayerful commitment, it can be accomplished. I encourage all my Christian brothers and sisters to take heed that faith becomes dogma when it is no longer shared as a gift but instead is enforced as a mandate. In reality, none of us completely know the heart, mind, and intention of God. We only make presumptions based on our interpretations of His written word, which itself has been interpreted and translated, potentially with inherent error.

> **Faith becomes dogma when it is no longer shared as a gift but instead is enforced as a mandate**

In Genesis 1, the Bible tells us that God created man in His image. Most Christians will agree that God is a spirit and not human. Most would also agree that if God is a spirit, He has no physical form. If the scripture is accurate in stating that man was created in the image of God, then when man was created, he too was without form. He was a spirit. This notion is supported by the very scripture in Jeremiah, which states that he was known by God before he had form.

The scriptures inform us that after God created man as a spirit, He gave man a physical form made from the dust of the ground (Gen. 2:7). That spirit, which had previously been created and endowed with dominion, was then placed in the form of a human body. Then *the Lord God formed man of the dust of the ground, and breathed into his nostrils the breath of life; and man became a living being* (Gen. 2:7 NKJV).

According to the scriptures, it can reasonably be argued that man didn't become a living soul, a human being until he had breath in his lungs despite being known of God as a spirit. It is, therefore, reasonable to argue that an embryo or fetus is not a living soul until he/she has air in the lungs. Medically speaking, that does not occur until after birth. While in the mother's womb, a fetus derives its source of oxygen via gas exchange across the placenta, drawing from the mother's blood.

I don't have to personally subscribe to this belief to accept it as a reasonable, Bible-based conclusion. Frankly, a debate over when life begins is unfruitful for reasons discussed previously. I present this argument simply as a rebuttal to the notion that because a fetus is known of God while he remains in the womb, the fetus is definitionally a human life.

In an effort, which has no eternal value, to define for humanity when life begins, Evangelicals are contemporarily thrown into the thralls of a heated debate in America about how to define human embryos. An embryo is formed when the sperm from the father fertilizes an oocyte (or egg) from the mother. The DNA from the two parental gametes fuse, and the fertilized egg is then a single-cell organism called a zygote. Bacteria are unicellular organisms that contain all their functions (e.g., metabolism, excretion, and reproduction) as a single cell. Humans, by contrast, are multicellular organisms, and a zygote doesn't develop into a viable human until much later in the pregnancy. Thus, it can be argued that a zygote is not human.

In its initial state, the zygote is considered totipotent. Totipotency is "the ability of a single cell to develop independently into a healthy organism in a permissive environment."[10] After fertilization, the zygote soon begins to replicate by dividing. These cell divisions occur within the egg and initially do not result in a change in the size of the egg until after the eighth division. During the first division, the two halves infrequently do not remain together but instead actually separate. This results in two zygotes, each with totipotency. They can each develop into an individual fetus, resulting in monozygotic twins, meaning they derive from the same zygote and consequently have identical DNA.

After a few cell divisions – about six days after conception – the zygote becomes a ball of cells called a blastocyst, and as it develops further, it loses

---

[10] Kejin Hu, "On Mammalian Totipotency: What Is the Molecular Underpinning for the Totipotency of Zygote?," *Stem Cells and Development* 28, no. 14 (July 15, 2019): 897–906, https://doi.org/10.1089/scd.2019.0057.

much of its totipotency.[11] How the blastocyst develops depends greatly on the cues that it receives from its environment. When the blastocyst implants into the wall of the mother's uterus, cues from the womb, including physical contact and hormones, induce the differentiation of the blastocyst into an embryo and, subsequently, a fetus and then an infant.

Totipotency of a zygote and early embryos is important for various scientific reasons. Most publicized is that the zygote can be frozen in its early stages of division. It can then later be induced *in vitro* (i.e., in a lab) to continue division and development until it is of sufficient maturity to be implanted into the uterus of a woman. This is called *in vitro* fertilization (IVF). *In vitro* fertilization has gained a lot of public attention lately, particularly since the Supreme Court of the United States (SCOTUS) reversed Roe v. Wade legislation in their Dobbs v. Jackson case. The Dobbs decision concluded that the Constitution does not confer a right to abortion. The authority to regulate abortion has consequently been returned to state-elected representatives and theoretically, the people.[12]

> *When zeal for legislation is fueled by voracious passion instead of logical contemplation, it creates an ethical conundrum*

Many states in America had laws already in the books or quickly enacted them that would prevent abortion at any stage of pregnancy. A major problem with some of these laws is that they attempt to define when human life begins. Those states, such as Alabama, who determined that life starts at conception

---

[11] Raul Artal-Mittelmark, MD, "Stages of Development of the Fetus - Women's Health Issues," Merck Manual Consumer Version, May 2021, https://www.merckmanuals.com/home/women-s-health-issues/normal-pregnancy/stages-of-development-of-the-fetus#Fertilization_v809169.

[12] "Dobbs v. Jackson Women's Health Organization," National Constitution Center, 2022, https://constitutioncenter.org/the-constitution/supreme-court-case-library/dobbs-v-jackson-womens-health-organization.

were then faced with an ethical dilemma that they were not prepared to handle. On February 16, 2024, the Alabama Supreme Court issued a ruling declaring that embryos created through IVF should be considered children. Several of the state's IVF clinics have since paused services while doctors and lawmakers determine what to do with the thousands of 'children' (according to Alabama law) that are being held captive in freezers.[13]

I refer to the embryos as frozen children, not to be insensitive, but to emphasize the lunacy of poorly contemplated legislation. When zeal for legislation is fueled by voracious passion instead of logical contemplation, it creates an ethical conundrum, such as what we see in this situation. When states consider embryos children, at least four aspects of IVF face scrutiny and inevitable restriction. In addition to embryo cryopreservation, as mentioned above, other factors include embryo disposal, preimplantation genetic testing (PGT), and selective reduction of multiple pregnancies.

Selective pregnancy reduction is the practice of targeted reduction of embryos that have successfully implanted into the uterine wall. During IVF, multiple embryos might be implanted to ensure a successful pregnancy. After the mother is assured that a sufficient or desirable number of implants have been successful, the other implanted embryos are selectively reduced. This is becoming a much less common practice, but it still needs to be considered because there are inherent risks of multiparity – a multiple-birth pregnancy.

Disposal of embryos occurs for a variety of reasons. The parents could have had successful pregnancies and no longer need to have a store of additional embryos because they plan to have no more children. Equally challenging to the ethics of some, embryos may be discarded after genetic testing reveals genetic defects that will produce known diseases. And there's always the hyperbolized fear that parents will, in vanity, discard embryos because they might not like something as menial as eye or hair color when determined in advance by genetic

---

[13] Perrine Ginod and Michael H Dahan, "Embryos as Unborn Children: The Alabama Supreme Court's Ruling and Its Possible Impact for Legal Rulings in Other States.," *F&S Reports* 5(2) (April 1, 2024), https://doi.org/10.1016/j.xfre.2024.03.006.

testing. Now, IVF clinics in Alabama are not able to destroy the embryos for any reason without the threat of legal prosecution.

Even the staunchest pro-life advocates are now confronted with an ethical dilemma that was unforeseen in their zealous support. Any resolution they support will necessarily result in an embarrassment of hypocrisy. You must either succumb to the option of 'killing embryo babies' or holding them hostage in freezers. These are the challenges that we encounter when technology outpaces our morality. We discover that we can do something long before we rationalize whether we should do it.

The most logical solution is to resist the urge to let our morality inform our legislation, especially when there is broad and passionate public disagreement about what is or isn't moral. Moreover, when the majority opinion is one that offends our Christian sensibilities, our response should not be to revolt and certainly should not involve unscrupulous tactics to enforce our will (or God's will) on a people who outright reject it. Paul encouraged us, in Romans 12:18, to *"If it is possible, as much as depends on you, live peaceably with all men"* (NKJV).

Some people may consider it a cop-out, but I conclude that regardless of one's position about when life begins, it doesn't change the immutable preeminence of integrity, honesty, and obedience over mortal life in the eyes of God. There are weightier matters that we as Believers should be more concerned about. Jesus admonished the Pharisees to do just that, *"Woe to you, scribes and Pharisees, hypocrites! For you pay tithe of mint and anise and cummin, and have neglected the weightier matters of the law: justice and mercy and faith. These you ought to have done, without leaving the others undone"* (Matt. 23:23 NKJV).

Throughout the centuries, the pervasive leaven of Evangelicalism has recruited many well-intentioned Christians into the doctrine it espouses. Using what seems to be a logical conclusion, Evangelicalism expands the reach of its loyalists. The arguments made by its most loyal ambassadors make what seem to be prima facie irrefutable arguments because they make common sense. However, we must recall that the message Jesus taught and the ways of God don't always comport with common sense. *"There is a way that seems right to a man, but its end is the way of death"* (Prov. 14:12 NKJV).

It requires a bit more faith to resist being sucked into what seems to be a very logical argument but just doesn't feel right. People enticed by their fervent commitment to ideals that seem on the surface to be honorable find themselves unable to break from the clutches of Evangelical influence. Even the explicit word of God seems unable to open the eyes of those so entranced by the deceptive virtue of Evangelicalism. The Apostle Paul said it best in Galatians 3:

> *"O foolish Galatians! Who has bewitched you that you should not obey the truth, before whose eyes Jesus Christ was clearly portrayed among you as crucified? This only I want to learn from you: Did you receive the Spirit by the works of the law, or by the hearing of faith? Are you so foolish? Having begun in the Spirit, are you now being made perfect by the flesh? Have you suffered so many things in vain—if indeed it was in vain? Therefore He who supplies the Spirit to you and works miracles among you, does He do it by the works of the law, or by the hearing of faith?" (Gal. 3:1-5 NKJV)*

Paul goes further to explain how inept the law is in giving life or producing righteousness. He explains that *"before faith came, we were kept under guard by the law, kept for the faith which would afterward be revealed"* (Gal. 3:23 NKJV). It isn't terribly peculiar that Paul would use the word imprisoned. This is what the law does; it imprisons those who are strictly bound by it. *"But when the fullness of the time had come, God sent forth His Son, born of a woman, born under the law, to redeem those who were under the law, that we might receive the adoption as sons"* (Gal. 4:4-5 NKJV).

CHAPTER 6

THE OTHER GODS

Offering A Strange Fire

Activism has become the strong root of evangelicalism. The context in which evangelicalism is even mentioned today is almost exclusively within the context of politics. While it has accomplished some good for humanity, the harm it has done to the Christian witness is far-reaching. What began as a common belief or passion for a singular issue, such as anti-abortion legislation, has expanded its reach to various other areas. It now also demands loyalty to those ancillary issues. Among them are issues relating to patriotism and capitalism. Like Pro-Lifeism, these have become idols that demand unconditional sacrifice. The mascot for these activist pursuits has taken the form of an elephant, the Republican Party.

It is curious that the Republican Party has fashioned itself as the 'party of values' over the past five decades or so. While some of the political platform issues they support do align with God's heart and values, not all of them do. In fact, some are in stark opposition to the priorities of God – at least as supported by scripture. Similarly, while there are some Democratic platform issues that oppose God's precepts, there are others that align with them. The reality is that no political party (or any contrivance of man) can ever be perfectly aligned with

God. In fact, they cannot be satisfactorily or even acceptably aligned with God. Sacrifices that are contrived by man and subsequently offered to God are often offensive and repulsive to God.

Sadly, some people have come to consciously or unconsciously consider our political offerings as sacrifices unto God. Many Evangelicals felt that their support of an unabashedly morally bereft presidential candidate could be atoned for by the offering of legislation they perceived would be desirable to God. Similarly, any person who believes that the apostasy of a Democratic candidate could be ameliorated by the promise of policy that extends kindness and welfare to the poor or to foreigners is deceived. These political platforms are carnal from the beginning and cannot be converted to a righteous cause, no matter how desperately we might wish it so.

In Exodus 20, the Lord advises His people on the importance of keeping the work of their hands from polluting the sanctity of His altars of sacrifice. In the 25th verse, He cautions, *"And if you make Me an altar of stone, you shall not build it of hewn stone; for if you use your tool on it, you have profaned it"* (Exod. 20:25 NKJV). God never desired sacrifices fabricated by man's hands. He has always desired the product of the heart. The creator of all things could never be impressed by man's manipulations of His creation that are repurposed as a sacrifice.

When sacrifices are executed according to our own prescriptions, we profane the sacrifice and the altar

---

There is no other scripture where this is more poignantly demonstrated than in 1 Samuel 15. God commanded King Saul to slay all the Amalekites, including children and women. He also advised him to kill all the oxen, camels, sheep, and donkeys (vs. 3). *"But Saul and the people spared Agag and the best of the sheep and of the oxen and of the fattened calves and the lambs, and all that was good, and would not utterly destroy them. All that was despised and worthless they devoted to destruction"* (1 Sam. 15:9 ESV).

Using his human rationale, Saul presumed it to be wasteful if he needlessly slaughtered such valuable creatures. He rationalized that it would be much better to offer these things to God as a sacrifice, or at least that was his justification for the act. This fallacious thinking and its consequent action prompted God to regret that He ever ordained Saul as king. God instructed His prophet, Samuel, to admonish King Saul:

> *"Has the Lord as great delight in burnt offerings and sacrifices, as in obeying the voice of the Lord? Behold, to obey is better than sacrifice, and to listen than the fat of rams. For rebellion is as the sin of divination, and presumption is as iniquity and idolatry. Because you have rejected the word of the Lord, he has also rejected you from being king"* (1 Sam. 15:22-23 ESV).

Saul's presumption, using his very human intellect, instigated his disobedience. His disobedience cost him his influence.

We often quote the part of that scripture that says obedience is better than sacrifice, but we overlook the part that says presumption is as iniquity and idolatry. Our humanistic presumptions predispose us to offer sacrifices that are wholly unacceptable to God. If God did not specifically command it of us, we should not do it – at least, we shouldn't purport it to be a sacrifice unto God after we've already done it. Instead, we should let it be exactly what it is – a self-gratifying act or one that helps us to feel better about our human condition in some small or great way.

If, however, we seek to offer an acceptable sacrifice to God, it must be according to His precise instruction. When sacrifices are executed according to our own prescriptions, we profane the sacrifice and the altar upon which it was sacrificed. God considers it a strange fire, just as He did the sacrifice of Nadab and Abihu.

> *"Now Nadab and Abihu, the sons of Aaron, each took his censer and put fire in it and laid incense on it and offered unauthorized fire before the Lord, which he had not commanded them. And fire came out*

from before the Lord and consumed them, and they died before the Lord. Then Moses said to Aaron, 'This is what the Lord has said: "Among those who are near me I will be sanctified, and before all the people I will be glorified."' And Aaron held his peace" (Leviticus 10:1-3 ESV).

Aaron was the High Priest of Israel. He and his sons were well-versed in and knowledgeable about the process of offering sacrifices to God. As part of his duties, Aaron made intercession to God on behalf of the people. He was permitted to come into the Holy of Holies once a year to make sacrifices. Nadab and Abihu were the two oldest of Aaron's four sons. They would certainly have known the appropriate protocols for offering sacrifice to God. After all, they had previously participated in an acceptable manner (Lev. 9).

For reasons that are not clear in the scriptures, on this particular day, they felt compelled to offer God a sacrifice according to their own prescription. They presumed it would be acceptable to God but were swiftly and definitively reprimanded by God for such an unholy sacrifice. The fire from the censer they lit came out to kill them. They were consumed and killed by the very product of their unholy sacrifice. The Bible says that their sacrifice was unauthorized and not commanded by God. The King James Version of the Bible calls it a "strange" fire. That means it was not what was usually offered to God, and moreover, God never commanded them to change the method by which they sacrificed.

God knows exactly what He desires from His people and is quite capable of explicitly stating such. Our arrogance causes us to presume that we could fabricate an unsolicited sacrifice that would somehow be acceptable to God. We cannot. God is explicit about the sacrifices He requests. Recall that atonement isn't the sacrifice itself, but rather the obedience in following His prescription for sacrifice. The evangelical mindset wrongly supposes that although God hasn't specifically requested it, our presumptively generous offerings to Him would be acceptable.

God is not impressed by our commitment to augmenting His laws by writing our own laws. While it is a reasonable civic duty to exercise, when we try to ascribe a Godly purpose or benefit to it, we have profaned God's altar and offered a strange fire. I've seen these very sacrifices consume evangelical leaders. Some have literally lost their lives as a result, while others have lost their influence and witness.

Another key correlate to Saul's disobedience and the leaven of evangelicalism is self-supremacy. 1 Samuel 15:12 quickly mentions an important observation and then seems to quickly move on. It was told to Samuel that Saul went to Carmel and set up a monument unto himself. Before he feigned an intention to sacrifice unto the Most High God, he prioritized the erection of a monument to celebrate his own greatness. From the scripture, I cannot confidently conclude whether self-supremacy was the consequence of or the impetus for Saul's disobedience. Either way, there is a definite association between the two.

Early in his rebuke, Samuel reminds Saul that the greatness he achieved was only because of God's generosity toward him. Instead of following through with God's explicit instruction, he proceeded to usurp God's omniscient sovereignty and presume himself to know more than the Creator. The erection of the monument was only a physical manifestation of the hidden sentiment.

> ***Our natural aspiration is to acquire knowledge, autonomy, and authority equal to or exceeding God's***

Like many of us, Saul inwardly sought to dictate his own behaviors, goals, and exploits. He sought to be the master of his own fate. He lacked the humility that inspires submission to the sovereignty of God, especially when the instructions seemed to be nonsensical in his eyes. This human flaw manifested by Saul's, and our own, obstinance has existed since the creation of man. Satan was able to tempt Eve with the promise of knowing as God knows. Unless actively squelched, our natural aspiration is to acquire knowledge, autonomy, and authority equal to or exceeding God's. This susceptibility marks a lot of the aspiration of Evangelical ancillary activism.

Love of Country

I liken the influence of Evangelicalism to metastases because it does exactly that. Like an aggressive cancer, it spreads to and impacts areas remote from its primary site of origin. Evangelicalism wins an easy fight with those who are passionate about anti-abortion and anti-LGBTQ+ causes. It exploits passion to extend its prongs broadly to demand loyalty in other unrelated areas of sociopolitical discourse. Patriotism is one such example.

The devotion and vigorous support of one's country seem to be a reasonably admirable trait. What red-blooded American wouldn't venerate the love of country and those who have dedicated their lives to the defense of that country? In fact, the mantra "love of God and country" is frequently espoused by many Evangelicals. The pulpits of many Evangelical churches are adorned by an American flag. Often, these churches orchestrate special services, remembering the sacrifice of veterans and extolling their love for the country on Veteran's Day and/or Memorial Day.

These services feature moving videos remembering the sacrifice of servicemen and servicewomen. Often, military veterans may be asked to stand for special recognition amid emphatic rounds of applause. Their devotion and sacrifice are heralded as Christ-like in that they resemble the greatest love of all—one who would lay down his/her life for a friend.

I am not suggesting that servicemen and servicewomen should not be honored. On the contrary, I wholeheartedly believe the men and women who serve in the armed forces rightly should be celebrated. There are biblical examples of worthy men and women receiving double honor (1 Tim. 5:17). While this scripture relates specifically to those who teach the word of God well, it seems a reasonable endeavor to show appreciation for the sacrifice of brave soldiers.

A common practice of the children of Israel was to celebrate victories when soldiers returned from war by singing and dancing. Most notably, *"when David returned from striking down the Philistine, the women came out of all the cities of Israel, singing and dancing, to meet King Saul, with tambourines, with songs of joy, and with musical instruments. And the women sang to one another as they celebrated, 'Saul has struck down his thousands, and David his ten thousands'"* (1 Sam. 18:6-7 ESV).

These men and all the warriors were certainly worthy of honor. My contention, however, is that they should not be idolized. The worship service is perhaps not the most appropriate setting for such honor, as it distracts the glory and focus of the service away from God and onto humans. Such presentations easily and subconsciously confuse attendees and almost deify patriotism and service to the country.

Without question, I believe the United States of America is by far the best country in which to live. I am grateful for the liberties and economic prosperity we enjoy as citizens. These have been provided to us through a beautifully (but imperfectly) crafted constitution. These rights are, and should be, vigorously defended by our service men and women, as well as by our elected officials. While the U.S. Constitution is an impressive creative work to establish a system of government, and it has endured 235 years of scrutiny and defense, it is not the Bible!

Although some of the ideals presented in the Constitution might resemble precepts of the Bible, we must be cautious to always recognize that the writ of man should never be made comparable to the Holy Writ of God. Nor should we ascribe its writing to the inspiration of God. Even if the Constitution were perfectly inspired by God, its execution by man will always be fallible. In a theological defense of the Constitution, some argue that it was written by men who alleged to have a relationship with God. Still, there's no mistaking the numerous flaws of its original writing and many aspects that persist today that make clear that it is not the work of godly inspiration.

Yet, a common refrain of the Evangelical hymnal is the claim that our rights are 'God-given,' that the United States is a Christian nation, and that our country was founded on Christian principles. These assertions are simply false and result from the systemic indoctrination of patriotism as a righteous ideal.

The rights we enjoy as American citizens are provided to us under the Constitution, not the Bible. There are various components of the Constitution and its amendments that are in stark contradiction to the word of God. The First Amendment is the most evident of all. It states: "Congress shall make no law respecting an establishment of religion, or prohibiting the free exercise thereof; or abridging the freedom of speech, or of the press; or the right of the people peaceably to assemble, and to petition the Government for a redress of grievances."[14]

The first commandment of God forbids the worship of any other god, while the First Amendment allows us to freely worship any god we choose or none at all. Jesus said this was the first and one of the two greatest commandments of all (Matt. 22:37-38). We have God's law telling us that we cannot worship any other god and man's law saying we can. I'm grateful that the Constitution offers this freedom because if the predominant religion of this country was something other than Christianity, I would not want the government to force my submission to its precepts.

The oblivion of our arrogance causes many Christians and Evangelicals to remain blind to the consequences of their pursuit of laws that reflect our Christian beliefs. They have no problem imposing on other people constraints similar to those that they themselves would reject if Christianity were not the majority religion. They claim that their attempts to force the display and reading of the Ten Commandments in public schools, such as the recent legislation passed in Louisiana and Oklahoma, are done to help restore America to the feigned righteousness of its former years. They allege it to be an act of patriotism. While Evangelicals purport that those who defend sexuality-related liberties granted them under the Constitution attempt to indoctrinate our children, I submit that the patriotism they venerate is more accurately a strategic indoctrination of the children.

---

[14] Congress, "U.S. Constitution - First Amendment," constitution.congress.gov (Library of Congress, December 15, 1791), https://constitution.congress.gov/constitution/amendment-1/.

The Continental Congress approved the American flag on June 14, 1777, which became known as Flag Day.[15] The flag's original purpose was not to symbolize affection and devotion to the country but to designate and protect U.S. ships at sea. It served as a banner, not for fealty but for a very practical purpose. It wasn't until after the Civil War that it became a widely used and generally popular symbol of patriotism.

In the following decades, there was a growing perception that the flag would be misused for commercial and political causes. By the late 1800s, an organized flag protection movement was born, and the snowball of flag worship gained momentum. After failing to obtain federal legislation, the states of Illinois, Pennsylvania, and South Dakota were the first to adopt flag desecration statutes. These laws made it illegal to desecrate the flag and consequently elevated its status to a symbol of American patriotism. This trend extended to other states, and by 1932, all of the States had adopted flag desecration laws.[16]

The fealty to the flag had become so profound that the state of California sought to prevent individuals from waving a solid red flag, which had become a symbol of opposition to organized government. Love of the country continued to grow, but not without some opposition that seemed to slow its progress. The Supreme Court held, in Stromberg vs. California, that a state's prohibition of waving the oppositional red flag violated an individual's First Amendment rights of free speech.[17]

The battle over an individual's free speech rights and flag desecration would be tested during anti-Vietnam War protests, during which US flags were burned. Motivated by these highly publicized events, Congress adopted the first federal flag desecration law in 1968. It made it illegal to "knowingly" cast

---

[15] "Facts about the United States Flag," Smithsonian Institution, September 2001, https://www.si.edu/spotlight/flag-day/flag-facts.

[16] Muriel Morisey, "Flag Desecration, Religion and Patriotism," *SSRN Electronic Journal* 9.1 (October 25, 2007).

[17] "Stromberg v. California, 283 U.S. 359 (1931)," Justia Law, n.d., https://supreme.justia.com/cases/federal/us/283/359/.

"contempt" upon "any flag of the United States by publicly mutilating, defacing, defiling, burning or trampling upon it."

By this time, the flag had been so highly venerated that wearing a replica of the flag on the seat of the pants was considered by many to be so egregious that it should be outlawed. New York prosecuted a gentleman named Street for burning his own flag and exclaiming to a small crowd that if the government could allow civil rights leader, James Meredith, to be killed, "we don't need no damn flag."[18]

Other nonsensical prosecutions proceeded over the ensuing two decades. These were all pursued by the states against citizens who would defame the flag even in minute ways. Actions such as affixing removable tape in the form of a peace sign to the flag were prosecuted. Eventually, the Supreme Court intervened and limited the infringement of flag desecration laws on citizens' free speech.

The reverence of the American flag by laws is evident, as previously outlined. However, its deification has been advanced by various social practices. Chief among them is the Pledge of Allegiance. The Pledge of Allegiance was written in August 1892 by Francis Bellamy. It was originally published in a widely distributed family magazine, The Youth's Companion, on September 8, 1892.[19] It was initially intended to be used by citizens in any country. In its original form, it read:

> "I pledge allegiance to my Flag and the Republic for which it stands, one nation, indivisible, with liberty and justice for all."

In 1923, the words "the Flag of the United States of America" were added. In response to the Communist threat of the times, President Eisenhower in

---

[18] "Street v. New York, 394 U.S. 576 (1969)," Justia Law, n.d., https://supreme.justia.com/cases/federal/us/394/576/.

[19] Jeffrey Owen Jones, "The Man Who Wrote the Pledge of Allegiance," Smithsonian, 2014, https://web.archive.org/web/20180131235459/https://www.smithsonianmag.com/history/the-man-who-wrote-the-pledge-of-allegiance-93907224/.

1954 encouraged Congress to add the words "under God," creating the pledge we say today:

> "I pledge allegiance to the flag of the United States of America and to the republic for which it stands, one nation under God, indivisible, with liberty and justice for all."

Section 4 of the Flag Code states that the Pledge of Allegiance "... should be rendered by standing at attention facing the flag with the right hand over the heart. When not in uniform, men should remove any non-religious head-dress with their right hand and hold it at the left shoulder, the hand being over the heart. Persons in uniform should remain silent, face the flag, and render the military salute." These acts and the recitation of the pledge hold both the flag and the Republic in high reverence.[20]

The evolution of the composition and stance for recitation of the Pledge of Allegiance is noteworthy. Francis Bellamy was a Baptist Minister. Considering the anti-socialism rhetoric of many conservatives and Evangelicals who insisted that homage be paid to the flag and national anthem, it is ironic that Bellamy was a self-proclaimed socialist. It is also curious that a Baptist Minister would commit two glaring errors. First, he would pledge allegiance to an object such as a flag, and second, he ominously excluded the language "under God" from the original writing. Presumably, a minister of the Gospel would have a devotion to God at the forefront of his consciousness. If that devotion had to be shared, one would expect that it would at least be alleged to have been sanctioned by God. But he did neither. It is essential to understand his motive.

At the time of the writing of the Pledge of Allegiance, Bellamy recalls that America was experiencing a crisis of civil loyalty.[21] Among the causes was a developing theory that America should subjugate its self-interest in favor of

---

[20] "[USC02] 4 USC Ch. 1: THE FLAG," uscode.house.gov, n.d.,
https://uscode.house.gov/view.xhtml?path=/prelim@title4/chapter1&edition=prelim.

[21] "The Story of the Pledge of Allegiance to the Flag," Archive.org, 2024,
https://web.archive.org/web/20100504061201/http://www.lib.rochester.edu/index.cfm?PAGE=34
18.

world interests – a theory opposite the America First policy of today. After the publishing of a Boston Herald article entitled "The Worship of a Textile Fabric." James B. Upham, a marketer for The Youth's Companion magazine, began a campaign to instill American nationalism in school-age students. According to Bellamy, Upham had "a grim determination to make the school children of the country understand that their country was first of all, and that the flag was worthy of their highest love." Upham enlisted the help of Francis Bellamy. Bellamy set to work arranging a patriotic program for schools to commemorate the opening ceremonies for the Columbian Exposition in October 1892, the 400th anniversary of Christopher Columbus' arrival in the New World. Upham envisioned that this would be the perfect time to revive a dying enthusiasm for nationalism. He successfully lobbied Congress for a resolution endorsing the school ceremony during which millions of schoolchildren recited this pledge.

Many ironies and hypocrisies reside in this brief recollection of the events. That children would be forced to recite a pledge of allegiance to an inanimate object should have been forthrightly objectionable. Francis Bellamy himself stated that the "pledge would seem far better adapted to educated adults than to children." Evangelicals should reasonably have been adamantly opposed to forcing children to offer any semblance of worship to any idolatrous image or ideal. But instead, it was the creation of a Baptist minister himself. And somehow, it became heavily ingrained and accepted in the cultural fabric of America. It was indoctrination in its most insidious form.

It is worth mentioning that as a socialist, Bellamy initially wanted to conclude the pledge with the words "with equality and fraternity" for all. However, he decided against it, knowing that the state superintendents of education on his committee were against equality for women and African Americans.

Much like the creation of the United States Flag and the Pledge of Allegiance, the National Anthem has had a curious rise to deity. After a series of trade disagreements, America declared war on Great Britain on June 18, 1812. In August 1814, British troops invaded Washington, D.C., and burned the

White House, Capitol Building, and Library of Congress before turning their target to Baltimore.[22] One of Francis Scott Key's friends was taken prisoner by the British. Key went to Baltimore to negotiate the release of his friend. However, they weren't allowed to leave until after the British bombardment of Fort McHenry. After the British could not destroy the fort and gave up, Key was relieved to see the American flag still flying over Fort McHenry and penned a poem to commemorate what he saw.

Key named the poem "The Defence of Fort McHenry." It was later set to the music of an English drinking tune called "To Anacreon in Heaven" by composer John Stafford Smith. In 1916, President Woodrow Wilson proclaimed the song to be the national anthem for all armed forces. It was played during flag-raising ceremonies.

One year into World War I, debate arose as to whether the World Series in 1918 should be played between the Boston Red Sox and the Chicago Cubs. Baseball officials suggested that out of respect for soldiers at war, the game should be canceled. However, servicemen abroad were anxious to know the outcome of the competition. Baseball officials decided to play the National Anthem during the seventh-inning stretch to honor the soldiers fighting in France. It was met with a warm reception and soon was played at almost all sporting events. It received yet another boost in 1931 when President Herbert Hoover adopted the "Star-Spangled Banner" as the official anthem of the United States of America through a Congressional act.

By 1942, the National Anthem was played at all regular season baseball games. As during World War I, nationalism stoked enthusiasm for playing the anthem during NFL games amidst World War II. At the conclusion of the war, the NFL commissioner suggested that the anthem should continue to be played.[23] At that time, most players were not present during the playing of the

---

[22] Wikipedia Contributors, "The Star-Spangled Banner," Wikipedia (Wikimedia Foundation, February 15, 2019), https://en.wikipedia.org/wiki/The_Star-Spangled_Banner.

[23] Becky Little, "Why the Star-Spangled Banner Is Played at Sporting Events," HISTORY, September 25, 2017, https://www.history.com/news/why-the-star-spangled-banner-is-played-at-sporting-events.

anthem. In most instances, the players would be in the locker rooms while it was played. On special occasions, the players would observe the anthem, such as during Super Bowl games and after the attack on September 11, 2001. In 2009, however, players were mandated to be on the field for the playing of the national anthem.

Between 2012 and 2015, the Department of Defense gave $6.8 million to various major sports teams in exchange for holding various military and patriotic events at their games, including the performance of the national anthem.[24] All of these coordinated efforts intended to stoke nationalism among American citizens. National codes were enacted to prescribe acceptable behavior that demonstrates a citizen's homage and allegiance to his country. These behaviors, if not initiated by, are fervently endorsed by many Evangelicals. Violations of them evoke an offense of the highest order.

In the 2016 NFL preseason, San Francisco 49ers quarterback Colin Kaepernick began sitting during the national anthem. He did this in protest of police brutality and racism. For two weeks, it went largely unnoticed. After much consideration and consultation with a retired Green Beret and former NFL player, they came to the conclusion that he should kneel rather than sit. He believed that kneeling still showed respect for the flag and national anthem. However, even the act of kneeling sparked a national debate and outrage that cost him his NFL career. Moreover, it revealed what I believe is an idolatrous devotion that many Americans and Evangelicals have for the country.

I reiterate that I love America and appreciate the ideals for which the flag stands. However, I stand adamantly against forcing any individual to pledge allegiance to an inanimate object, song, or even a country. If you pledge this type of devotion, it should be of your own volition. A citizen of a free country should not be castigated for refusing to bow in worship to what they perceive

---

[24] AJ Willingham, "The National Anthem in Sports (Spoiler: It Wasn't Always This Way)," CNN, 2017, https://www.cnn.com/2017/09/25/us/nfl-national-anthem-trump-kaepernick-history-trnd/index.html.

as an idol. More importantly, Christians should be the last people to require or demand this type of homage.

The first commandment of God states, *"You shall have no other gods before me. You shall not make for yourself a carved image, or any likeness of anything that is in heaven above, or that is in the earth beneath, or that is in the water under the earth. You shall not bow down to them or serve them, for I the Lord your God am a jealous God..."* (Exod. 20:3-5 ESV). The scripture is clear that we shall not make any image or likeness of anything to which we bow down or serve. It seems reasonable that a flag or a national anthem should be included.

I am certain many will claim that they don't bow down to, serve, or worship the flag. However, the great offense that people have taken to various professional sports players' kneeling during the anthem suggests otherwise. At the very least, the flag and the national anthem are highly esteemed by many of our Evangelical friends. To this, I refer them to the words Jesus spoke to the Pharisees, *"You are those who justify yourselves before men, but God knows your hearts. For what is exalted among men is an abomination in the sight of God"* (Luke 16:15 ESV).

Holding anything other than God in high esteem is yet another abomination that Evangelicals seem to assuage, minimize, or ignore. To them, it seems almost heretical for me to suggest that to extol one's country, an anthem, a pledge of allegiance, or a flag is abominable in the sight of God. Why? Because the leaven of Evangelicals have so tightly interwoven patriotism and nationalism with the love of God that they seem inextricable.

The publishing of such criticisms is almost a death sentence for anyone who might desire to pursue political office in the future. The inculcation of patriotism is so pervasive that one's unwavering love of the country must almost rival their loyalty to and love of God if they have political aspirations. Sadly, among them who would cast the first stone are Evangelicals. If we are not cautious and discerning of the insidious nature of evangelical indoctrination, we, too, will find ourselves endorsing heretical litmus tests of patriotism that compromise our devotion to and right standing with God.

Nationalism and Fear

Patriotism is a progenitor to nationalism. Nationalism, according to the Oxford Dictionary, is identification with one's own nation and support for its interests, especially to the exclusion or detriment of the interests of other nations. Patriotism is devotion to and vigorous support for one's country. To understand the progression from patriotism to nationalism, we must first understand the root word, nation. We often equate one's country with their nation. This is not always the case. A nation is a large body of people united by common descent, history, culture, or language who inhabit a particular country or territory. The United States is a melting pot of various ethnicities, cultures, histories, and even languages. Consequently, within one country, there can be several nations. When the love and devotion of one's country, or their fond memories of what the country used to be, becomes extreme, nationalism becomes more probable.

> *Exploitation of religious convictions is a powerful tool to solicit support for an otherwise unjustifiable cause*

Donald Trump, in his 2016 presidential campaign, tapped into the nostalgia of many White conservatives who longed for the day when America was great in their estimation. At that time, there was a clear societal hierarchy. More accurately, it was a White patriarchy where White men, particularly those of substantial wealth, controlled the levers of government. As women and minorities grew in political clout and as immigrants gained more prominence in society, the White patriarchy of America was weakened.

Like the United States of America, other industrialized nations have mandated the equal treatment of all citizens. Many are desperate to reclaim the authority that has been lost with the inclusion of other people groups in the social, political, economic, and judicial discourses of these societies. As mentioned in a previous chapter, the exploitation of religious convictions is a powerful tool to solicit support for an otherwise unjustifiable cause. From these exploitations, White Christian Nationalism was birthed.

In my opinion, there is no place where the hypocrisy of Christianity is more plainly evident and displayed than in America. The First Amendment of our Constitution promises that religious freedom extends to persons of all religions and nationalities. However, Christian Nationalism is fueled by fear that America is losing its Christian identity. Pew Research reported that in 2022, 48% of Republicans and 25% of Democrats believed that Christian faith was an important determinant of who should be considered truly American.[25] Fortunately, both are down from 2016, when the numbers were 63% and 41%, respectively. This might explain, in part, the appeal of Donald Trump among conservative Republicans. He recognized and capitalized on the fear that people who are more committed to their religion than the Christian majority are going to come into the country and force their ideals and laws on us.

It is ludicrous to believe that Muslims, which currently represent 1% of the U.S. population, are somehow going to be effective in coming to America to institute Shariah Law. Yet, this is a prevailing fear among many conservative Christians. They use the fear of terrorism as a cover for their discriminatory ideology. Search the internet, and you'll easily find veiled and sometimes blatant racist and Islamophobic references to the number of Muslim immigrant refugees brought to the country under President Barack Obama.

Some people allege that President Obama was involved in a covert initiative to help usher in Shariah Law as the prevailing law of the land - clearly Islamophobic but more subtly racist. They duly noted that 2016 was one of the years where the highest percentage of Muslim refugees were granted asylum in the U.S., but they failed to acknowledge that in 2006, President Bush permitted a similar percentage of Muslim immigrants relative to Christians. However, it was more evocative to promulgate the Islamophobic agenda by

---

[25] Aidan Connaughton, "In Both Parties, Fewer Now Say Being Christian or Being Born in U.S. Is Important to Being 'Truly American,'" Pew Research Center, May 21, 2021, https://www.pewresearch.org/short-reads/2021/05/25/in-both-parties-fewer-now-say-being-christian-or-being-born-in-u-s-is-important-to-being-truly-american/

prefacing it with a name like Barack Hussein Obama. At the helm of pushing these unfounded fears were Evangelicals.

If our Evangelical friends truly believed that Christianity is the world's greatest religion and that the greater God resided in them, then they would readily welcome the opportunity to introduce this great God to those who have been denied the prior opportunity. But instead, they hide their fear (really of diversity) under the cloak of fear that indoctrinated Jihadists hate all things American and Christian. Did not Jesus teach us to *"Love your enemies, bless them that curse you, do good to them that hate you, and pray for them which despitefully use you, and persecute you; That ye may be the children of your Father which is in heaven: for he maketh his sun to rise on the evil and on the good, and sendeth rain on the just and on the unjust"* (Matthew 5:44-45 KJV). Should this not also apply to Muslims, even those who might hate us because of our faith?

> ### *The imposition of faith in the absence of its compassionate demonstration subjects us to justified hatred*

Instead of responding in the gracious and courageous manner Jesus instructed us to, we retreat to our religious silos and castigate people with beliefs different than ours. We justify our failure to measure up to His standard by using carnal analogies like, "I put up a fence around my yard or a lock on my door to protect my loved ones within." In reality, it is merely a justification for biased immigration policies, not just for Muslims entering the country but also for Hispanic people seeking refuge at our southern border.

The truth is that Evangelicals don't desire to evangelize at all. They would be far more content in a country where everyone looked like them and professed, "Jesus Christ is Lord," before they entered the country. While to some, that might be ideal, it is not the way of Christianity. Christianity boldly goes into hostile territory to make disciples of all men. The problem here is that they are not true Christians; they are Christian nationalists.

A central component of nationalism is the exclusion or detriment of another nation's (or group of people's) interest. The America First mantra is rapidly denigrating into an America Only policy. The racial and religious biases of our citizens and legislators are quickly exposing us to the targeted ire of other nations. Representative Ilhan Abdullahi Omar, a Somali-American Muslim, once stated a truth that sounds more Christian in nature than much of the hateful rhetoric coming from professed Christians. She stated, "The best deterrent to fanaticism is a system of compassion. We must alter our attitude and approach; if we truly want to affect change, we should refocus our efforts on inclusion and rehabilitation." Our failure to do so will fuel a greater hatred for not only Americans but Christians in general.

Our Christian faith assures us that we will be persecuted for our faith. I've often wondered why such a faith that is so inclusive and so marked by compassion would make us targets. I'm increasingly discerning that it is not these characteristics that will cause us to be hated. The imposition of our faith in the absence of its compassionate demonstration subjects us to justified hatred. No amount of legislation or limitations on immigration will prevent this. In fact, my and others' admonishments to Christians to repent and love as Jesus instructed will also fail to prevent the persecution foretold by the Bible. My purpose in writing this is simply to identify the problem and compel Christians to repentance. Like many of the prophetic words given to God's people in the Bible, the people in large portion will disregard. That said, I encourage Christians also to stop trying so desperately to shield themselves from the persecution that is inevitable. More importantly, stop compromising on the guiding principles of our faith, attempting to thwart the persecution promised.

Matthew 5 advises us to count ourselves blessed when we are persecuted for the sake of righteousness and when men revile us, saying all manner of things falsely against us. The operative words here are 'righteousness' and 'falsely'. 1 Peter 2:20-21 admonishes us, *"For what credit is there if, when you sin and are harshly treated, you endure it with patience? But if when you do what is right and suffer for it you patiently endure it, this finds favor with God. For you have been called for this purpose, since Christ also suffered for you, leaving you an example for you to follow in His steps"* (NASB).

There's glory in our persecution, but only when it is for the sake of righteousness. There's an honor when we are reviled, but only when the accusations are false. However, I am more concerned that the disdain the world is developing for Christians is well-justified, especially when we subvert the laws of the land to achieve favor and to impose our personal statutes on a population unwilling to accept them. We must always remember that we are the salt of the earth (Matthew 5:13). If we allow the prongs of Christian nationalism and fear to pilfer our savor, we are good for nothing but to be trodden under the feet of men.

The scriptures remind us in various passages that, as Christians, we will always be a minority in a world full of perversion and apostasy. Jesus reminded his disciples, *"Enter through the narrow gate; for the gate is wide and the way is broad that leads to destruction, and there are many who enter through it. For the gate is small and the way is narrow that leads to life, and there are few who find it"* (Matt. 7:13-14 NASB). Romans 9:27 reiterates, *"Isaiah cries out concerning Israel, 'Though the number of the sons of Israel be like the sand of the sea, it is the remnant that will be saved'"* (NASB).

Jesus identifies a power other than God as the ruler of this world in John 14:30. He again references a ruler of this world in John 12:31, meaning that this power rules the systems and the kingdoms of this world. In the same passage, Jesus encourages his disciples that when he is crucified, "the ruler of this world will be cast out." Many confuse Jesus' proclamation in this passage to mean that Satan no longer rules the world and that we should, therefore, exercise dominion – and by any means necessary. This is not so.

Although the inference might or might not be accurate, Jesus doesn't specifically identify Satan as the ruler. In other scriptures, the devil is specifically named. Matthew 4 states specifically that the devil took Jesus up to the mountain and tempted him. In John 8:44, Jesus identifies the devil as the father of the Pharisees, who sought to kill him. He calls the devil a murderer, and the father of lies, but curiously, in this passage, Jesus does not ascribe to the devil any greater powers.

I am not refuting the possibility that Satan, or the devil, could be the power whom Jesus and Paul suggest is the ruler of this world. However, I believe that Jesus is intentional in not specifically identifying Satan as that ruler. Perhaps it could be a broader and more cunning but powerful ruler to which Jesus refers. We can readily identify and resist the devil. However, the recognition of our own will, greed, lust, and passions as rulers in this world is much more elusive. Jesus' death and resurrection give us power and authority over the influence of the devil, but it also gives us the same authority over our own bodies and lusts. However, it does not eradicate the influence of either.

Paul reminds us that *"the god of this world has blinded the minds of the unbelieving so that they might not see the light of the gospel of the glory of Christ, who is the image of God"* (2 Cor. 4:4 NASB). If the god of this world was physically cast out by the death and resurrection of Jesus and he has no authority in the earth, how then could he blind the unbelievers to the Gospel? I believe the answer can be inferred from another writing of Paul: *"For the wrath of God is revealed from heaven against all ungodliness and unrighteousness of men who suppress the truth in unrighteousness"* (Rom. 1:18 NASB). Taken together, we see that the truth can be suppressed by an unnamed 'ruler of this world' and by the ungodliness and unrighteousness of men.

Jesus encouraged his disciples that the god of this world and, by extension, the ungodliness of man have no spiritual authority over those who have accepted the gospel and submitted to the lordship of Christ. His exhortation was neither a mandate nor an authorization for Christians to commandeer the levers of worldly government to subjugate them to the authority of Christ. Paul clarifies the intention:

> *"Therefore, since we have this ministry, as we received mercy, we do not lose heart, but we have renounced the things hidden because of shame, not walking in craftiness or adulterating the word of God, but by the*

manifestation of truth commending ourselves to every man's conscience in the sight of God" (2 Cor. 4:1-2 NASB).

In this single writing, Paul profoundly enumerates what our focus, as Christians, should be. First, he identifies ours as a ministry granted by the mercy of God. In this context, ministry is service rendered at the command of God. Thus, only those things sanctioned and commanded by God should be undertaken. He emphasized that they refuse to tamper with God's word. God's word never instructed or authorized Christians to subjugate the world's systems to God. That is the role of Jesus. Revelation 11:15 informs us that the kingdom of this world would become the Kingdom of our Lord at the sound of the seventh trumpet at the end of the world. Until then, the prince of the power of this world maintains authority over those who do not submit to the lordship of Christ.

Paul additionally states that he and other Christ followers have renounced disgraceful and underhanded ways. They refused to practice cunning. While we have the tools of Democracy available to use, we should never manipulate those tools in a way to subvert the laws of this land, working them to enact our own, or even God's statutes. Jesus criticized the Pharisees for doing the very thing, *"They tie up heavy burdens, hard to bear, and lay them on people's shoulders, but they themselves are not willing to move them with their finger"* (Matt. 23:4 ESV). He rebukes them further, saying:

"But woe to you, scribes and Pharisees, hypocrites! For you shut the kingdom of heaven in people's faces. For you neither enter yourselves nor allow those who would enter to go in. Woe to you, scribes and Pharisees, hypocrites! For you travel across sea and land to make a single proselyte, and when he becomes a proselyte, you make him twice as much a child of hell as yourselves" (Matt. 23:13-15 ESV).

We must not be like the Pharisees who shut up the Kingdom of Heaven from people who would otherwise come in. When we employ disgraceful and underhanded tactics to force compliance with God's statutes, our gospel becomes repulsive. Jesus' intention in his sacrifice was that he would draw all men unto him. That cannot and will not happen when Christians engage in unscrupulous tactics.

A common fear is sufficient to unite people with divergent beliefs

Paul makes clear that the focus of our attention should be the 'conscience' of those whom we seek to evangelize. When we minister the Gospel of Jesus Christ to the conscience of the unbeliever, we endue them with the power granted by the death and resurrection of Jesus to overcome the ruler of this world and the ungodliness of man, including ourselves. Should conservative state legislators be effective in forcing unbelievers to read and submit to the Ten Commandments in school systems, the best they could hope to produce are products 'twice as much a child of hell' as they themselves are.

Christian nationalism derives its power from fear – fear that the political and economic influence that Christians (historically White Christians) once enjoyed unfettered will be diminished. As other people groups grow in number and influence, the fear intensifies. Those who share those fears are more susceptible to recruitment. Islamophobes, homophobes, antisemites, and a host of other people who fear losing influence are easy targets. The irony is that a common fear is sufficient to unite people with divergent beliefs. Generally, conservative Christians are the staunchest supporters of Israel. However, to consolidate political influence, they find themselves uniting politically with antisemites because of their mutual Islamophobic and homophobic values. An ancient proverb, 'the enemy of my enemy is my friend,' rings true in the motivations of Christian Nationalists.

Islam has been a historic enemy of Christian Nationalists. A new formidable enemy is emerging in the form of homosexuality. I will never excuse homosexuality as anything other than the sin the Bible declares it to be. As for me and my household, we will continue to serve God and submit to his statutes.

As Christians, we recognize that we have dual citizenship. First and foremost, we are citizens of the Kingdom of God. Anything God calls unholy is, therefore, unholy for us to practice or endorse. We are also citizens of the United States of America. The Equal Protection Clause of the Fourteenth Amendment to the Constitution grants those who practice homosexuality equal protection under the law against discrimination. Consequently, they should be granted every right and representation that we, as God-loving, right-living Christians, enjoy under the Constitution.

In recent years, an all-out assault on the rights of homosexuals in this country has been launched by conservative Christian communities and politicians. The irony is that it is wholly unnecessary. Moreover, it perpetuates the notion that Christians hate homosexuals. That is precisely the opposite message that we should be sending to people whom we hope to reach with the loving message of Christ.

Let me be clear! Another person's practice of homosexuality does not hinder or hamper my pursuit of righteous living. Homosexuality is not contagious. It escapes me why so many Christians fear that compassionate, respectful, and equitable treatment of fellow citizens who practice different sexual habits than we embrace will somehow pollute or indoctrinate us and our children into 'ways of the world.' Again, if we truly believed that the God we serve is greater than the god of this world, we would not be intimidated by the expressions or rule of the god of this world. After all, Jesus has given us power over its influence, correct?

Do I want my children to be taught that homosexuality is acceptable in the sight of God? Absolutely not! However, in the United States of America, homosexuality is wholly acceptable by law, and those who practice it are every bit as worthy of fair treatment and representation as my Christian brothers and sisters.

As an African American man, I recognize the importance of favorable representation in society. Growing up, the only representation I saw on television of Black Americans was that of a criminal, pauper, or buffoon. The incessant representation of Black people as subservient to White people has an indelible effect on the psyche of those who are exposed to it. Unless counteracted by the affirming words of parents or others in a community of love, Black children become more susceptible to growing up believing that they are less valuable than their White cohorts. No one ever has to explicitly state it; the ubiquitous representation in media and the world around us is more than sufficient to inculcate that notion.

Television shows like The Jeffersons and The Cosby Show planted the seed in the minds of little Black children, who might not have had parents who counteracted the negative societal representations that they too can be successful and achieve anything their White counterparts could. The gradual appearance of Black news anchors reinforced the idea that we could achieve great things. Yes, prior to these shows, there were Black people who achieved great exploits. However, there is power in repeated exposures, even if they only occur through the media of television.

People, I think myopically, believe that President Barack Obama did little to help the Black community. I believe President Obama's greatest contribution to Black people in America was not legislation but representation. It is impossible to measure the intangible benefit of viewing on television over the course of eight years, an African American man who was the most powerful man in the world. As importantly, he comported himself with the utmost dignity amid a constant barrage of insults and criticism. Although many Christians disagreed with his policy decisions, not once were they able to lay a legitimate charge against his personal integrity. This type of influence is immeasurable and is implemented solely through representation.

In my home, and hopefully, in millions of homes across America and this world, Christian values are emulated daily. Because I am confident of this representation in my home, I am unthreatened by any institution or power that seeks to challenge it in my children's schools. This is not the case with many conservative Christians who insist that the schools ban books that represent homosexuality in an equitable light, as a traditional family structure and values.

While I prefer not to see homosexual relationships on my favorite television shows, I must remember that I have the option to turn the television off. Children might not have the option of not reading a textbook with references to same-sex parents. I submit that their parents wouldn't have to fret about such if the demonstration of Christian values in the home were consistent and authentic.

However, I am concerned about little Billy, who is being raised in a loving family of two dads. I worry that the lack of representation of his family structure as 'normal' in the United States of America disadvantages him as a citizen of this country. I am not equating the plight of homosexuals in America with that of Black people in America. However, I am saying that representation matters! This country was founded after a war that started because the citizens grew intolerant of taxation without representation.

As Christians, we must be ever cognizant of our dual citizenship. Our obligations to the Kingdom of God are personal. As long as the laws of the United States of America do not inhibit the free exercise of my personal faith, I have little opposition to its laws because I'm governed by a higher law. We are to spread the Gospel of Jesus Christ, but our focus should be the conscience of man and not the letter of his law. Jesus urged us to maintain this perspective when he instructed his followers to *"Render to Caesar the things that are Caesar's, and to God the things that are God's"* (Mark 12:17 ESV).

In response to the Pharisees' attempts to entrap him, Jesus asked them to bring him a coin, the denarius. He asked them to look at the coin and describe whose likeness and inscription was written on it. They replied that they were both Caesar's. Jesus' instruction was broad enough to extend beyond whether the people of God should pay taxes. He was essentially stating that if Caesar's name, or any other ruler's or government's name, is on the instrument, whether it be a financial or legislative instrument, it belonged to that ruler or government. He had no expectation for his disciples to overthrow or subvert in any way those governmental institutions Instead, we are instructed:

"Be subject for the Lord's sake to every human institution, whether it be to the emperor as supreme, or to governors as sent by him to punish those who do evil and to praise those who do good. For this is the will of God, that by doing good you should put to silence the ignorance of foolish people" (1 Pet. 2:13-15 ESV).

The Cause of Capitalism

Like pro-lifeism, patriotism, and nationalism, I believe capitalism has become an idol to American Evangelicals. When analyzing the current political environment, it becomes immediately apparent that certain buzzwords trigger vitriolic responses and loyalties coerced by fear. A recurring allegation by the Republican Party in multiple presidential elections is that the Democrats intend to convert the United States into a socialist state like Venezuela or Cuba. These tactics are effective in part because people have a limited understanding of what these political and economic systems represent. More concerningly, people conflate the notion of social responsibility with authoritarian socialism.

It is first important to understand that in its purest sense, socialism is not a political system. It is an economic system that involves public ownership of the means of economic production. The key problem in these countries is not Socialism (the economic system) but rather the political system. In these countries, the political system is one of authoritarianism, where people's political rights are sacrificed. Their freedom of speech is also restricted because people fear opposing the power of a centralized authority. This would conceivably never happen in America because the First Amendment of the Constitution will always allow the freedom of the press, which is crucial in maintaining democracy. The press must be free to criticize elected and appointed leadership. This enables the consumer public to draw conclusions of their own based on information. Nonetheless, there are always political influences that determine how any economic system works.

In the United States, we have operated under a capitalistic economic system. The International Monetary Fund describes capitalism as "an economic system in which private actors own and control property in accord with their interests, and demand and supply freely set prices in markets in a way that can serve the best interests of society. The essential feature of capitalism is the motive to make a profit." The Oxford Dictionary defines capitalism as "an economic and political system in which a country's trade and industry are controlled by private owners for profit."

More accurately, in America, the economic system should be considered Political Capitalism. Professor of Economics at Florida State University, Randall G. Holcombe, describes Political Capitalism as: "an economic and political system in which the economic and political elite cooperate for their mutual benefit. The economic elite influences the government's economic policies to use regulation, government spending, and the design of the tax system to maintain their elite status in the economy.[26] The political elite are then supported by the economic elite, which helps the political elite maintain their status; an exchange relationship that benefits both the political and economic elite."

Indeed, the economic elite influence governmental policies in a self-serving way by making political contributions to candidates that are more malleable to their agenda. Each election cycle, we have the debate about how much the government should be involved in regulating private industry. Clearly, if left unchecked, the greed of the economic elite will create conditions that serve only their financial interests. In many cases, these interests can be harmful and abusive to the employees who depend on their companies or corporations for employment.

For capitalism to persist, it depends on a continual supply of workers. While most people are not entrepreneurial by nature, many more would be if they had the economic means to venture out into business on their own. The goal of capitalism and the perpetuation of the economic elite's wealth would be hampered by such endeavors. Thus, the elite must carefully titrate the dispensing of funds to the working class. The ideal strategy is to pay just

---

[26] Randall G Holcombe, *Political Capitalism: How Economic and Political Power Is Made and Maintained* (Cambridge: Cambridge University Press, 2018).

enough to meet their basic financial needs with a few indulgences. However, if the workers have too much expendable funds, the risk of them leaving the workforce to become entrepreneurs increases. Such a depletion of the workpool threatens the wealth of the elite.

Karl Marx postulated about the dangers of continued exploitation of the working class.[27] He first posited that the foundation of any society was created by its economic structure. On that basis, legal and political systems were built. The elite, or the bourgeoisie as he called it, were the owners of the means of production. The product is made by the worker or the proletariat. He surmised that the value of the product (e.g., gross profit) exceeded the value of the worker (e.g., wages). The difference in these values permitted the owner of production the ability to allocate the profit as he saw fit. Often, that would be to invest in supplies needed to increase production.

He surmised that when the proletariat became aware of the class divide, they would eventually revolt against the bourgeoisie, resulting in eventual communism. One form of such, he postulated, would result in a transfer of legal and political power from the bourgeoisie to the proletariat. It is for this reason that Marx is often sharply criticized by proponents of capitalism. The mere reference to the name Karl Marx elicits a reflexive rejection of everything that follows thereafter without an objective assessment of its legitimacy. They assert that communism was the desired end goal of Marx and consequently must be the end goal of Democrats and people who believe that the government has an obligation to protect its citizens from exploitation and unfair treatment from the elite.

To be clear, there are societal and economic structures that the Bible presents that would be readily rejected by lovers of capitalism who ironically also identify as Christian. At the foundation of the Christian church, the Bible says that there were devout men from every nation under heaven dwelling in Jerusalem. At the time of Pentecost, when the Holy Spirit filled the room, there

---

[27] Karl Marx and Friedrich Engels, *The Communist Manifesto* (Workers' Educational Association, 1848).

were three thousand added to the church in one day. *"And they were selling their possessions and belongings and distributing the proceeds to all, as any had need"* (Acts 2:45 ESV).

Some will argue that this is a unique situation in part because it deals with the founding of the church. The reality is that men from a multitude of nations came together with a common idea, culture, and beliefs to form a nation within a nation. The way they ensured that all members of that nation had adequate provisions was that each member sold what he had and distributed it among those who did not have the resources they needed for survival. This would be considered socialism, an economic structure that is profoundly rejected by conservative Evangelicals.

Caring for the poor has always been a high priority of God and consequently was one of Jesus' priorities. In Matthew 19, a rich man who professed to have upheld all the law since childhood inquired of Jesus what he must do to enter the Kingdom of God. Jesus replied, *"If you would be perfect, go, sell what you possess and give to the poor, and you will have treasure in heaven; and come, follow me"* (Matthew 19:21 ESV).

When God established His initial law, giving them to Moses, He instructed the people, *"And when you reap the harvest of your land, you shall not reap your field right up to its edge, nor shall you gather the gleanings after your harvest. You shall leave them for the poor and for the sojourner: I am the Lord your God"* (Lev. 23:22 ESV). There are numerous other scriptures that would support what might be considered socialistic activities. An enumeration of them is needless because they will all be patently rejected by those who love capitalism and its benefits.

I am not suggesting that capitalism is inherently evil. I'm certainly not suggesting that socialism is divine. They both are potentially flawed because they are implemented by fallible humans. I do contend, however, that in Acts 4, when the people were all one and no one claimed possessions as their own, *"with great power the apostles were giving their testimony to the resurrection of the Lord Jesus, and great grace was upon them all. There was not a needy person among them, for as many as were owners of lands or houses sold them and brought the proceeds of what was sold and laid it at the apostles' feet, and it was distributed to each as any had need"* (Acts 4:33-35 ESV).

Even though God was moving mightily in this environment, there were still those who attempted to game the system. A man named Ananias and his wife Sapphira sold some property, and instead of donating all the proceeds, they withheld some portion of it and subsequently lied about donating it all. Greed crept in and inspired the lie, which would eventually lead to both of their sudden deaths (Acts 5:1-10). Perhaps one of the reasons we have not seen God move in such a manner today is that we have neglected the poor.

Ecclesiastes 5:19 informs us that God has given man wealth and possessions and the power to enjoy them. Proverbs 31 describes the virtuous woman who recognizes that the merchandise that she works hard to create is profitable (vs. 18). The problem isn't having wealth. In fact, God gives us the power to gain wealth (Deut. 8:18). The problem is what we do with that wealth and how that wealth impacts our behavior and spirit. The virtuous woman mentioned in Proverbs 31 *"opens her hand to the poor and reaches out her hands to the needy"* (Prov. 31:20 ESV).

In Amos 8, the Bible sharply rebukes those who trample on the needy and abuse the poor, disregarding holy days so that they might return to making more money. Those who deal deceitfully, create false balances, and cheat people out of their goods will be dealt with by the Lord. These traits are not inherent to capitalism, but the structure of capitalism is ripe for cultivating these behaviors. The elite makes more profit by working the laborer strenuously and providing meager wages. Only the owners know the extent of the profit they make and whether they could more fairly reward the laborers who help them to obtain that wealth.

Often, what is seen in American capitalism is that the rich get richer, and the poor get poorer. The wealth gap in America has progressively widened over the past several decades. Pew Research has reported that the share of U.S. aggregate wealth owned by the top 5% of income earners grew from 60% in

1983 to 79% in 2016. The portion owned by the middle class, during the same time, declined from 32% to 17%, underscoring the widening gap between the haves and the have-nots.[28]

It is inconceivable that God is pleased with such disparities. And this is considering only those people who live in the United States. When we consider the poverty experienced around the world, the greed of America, fueled by capitalism, must be a stench in the nostrils of God. The US has approximately 5.5% of the world's population but is home to 37% of the world's millionaires. Currently, there are 5.5 million people in the US who have at least $1 million in liquid investable income on hand. This number has grown by 62% over the past decade, compared to the worldwide growth rate of 38%. Is there any wonder why foreigners from impoverished nations seek to migrate to the US despite the incredible risk to their health and safety?[29]

Capitalism is not inherently evil, but it does predispose those who embrace it to forsake the poor. This predisposition extends to how capitalists perceive immigrants. If we embraced biblical precepts for handling wealth, we would be more accustomed to freely giving to the poor and aiding foreigners who migrate to our land. We would have practiced benevolence, and when we find that it is truly needed, we would not be hesitant to engage.

This is not to suggest that Americans are not benevolent. According to the Charities Aid Foundation's World Giving Index 2022, the US is third in charitable giving, behind Indonesia and then Kenya. Of note, the US is considerably wealthier than either of these countries. When analyzed over time, high-income countries have consistently had a giving index that ranged from 46% to 52%. It reached a high in 2017. In 2018, that number sharply dropped

---

[28] Juliana Horowitz, Ruth Igielnik, and Rakesh Kochhar, "Trends in U.S. Income and Wealth Inequality," Pew Research Center (Pew Research Center, January 9, 2020), https://www.pewresearch.org/social-trends/2020/01/09/trends-in-income-and-wealth-inequality/.

[29] Henley Partners, "USA Wealth Report 2024: America Remains the World's Top Wealth Hub but Faces Uncertain Future," Prnewswire.com, March 19, 2024, https://www.prnewswire.com/news-releases/usa-wealth-report-2024-america-remains-the-worlds-top-wealth-hub-but-faces-uncertain-future-302090201.html#:~:text=The%20USA%20is%20currently%20home.

from 11% to 41%. It is difficult to determine the exact causes of this. However, it can be reasonably inferred that representation matters. When leaders of these high-income countries demonstrate selfish behaviors, the people typically will follow. Interestingly, in 2021, the giving index excelled to its highest level, 56%. While the pandemic and the compassions it ignited in people worldwide likely contributed to this, it cannot be underestimated that when the leaders of the free world model benevolence, the people emulate it.

Those who prosper to the peril of the poor poorly represent Christ

As a nation, we stand at an impasse. We must determine whether we will succumb to the pollutive influence of capitalism or if we will continue to be found moving in benevolence. A lot of this depends on the people we elect and place in positions of influence. As mentioned previously, the character of our elected leaders matters. Many people argue that they would prefer to have a Commander-In-Chief who has experience as a businessman. However, as an entrepreneur myself, I recognize and often warn people that business has no compassion. As leaders of the free world, we cannot be so moved by finances that we forsake weightier matters.

Those who prosper to the peril of the poor poorly represent Christ. Let us not be compared to the merchants and business owners referenced in Amos 8 who trample the needy and are so driven by profits that they forsake their obligations to the poor. If not for the fear of the wrath of God, let us at least remember that the economic structure is the foundation for other societal structures, including the legal and political systems. If the elite continues its self-serving exploits, the working class will eventually revolt, resulting in the destabilization of Democracy. Let us not elevate capitalism to a position of idolatry. Rather, let's make America charitable and benevolent in every endeavor – financially and socially.

CHAPTER 7

THE FULLNESS OF TIME

Up to this point, a reader of this manuscript might easily conclude that Evangelicalism needs to be stopped or eradicated. To be clear, I am not advocating for this. My prayer is that you will realize, as I have, that the evangelical mindset and the ascent of Evangelicals to power are instrumental in the fulfillment of God's plan. In the following chapters, we will explore biblical predictions of the impending apocalypse, the evolution of events, and how evangelicalism plays a necessary role in its fulfillment.

In full disclosure, I am not a scholar of apocalyptic studies. Herein, I merely present the prophetic revelation I believe God has given me concerning the present times and the times to come. These are offered so that as you see them happening, you won't be disheartened, knowing that Jesus and his apostles warned us so that we might be prepared. As Jesus said, *"I have said all these things to you to keep you from falling away... that when their hour comes you may remember that I told them to you"* (John 16:1, 4 ESV).

175

The Preference of the Prophet

As I consider the very charged and polarized climate of today, it occurs to me that we are dysfunctional either by choice or by ignorance. Consider that each member of the body has unique functions, positions, and sensitivities. The feet, for example, are specifically designed for strength and stability. While they possess the ability of tactile sense, it is less discriminative than the hand. Though the foot also has some measure of dexterity, it is less dexterous than the hand. The position of the feet on the body affords them a sensitivity to more readily detect things that are destabilizing than any other part of the body.

Would it not be foolish for the hand to disregard the warning from the foot that a destabilizing force is present merely because the hand presumes to be more sensitive than the foot? Such a dismissal predisposes the body to falls and injury. But when the hand heeds the warnings of the feet, it prepares the body for an impending fall. The body then instinctively extends the hand to prevent or at least soften the blow of the fall and protect more vulnerable parts of the body from potentially fatal injury. When the body is connected and functioning as created, these protective functions are instinctively present and active. For the maximum protection of the body, the signals of impending harm must be effectively communicated and received.

The Bible tells us that God gave us apostles, teachers, pastors, evangelists, and prophets for the edification or building up of the body of Christ (Eph. 4:11-16). When each of these ministries is operational, the body can be adequately prepared to endure the persecution the Bible foretells will eventually befall His Church. God does not do anything unless He reveals it first to and through His prophets (Amos 3:7). The challenge, however, is two-fold.

First, the prophetic word of God is often not heeded. It is rejected as lunacy by many who do not perceive the voice of God speaking through His prophets. The prophets are sent so that we might prosper, as iterated in 2 Chronicles 20:20 – *"Believe in the Lord your God, and you will be established; believe his prophets, and you will succeed"* (ESV). Unfortunately, people who are led by their own wills or consumed by their own desires will rarely subjugate their perceptions to the prophetic word of God. Throughout the scriptures, God sent prophets to warn the people of impending judgment, but they failed to heed the admonishment and repent. Instead, they continued in the indulgence of their lusts until the anger of the Lord was kindled against them.

The second obstacle to the proper functioning of the prophetic word of God is that some prophets speak false prophecies. *"Thus says the Lord God, Woe to the foolish prophets who follow their own spirit, and have seen nothing! Your prophets have been like jackals among ruins..."* (Ezek. 13:3-4 ESV). When the Lord issued a strong rebuke of the children of Israel, He started with the prophets. He warned that in their delivery of false prophecies, they had left the city vulnerable to attack, *"You have not gone up into the breaches, or built up a wall for the house of Israel, that it might stand in the battle in the day of the Lord"* (Ezek. 13:5 ESV).

God proceeded to admonish the prophets that because they had uttered falsehoods and lied about visions they had seen; He was against them. He was infuriated with the prophets because they misled the people by declaring, "Peace, peace!" where there was no peace. In essence, the prophets provided the comforting words that the people wanted to hear. In doing so, they failed to fortify the city against attack.

Jeremiah gives a similar account of the apostasy of the prophets. God proclaimed that, *"Both prophet and priest are ungodly; even in my house I have found their evil"* (Jer. 23:11 ESV). He accused the shepherds of scattering the sheep, leaving them unattended and even driving them away. He further accused the prophets from Samaria of prophesying by a false god, Baal, and the prophets in Jerusalem of adultery and walking in lies. In so doing, *"they strengthen the hands of evildoers, so that no one turns from his evil"* (Jer. 23:14 ESV).

In the religious sphere today, prophets rarely speak the corrective word or rebuke of the Lord, as they did in the Old Testament. They are marked by feel-good words of prosperity, which are often rewarded with celebrity and wealth. Falling into the trap of offering only fanciful exhortations, the prophets misinterpret their purpose in edifying the Body of Christ. While words of affirmation are essential, and the Bible encourages us to lift each other up with psalms and hymns (Eph. 5:19), it does not delegate that function to the prophets. The words of affirmation are intended to be how we, as brothers and sisters in Christ, encourage each other. The prophet, however, communicates the word of God. While that word might include words of affirmation, they often are characterized by corrective admonishments.

The reproof of the prophet is an absolute necessity for the edification or fortification of the body of Christ. Without it, the Church is unable to grow in strength, courage, tenacity, and endurance. To achieve the desired effect of edification, the hearer of the rebuke must embrace a paradigm shift. We often view correction as denigrating or negative. But God's perspective is clearly that His chastening is a symbol of His love (Heb. 12:6). Because God's perspective is eternal, the temporal negative emotional response to the reprimand is insignificant compared to the good that will result if the rebuke is heeded. His love is also demonstrated in corrections that prevent us from pursuing a path that eventually leads to our inevitable harm.

Throughout history, prophecy has been perverted. This current age is no exception, and the practice continues today. I believe there are individuals who have clearly been called by God to be His prophets but who have prostituted the gift in pursuit of personal gain or under the influence of personal preference. Such perversions are particularly harmful today because these pimped-out prophets have a much broader platform of influence due to the reach of social media.

In 2 Timothy 4:3, we are warned that in the last days, men with itching ears would heap unto themselves false prophets. They would seek and reward those who speak the words that their followers and supporters desire to hear. Consequently, the false prophets grow in celebrity and wealth. I am not suggesting that this is their goal. I am, however, saying that this is a predictable consequence – one that has a self-perpetuating effect. It then becomes increasingly tempting to continue with their fanciful prophecies because they

get positive feedback from those who receive the prophetic word they offer –
those whose ears are itching, not for the truth, but for affirmation of their own
predilections and aspirations.

As the Lord was training me in the gift of prophecy, He allowed me to
identify many of the pitfalls that I and others fall into while delivering a
prophetic word. Among them are seeking affirmation from people that the
word we're speaking is accurate. In one instance, He revealed to me that a
particular woman and her husband were enduring marital hardships. No
sooner than He told me this, without any further instruction, I glanced at the
woman's hand to see if she wore a wedding band. Indeed, she did, but what
followed immediately was a rebuke from the Lord. He reminded me that if He
speaks a word to me, I should immediately trust it and not try to confirm His
word using carnal clues.

In another instance, I prophesied to a woman, and in the midst of the exhortation, I looked at her face to see if what I was speaking resonated with her.
In that instance, I became distracted and proceeded to speak more about that
topic than the Lord authorized. Again, God immediately corrected my very
natural inclination to be misled by affirmations that merely appeased my own
insecurity about the accuracy of what I was hearing from God. It is imperative
that the prophets of God be able to distinguish that which is inspired by God
from that which is inspired by our own insecurities, preferences, or predilections.

As the world seems to be plummeting into moral decadence, Christians
and Evangelicals seem to be growing desperate for a solution to prevent further
decline. Motivated by a fear of losing the religious liberties afforded to us under
the Constitution, many evangelicals clung to the hope that, somehow, a
political leader could shield us from the loss of religious freedoms. They
understandably lament societal attempts to influence our children to accept
unholy practices as moral.

In their desperation, I believe they have aligned themselves with individuals who exploit their earnest and laudable passions as part of their strategy to
gain political influence and power. The requirement of repentance for one who

is allegedly God's chosen instrument is overlooked because of the promise of political or legislative dominance. They've quieted their discernment of good fruit and bad fruit. In doing so, the fruit has been defined by legislative promises and victories instead of the fruit of the Spirit, such as love, joy, peace, gentleness, longsuffering, and patience (Gal. 5:22-23).

The carnal laws of man can never produce a spiritual result

To appease the voice of conviction that the Holy Spirit undoubtedly whispered to those who formerly attentively listened, they contrived prophecies to conform to their preference. Yet, others even gave new prophecies that likely reflected more of the prophet's personal desire than the immutable word of God. Consequently, many well-intentioned evangelicals have succumbed to the notion that if an individual institutes what they perceive as righteous legislation, the lawmaker or executive is the ordained instrument of God.

They have, as Jeremiah wrote, strengthened the hands of some people who are historically and currently evildoers, presuming to justify them by their legislative works. Their silence about the evil works and ungodly acts is purchased by the promise of conservative legislation and judicial appointments. The consequence of their purchased silence is that neither the purchasers nor sellers of silence turn from their evil works.

For years, Evangelicals prayed fervently and believed honorably to see the laws of this land reflect the laws of God. While that is a laudable petition, I don't believe it is consistent with Biblical principles. The carnal laws of man can never produce a spiritual result that even the preeminent law of God was incapable of producing. While it seems to be a worthy pursuit, it is not theologically sound. Thus, in their seemingly righteous pursuit, they are led astray. Their prophets are, in part, to blame.

The remedies to abortion and homosexuality are not more laws! The solution is the church being the church and ministering to the underlying spiritual root that produces this bad fruit. If we advocate for carnal laws, we must recognize that these are man's mechanisms and should not be ascribed any divine mandate or authority. Likewise, we should not try to manipulate or create a prophecy to justify our pursuit of these legislative goals.

The deception has gotten so bad that during the 2020 election, many evangelicals asserted that one could not be Christian and vote Democratic. In doing so, they deified a political cause or platform. Exodus 20:24-25 makes clear that God has a specific prescription for how sacrifices made to Him should be offered. This passage tells us that God desires that an altar of earth be made unto Him, and if stones are used, they should not be stones cut or crafted by the hand of man. Verse 25 states that *"if you use your tool on it, you have profaned it."* In contrast, if the sacrifice is offered in the manner prescribed by God, He said He will record His name in that place and come thereunto and bless the people who offered the sacrifice. Jesus warned us, *"Every plant which My heavenly Father has not planted will be uprooted"* (Matt. 15:13 NKJV).

God will ascribe His blessing on sacrifices offered only according to His precise prescription and which bear His inscription. Any machination of man that imposes on the process defiles the sacrifice. As will be discussed in greater detail later, Nadab and Abihu, the sons of Aaron, offered unauthorized sacrifice unto God (Leviticus 10). By man's standards, the act would have been deemed honorable. However, in the Kingdom of God, obedience in the process is more important than the splendor of the product. Nadab and Abihu were killed by God for offering a "strange," or unauthorized, fire as a sacrifice. Because many of the modern-day prophets were so inspired by their personal preferences and what seemed right to them, I fear that many have defiled the sacrifice they sought to offer unto God. In doing so, they offered strange fire to God.

There are many Evangelicals, desperate to see righteousness prevail, who have cited prophecies from Kim Clement and others as evidence that God intended to use Trump to usher in a season of righteousness and victory for the church. They have contorted the words that were spoken and interpreted them, often erroneously, to suggest outcomes that they desired to see manifest. For example, in April 2007, Clement prophesied:

"The Spirit of God said, this is a moment of resurrection. For the Spirit of God says, honor Me with your praise and acceptance of this that I say to you. This that shall take place shall be the most unusual thing, a transfiguration, a going into the marketplace if you wish, into the news media. Where Time Magazine will have no choice but to say what I want them to say. Newsweek, what I want to say. The View, what I want to say. Trump shall become a trumpet, says the Lord! No, you didn't hear me. Trump shall become a Trumpet. Are you listening to me? I will raise up the Trump to become a trumpet and Bill Gates to open up the gate of a financial realm for the Church, says the Spirit of the Living God! For God said, I will not forget 911. I will not forget what took place that day, and I will not forget the gatekeeper that watched over New York who will once again stand and watch over this Nation, says the Spirit of God. It shall come to pass that the man that I place in the highest office shall go in whispering My name. But God said, when he enters into the office, he will be shouting out by the power of the Spirit for I shall fill him with My Spirit when he goes into office and there will be a praying man in the highest seat in your land. And God says, even a greater move of the Spirit shall take place and your enemies will finally be subdued by the year 2009."

Earlier that year, in February, Clement prophesied, "In the next two terms, there will be a praying President, not a religious one, for I will fool the people, says the Lord." He prophesied further, saying, "Yes, he may have hot blood, but he will bring the walls of protection on this country in a greater way, and the economy of this country shall change rapidly." An exhaustive list of the various prophecies concerning Donald Trump and his election as president is beyond the scope of this publication and can be found in the book *God's Man in the White House* by James A. Beverley and Larry N. Willard.[30] I've highlighted these because I believe they illustrate very important lessons we must learn about prophecy.

As mentioned previously, prophets are fallible and can be easily misled by their own fervent passions. If they are not careful, they will attribute a prophetic word to God, which God has not said. Though they may be well-intentioned, such an error is a punishable offense to God. The second lesson we should learn is that prophesies are often incomplete. Paul said, *"For we know in part and we prophesy in part, but when the perfect comes, the partial will pass away"* (1 Cor. 13:9-10 ESV).

We must be careful not to read more into what the prophetic word says and resist the urge to contort the prophetic word to conform to our paradigm or desired meaning. Certain words spoken in prophecy might be symbolic, while others might be literal. When that which is perfect comes, when the Spirit of God determines the time is right, the entire meaning will be made immutably clear.

Until then, we are cautioned, *"Do not despise prophecies, but test everything; hold fast what is good"* (1 Thes. 5:20-21 ESV). Not only should we judge the prophetic word, but also the spirit in which it was delivered. *"Beloved, do not believe every spirit, but test the spirits to see whether they are from God, for many false prophets have gone out into the world"* (1 John 4:1 ESV). Finally, we should be cautious, both as prophets and as those who receive prophecies, not to place too much emphasis on timelines. Unless God explicitly gives a date or timeframe, the prophet must guard against providing one.

Hananiah was a prophet from Gibeon who prophesied in the company of Jeremiah, the priests, and all the people that the Lord said in two years he would bring back all the vessels of the LORD's house which Nebuchadnezzar, king of Babylon, took away (Jeremiah 28). He went further to state that the Lord said he would also restore Jeconiah, who was dethroned by Nebuchadnezzar,

---

[30] James A. Beverley and Larry N. Willard, *God's Man in the White House: Donald Trump in Modern Christian Prophecy* (Burlington, ON, Canada: Castle Quay Books, 2020).

as king of Judah and that all the exiles from Judah who went to Babylon would be returned. In this prophecy, Hananiah was really led by his selfish desire. Jeremiah respectfully honored the prophecy and prayed that God bring it to pass. Jeremiah further warned him, *"The prophets who preceded you and me from ancient times prophesied war, famine, and pestilence against many countries and great kingdoms. As for the prophet who prophesies peace, when the word of that prophet comes to pass, then it will be known that the LORD has truly sent the prophet"* (Jer. 28:8-9 ESV).

Hananiah confidently doubled down on the prophecy, making a show before all the people and the priests. Jeremiah quietly walked away. Sometime after that, the Lord told Jeremiah to go back and rebuke Hananiah, telling him, *"The LORD has not sent you, and you have made this people trust in a lie. Therefore thus says the LORD: 'Behold, I will remove you from the face of the earth. This year you shall die, because you have uttered rebellion against the LORD'"* (Jer. 28:15-16 ESV). In the seventh month of that same year, Hananiah died.

Like Jeremiah, I do not refute God's prophecies of blessings and peace. We just need to be extra careful when the prophetic word is such to ensure that we are not moved by our own passions and desires to encourage those who are oppressed. Sometimes, the Lord sanctioned oppression as a punishment for his disobedient people. For this reason, the people of Judah fell under the oppression of Nebuchadnezzar.

In the prophecy of February 2007, Clement mentioned specifically that for the next two terms, the president would be a praying man with hot blood. His election to that office would fool the people because he was God's chosen. Evangelicals focus on the 'hot blood' reference to signify Trump's temper and fierce fighting style. But they fail to acknowledge that the president for the next two terms following this prophecy was Barack Hussein Obama. Could it be that what America stereotypes as an 'angry Black man' might be another reference to hot blood? Was not America fooled by the election of its first Black president? Would they not also be fooled that a man with a Muslim name might quietly pray to God, one who, as opposed to Trump, at least admits that he prays to God?

Under the presidency of Barack Obama, the unemployment rate and the economy grew at a faster rate than they did under the four years of Donald Trump. The gross domestic product (GDP) grew 70% higher under Obama than it did under Trump.[31] The unemployment rate went from a high of 10% in 2009 to 4.6% in 2016, at the end of Obama's presidency. Trump inherited an unemployment rate of 4.6%, but at the end of his term, it was 14.7%. I present these numbers not to make an assertion about who might have been the better president but rather to demonstrate how people can ignore key facts of the prophesy and contort them to fit a desired narrative. I am also not contending that the prophecy more accurately referenced Obama. I am merely pointing out that despite the more compelling evidence that the February 2007 prophecy might have referenced Obama, Evangelicals would never lend any credence to this possibility because it directly contradicts their paradigms concerning Democrats.

Admittedly, I don't know for sure whether the prophecy references either of the two. If, according to Jeremiah 28, Kim Clement was a true prophet of God, it would mean that it referenced Obama, the president who occupied the office for the next two terms, since he prophesied a specific timeframe. Otherwise, based on scripture, we might conclude that Clement was not a true prophet of God and should, therefore, disregard his other subsequent prophesies.

When Donald Trump won the presidency in 2016, Evangelicals presumed it must be the prophetic word and will of God. They often referenced Clement's prophecy of April 2007 when he stated, "Trump shall be a trumpet." They emphatically asserted that the prophecy was a foreshadow of his presidency. Like Jeremiah, I will not hold this prophecy or such an interpretation in contempt, unless and until the Lord reveals its veracity completely. However, I do think it is important to consider the context and the meaning of trumpet in the context.

---

[31] Wayne Duggan, "How GDP Growth under Trump Compares to Clinton, Obama and Other Presidents," finance.yahoo.com, October 29, 2020, https://finance.yahoo.com/news/gdp-growth-under-trump-compares-121008953.html.

The context of the prophecy was that there would be a transfiguration of the marketplace and in the media. It appears that he was prophesying a redistribution of wealth and influence, respectively. He curiously identifies three historically liberal publications, Time Magazine, Newsweek and The View, and declares that they will have no choice but to use their influence to speak only what God says to speak. He then turns his attention to the marketplace and states that Trump shall be a trumpet and Bill Gates shall be a financial gate for the church. The context suggests that Trump, like Bill Gates, should be providing some financial benefit to the church.

Let's first consider that among certain Evangelical and conservative camps, Bill Gates is absolutely despised for his role in philanthropic work in vaccine development and distribution. These activities make him *persona non grata* among many conservative religious camps. If these Evangelicals esteemed the prophetic word of God, perhaps they should esteem the entire prophecy and pray for the fulfillment of the word. Instead, they select the portions of the prophecy that tickle their ear and herald it as divine. How the phrase "Trump shall be a trumpet" could be interpreted to mean he will become the president is beyond my expertise and discernment.

As previously mentioned, prophecy often uses metaphoric or symbolic imagery. In the Bible, trumpets serve various purposes. Blowing the trumpet was used to praise the Lord (2 Chron. 5:13). In Numbers 10, God instructs Moses on how to make and use the trumpet for its various purposes. The number of trumpets to be blown, the number of times they are blown, and the duration of the trumpet blowing each signified a different thing.

Briefly, the trumpets were used for assembling the congregation at the tent and for breaking camp. At times they were used for assembling only the elders. When they were preparing to go to war, the trumpets would sound an alarm, and they would again blow the trumpets when they returned from war victorious. The trumpets were supposed to be blown during certain feasts and to remind them of their devotion to God and His to them.

The blowing of the trumpet was also intended to warn the people of impending danger or potential doom. In Ezekiel 33, God likened the voice of the prophet to a trumpet. He told the prophet that he was like a watchman in a tower who would blow the horn when he saw the enemy coming. If he blew the trumpet and the people did not heed the warning, the blood would be on the heads of the people. However, if the watchman saw the evil coming and did not blow the trumpet, the blood would be on his hands. God told the prophet, *"Whenever you hear a word from my mouth, you shall give them warning from me"* (Ezek. 33:7 ESV). Thus, the reference to the trumpet has prophetic implications as well.

Of significant concern, the blowing of the trumpet was used to signify the impending day of the Lord, spoken of prophetically. *"Blow a trumpet in Zion; sound an alarm on my holy mountain! Let all the inhabitants of the land tremble, for the day of the LORD is coming; it is near"* (Joel 2:1 ESV). Most notably, in Revelation 8-11, we learn that the trumpets were blown to release God's final judgment on the earth and the people who had rejected him.

When interpreting Clement's prophecy about Trump being a trumpet, we see that there is much to consider based on the context, as well as biblical and prophetic references to the trumpet. If Trump were to be a trumpet like Clement prophesied, is it possible that he could have been the instrument in the mouth of one of God's angels, being used to herald the first round of God's judgment of the earth? Again, I have not been authorized by God to assert that this is so. I only offer judgment on how the prophetic word is bent to appease the pleasures of man and announce God's displeasure with this practice.

Finally, I want to mention a prophecy by Kim Clement that was given in January 2006. Clement prophesied the following concerning Hillary Clinton:

> *"And some of you said, when the Spirit said Hillary Clinton, some of you shouted out 'yes.' God said, I have already dealt with her heart, not to be President of this Nation but to be president in a Christian world. She will have a testimony second to none and will eventually come out with it and make declaration that Christ Jesus saved her marriage,*

saved her child, and saved her life. And when this happens there will be a shaking in the Democratic Party so powerful. They will say, what choice do we have? And God says, one of the Kennedy sons who has lost a limb will come into the Kingdom and break the Kennedy curse once and for all, says the Spirit of God."

That Evangelicals would completely ignore and discredit this prophetic word from their trusted major, contemporary prophet, exemplifies the soulish motives behind their receipt of prophecy. More accurately, it identifies political affiliation as a measuring stick for their assessment of righteousness. They have conflated the affiliation of political party with the sanction of God. This is blasphemous!

Prior to the 2016 election season, relatively few prophecies had been made concerning Trump and his ascent to the presidency. In his book *God's Man in the White House*, James Beverley astutely notes, *"Prophecies about Trump increased with a frenzy during 2016, leading up to the November election. Prophets also issued divine warnings about Barack Obama, Clinton, and the Democrats in general."*[32] Beverley attempts to remain impartial in his presentation and itemization of the various prophecies concerning Donald Trump and his presidency, which is much more exhaustive than I have provided herein.

He concludes at least two perspectives in answering the question, "Is Donald Trump God's man in the White House?" First, there are many Christian prophets who believe God chose Trump to make America great again. These prophets enjoy the support of millions of Evangelicals, Pentecostals, and charismatics. Second, he asserts that "a few Christian prophets say that Trump represents God's judgment on America and that he is part of an unfolding apocalyptic scenario, either wittingly or not. From this perspective, Trump is a sign that things will get worse as the world awaits the return of Jesus Christ."

---

[32] James A. Beverley and Larry N. Willard, *God's Man in the White House: Donald Trump in Modern Christian Prophecy* (Burlington, ON, Canada: Castle Quay Books, 2020).

Each person must determine for themselves what their convictions are. Knowing that our strong convictions and passions can influence our perceptions, even of God's prophetic word, we must ask God to examine and reveal our hearts so that we would not be misled by false prophecy. Prophesies can be God's message of protection for his people. When they are given by false prophets, they can also be the entrapments of the devil to deceive the people of God, As Christians, we must remain diligent to discern the difference. When the prophecy is one that reinforces my paradigm, I am doubly cautious to watch patiently to determine if it is the genuine communication of God. As the day of the Lord's coming approaches, the discernment of truth, even in our own hearts, becomes more difficult. If the prophet Jeremiah took such a cautious approach when scrutinizing Hananiah's prophecy, it seems to be a prudent strategy for the rest of us.

The Extinction of Truth

In January 2018, the Lord gave me a prophetic warning about the deception and strong delusion that would ensue. The following is the word that was given to me, as was published at the time:

> *In 2018 there will be an Acceleration of Deception and a Deception of Acceleration. I strongly encourage you to read the entire 2nd chapter of 2 Thessalonians, but here I highlight verses 11-12, "And for this cause God shall send them strong delusion, that they should believe a lie: That they all might be damned who believed not the truth, but had pleasure in unrighteousness" (KJV).*
>
> *The scripture suggests that God will allow many to suffer "strong delusion" such that they believe a lie. I have often been confounded how so many seemingly mature Christians could not see a lie that is so plainly set before them. The scripture clarifies it, revealing that those who choose the pleasure of unrighteousness will not believe the truth. The pleasure of unrighteousness is not immediately obvious because it is disguised as*

"benefits" through the demonstration of power, signs, and lying wonders (vs. 9). If we fail to discern the truth and be deceived by the benefits and "deceivableness of unrighteousness," (vs. 10), we too will believe the lie.

The Deception will be Accelerated unlike ever before in our history. In this Age of Information, information is so readily available to us. However, we are now challenging the veracity of the information. It is becoming increasingly difficult to know what to believe as truth. As believers in Christ, we must sharpen our ability to discern the truth and the one by whom truth is revealed. A simple litmus test may be to determine if the one by whom the report comes is born again of Christ and submitted to the Lordship of Christ. Beware of him "Who opposeth and exalteth himself above all that is called God, or that is worshipped; so that he as God sitteth in the temple of God, shewing himself that he is God" (2 Thes. 2:4 KJV) as he will be revealed to those who do not revel in the pleasures (e.g., benefits) of his unrighteousness.

There will be the appearance and tangible perception of an Acceleration in 2018. By all earthly measures, the benefits of this acceleration will be palpable. However, the acceleration (mostly economic) will be Deceptive. Many will abandon their spiritual gift of discernment for the benefit of acceleration and will consequently be given a "strong delusion" that will realign their allegiance and determine a course of inevitable spiritual destruction. But take heed that the times we are living in are not to be taken lightly. There is a real battle for the souls of man, and the deception that will descend on the Christian community will separate the wheat from the tare - the "Christians" from the true "Church."

Be prayerful and discerning in 2018. Discern not only the end result but, as importantly, discern the process. Be spiritually skeptical of what appears to be Acceleration because it is easy to get caught up in its Deception. Pray for greater discernment and the fortitude to not excuse Deception for the benefit of Acceleration.

This warning was written and published long before the 2020 election, and the massive deception consumed many Christians because they were persuaded by the acceleration. Many people were so moved by economic and political victories that they would succumb to a lie. Today, this holds true more than ever, and it extends far beyond the political realm, permeating almost every aspect of our lives.

Mankind is consumed by its own inventions

The original sin of Adam and Eve was disobedience, but this disobedience was motivated by a desire for more knowledge – more information. The tree from which they ate was the Tree of Knowledge. They desired to know good and evil as God did. Thus, their thirst for knowledge and information was the Achilles heel through which the devil tempted and persuaded them.

We are living in the Information Age, where information instructs the marketplace, education, healthcare, politics, civics, and religion. Information is constantly collected about our preferences, biases, interests and affiliations. This information is processed and utilized to force-feed us with more information that suits our proclivities. The problem is that this information is hardly scrutinized. Moreover, we don't demand that it be, in part, because it supports or reinforces the very ideals we already hold dearest. The fact that it comports with our paradigms then serves as its validation – at least in our minds. In this way, the thing that God intended to shield us from will become the very thing that destroys us.

Mankind is consumed by its own inventions. The things we imagine in our hearts and minds, we eventually bring to reality because we were created in the image of God. What God imagines in his mind, He speaks, and it comes to existence. In a like manner, but certainly over much longer periods of time, what we imagine eventually manifests. I acknowledge that our imaginations have created many inventions that have been beneficial to humanity. However, the eventual fate of human inventions will be an evolution of corruption and evil. The more apt humans become in our inventions, the more self-reliant and secular we become. We do well to remind ourselves of Paul's faithful words to Timothy:

"But godliness with contentment is great gain. For we brought nothing into this world, and it is certain we can carry nothing out. And having food and raiment let us be therewith content. But they that will be rich fall into temptation and a snare, and into many foolish and hurtful lusts, which drown men in destruction and perdition. For the love of money is the root of all evil: which while some coveted after, they have erred from the faith, and pierced themselves through with many sorrows" (1 Tim. 6:6-10 KJV).

I don't intend to be fatalistic in my assessment, so let us first consider God's perspective on the matter. In the early part of creation, evil was multiplying on the earth. The Bible says:

"And GOD saw that the wickedness of man was great in the earth, and that every imagination of the thoughts of his heart was only evil continually. And it repented the LORD that he had made man on the earth, and it grieved him at his heart" (Gen. 6:5-6 KJV).

The Lord then determined that he would rid the earth of this creation whose imaginations were continually evil. The story of Noah and the Great Flood is a very familiar one and does not warrant elaboration in detail. After the flood waters receded:

"And the LORD smelled a sweet savour; and the LORD said in his heart, I will not again curse the ground any more for man's sake; for the imagination of man's heart is evil from his youth; neither will I again smite any more every thing living, as I have done" (Gen. 8:21 KJV).

That we have not been destroyed again is not evidence that the imaginations of our hearts, our intentions, have miraculously become pure. They remain evil continually. Jeremiah 17:9 reminds us, *"The heart is deceitful above all things, and desperately wicked: who can know it?"*

I concede that not every imagination is evil at its inception. However, the eventual implementation and exploitation of the invention are always executed by mankind. Eventually, the invention will be employed for less noble or even evil causes. The passage in Jeremiah 17 continues:

"Like the partridge that hatches eggs which she has not laid, So is he who makes a fortune in ways that are unjust. It will be lost to him before his days are over, And in the end he will be [nothing but] a fool" (Jer. 17:11 AMP).

This metaphor makes clear that once an invention is manifested, it is accessible to others who will utilize it for their own good. Often, this is due to man's love for money. Because the heart is deceitful, even our own motives in the creation and deployment of the invention may remain hidden from us. But God, who searches and tests the heart, rewards each person according to his ways and his actions (Jer. 17:10).

While there are numerous human inventions that could be discussed in the context of their exploitation for evil purposes, I will limit the discussion to those that help accelerate deception. Among them are the internet, social media, and artificial intelligence. The foundation upon which the evils of these inventions are built is the notion of 'free speech.' Regarding the notion of free speech, I submit that speech is never free, nor should it be to the Believer. The Bible warns us that the tongue is an *"unruly evil, full of deadly poison"* that no man can tame (James 3:8 KJV). Earlier in the same passage, the tongue is likened to the rudder of a ship. Though it is small in size, it has the ability to direct the path of a massive ship. Speech should never be underestimated for its power and influence.

The free wielding of such a powerful weapon was never the intention of God – it was an invention of man. In the United States, we enjoy constitutional protection of our speech. Some mistakenly presume it was a God-given right. This right is granted to you under the Constitution of the United States, not by God! Yes, God allowed the founding fathers to incorporate this right into the language of the Constitution, but it was never the perspective of God that speech should remain uncensored. In fact, His word says, *"If anyone thinks he is religious and does not bridle his tongue but deceives his heart, this person's religion is worthless"* (James 1:26 ESV). God expects us to exercise control over that which we say, realizing that our words have creative power endowed by the Creator himself.

Unified speech is unstoppable

Even the Constitution understands that there are circumstances under which speech must be censored or constrained. The government may generally restrict the time, place, or manner of speech if the restrictions are unrelated to the content of the speech and if people are left with enough alternative ways of expressing their views. For example, the government can and will restrict the use of loudspeakers in residential areas at night. They limit all demonstrations that block traffic and can ban all picketing of people's homes. Additionally, the government can restrict speech that falls into categories such as incitement, defamation, fraud, obscenity, child pornography, fighting words, and threats.[33]

Importantly, the Constitution's First Amendment limits the government's ability to censor or restrict speech to these categories. It imposes no restriction on private individuals or entities. Therefore, corporations or other companies can more strictly constrain the extent of harmful speech without infringing on an individual's constitutional rights. Consequently, members of Congress and socially conscious individuals have collectively petitioned social media companies and those who engage in the massive dissemination of knowledge to more responsibly scrutinize the information they distribute. Failure has the deleterious consequence of accelerated deception and the eventual extinction of truth.

---

[33] Eugene Volokh, "First Amendment - Permissible Restrictions on Expression," in *Encyclopedia Britannica*, 2019, https://www.britannica.com/topic/First-Amendment/Permissible-restrictions-on-expression.

Individual speech is powerful, especially when it is delivered by persons of influence. Unified speech is unstoppable. Genesis 11 beautifully demonstrates how unified speech fosters invention that is eventually defiled by human intentions. The passage begins with the observation that *"the whole earth had one language and the same words"* (Gen. 11:1 ESV). The scripture continues:

"And they said to one another, 'Come, let us make bricks, and burn them thoroughly.' And they had brick for stone, and bitumen for mortar. Then they said, 'Come, let us build ourselves a city and a tower with its top in the heavens, and let us make a name for ourselves, lest we be dispersed over the face of the whole earth.' And the LORD came down to see the city and the tower, which the children of man had built. And the LORD said, 'Behold, they are one people, and they have all one language, and this is only the beginning of what they will do. And nothing that they propose to do will now be impossible for them. Come, let us go down and there confuse their language, so that they may not understand one another's speech.' So the LORD dispersed them from there over the face of all the earth, and they left off building the city" (Gen. 11:3-8 ESV).

The people had a legitimate need for brick. It was used for shelter and protection. Once they accomplished the invention of brick, then they imagined that they would use the technology they developed in brick making to build a city and a tower. Eventually, their true motives were uncovered. They desired to make a name for themselves and to become more secular, no longer relying on God for protection but on their own inventions. The nidus for the evil that would eventually proceed had the Lord not intervened was unified speech.

In 1436, a German goldsmith by the name of Johannes Gutenberg invented a device that would forever change the dissemination of knowledge and the unification of speech: the printing press. His invention provided a means to inexpensively mass-produce books on every imaginable topic. Revolutionary ideas and priceless ancient knowledge were placed in the hands of every literate person who had access.

It is said that knowledge is power. He who was kept illiterate would thereafter be rendered effectively powerless. He who was literate and had access to knowledge attained at least a modicum of power. But he, who controlled the dissemination of knowledge, was most powerful. Gutenberg's greatest accomplishment was the publishing of 200 Bibles in Latin. It took him three years to do it, but it was no small feat. He then had the problem of distributing these Bibles in addition to the problem that most people were illiterate at the time.[34]

Remember, wherever there's an egg laid, there's a partridge, who didn't lay the egg but who stands ready to sit on it and derive benefit. Gutenberg died penniless, but others with wealth soon found ways to turn a profit from the invention Gutenberg initially sought to use for good – the printing of Bibles.

Because many people were illiterate, they would gather around in pubs and listen to paid readers recite the latest news. According to historian Ada Palmer, this radically changed how people consumed news. Knowledge, which was initially a tool available to only the wealthiest of citizens, became more broadly available.

The religious reformer Martin Luther is attributed to have said, "Printing is the ultimate gift of God and the greatest one."[35] While he was not the first theologian to challenge the Roman Catholic Church, he was the first to widely publish his works thanks to the printing press. Eventually, his writings would account for over a third of all books sold in Germany. He also printed Bibles in German and sold them. This widespread dissemination of his writings and the Bible helped to found Protestantism, what we broadly refer to as Christianity today.

The ability to obtain knowledge and inspire unified speech helped to form the basis of religion. The same could be said of science. Francis Bacon, the man

---

[34] Dave Roos, "7 Ways the Printing Press Changed the World," history.com (A&E Television Networks, March 27, 2023), https://www.history.com/news/printing-press-renaissance.

[35] Dave Roos, "7 Ways the Printing Press Changed the World," history.com (A&E Television Networks, March 27, 2023), https://www.history.com/news/printing-press-renaissance.

credited with developing the Scientific Method, is said to have claimed the three greatest inventions that forever changed the world are: gunpowder, the nautical compass, and the printing press.

For thousands of years, great philosophers, mathematicians, and scientists were separated by geography and language. It was time-consuming and expensive to hand-write scientific data. Furthermore, the transcription was prone to error. These obstacles greatly hampered the advancement of science. There is nothing that is new under the sun (Eccl. 1:9). The thoughts and inventions that come to one person are not unique to that person. There are people who would never meet or interact because of geography and language, but who have the very same imagination. The sharing of printed media and scientific data facilitated the rapid expansion and acquisition of scientific knowledge.

As access to printed materials and people's abilities to print materials increased, persons who previously had no voice or audience gradually developed one. Just as with any invention, there are always some who would exploit that which was intended for good and use it for selfish gain, whether money, power, or influence. When knowledge, be it truthful or fabricated, is distributed in printed form and on paper, it travels more slowly and to a much more restricted audience. Although its reach is far greater than that which is passed on by oral tradition, it still requires substantial expense and time to reach its intended audience. The invention of the internet and its availability for use by almost anyone greatly impacted the dissemination of information.

The information age is said to have started in the mid-twentieth century. Early versions of the Internet were employed by the U.S. government in the 1960s to help researchers share information.[36] Prior to then, digital data, like printed information, had to be transported from one huge computer in one location to a huge computer in another facility. Alternatively, it could be sent

---

[36] "A Brief History of the Internet," www.usg.edu, n.d., https://www.usg.edu/galileo/skills/unit07/internet07_02.phtml#:~:text=ARPANET%20and%20the%20Defense%20Data.

through the postal service. Still, it was an inefficient process. With the advancement of technology, this digital information was able to be transferred through wires and eventually through air to another location in seconds. January 1, 1983, is considered the official birthday of the internet. A universal language called Transfer Control Protocol/Internetwork Protocol (TCP/IP) was created. This unified speech or language allowed computers to communicate with each other from remote locations.

Gradually, consumers of information swapped the local library, newspapers, news channels, and magazines as their source of information for the Internet. The internet offered a great convenience for these consumers because they no longer had to leave their physical location and conduct a scavenger hunt through libraries to find an article or book of interest written by an expert in the field and published by a reputable company. Instead, they could readily type a string of characters and words in a search window, and in a matter of seconds, they would have a plethora of information available at their fingertips.

In its earlier stages, people often cautioned that the internet is full of false information and that the information derived therefrom should be scrutinized with trepidation. There was no good way of policing the internet for false information and even if there were, agencies who performed this task would be criticized for attempting to censor the information and thereby manipulate public perception and behavior.

Today, people almost universally always have a computer in their hands. With little effort, they can obtain an answer to almost any question they ask. It is curious that the warnings of the internet's propensity for producing misinformation seem to be quieting. I suspect this is because of a relatively new invention called algorithms.

An algorithm is a series of instructions designed to solve specific problems, perform tasks, or make decisions. In computer programming, algorithms direct the computer's actions, such as sorting elements, locating data, or identifying objects. Every interaction with a computer generates data.

Computer algorithms identify, compile, and analyze that data. When sufficient data is obtained from large groups of people, algorithms can identify commonalities. Those commonalities identified by algorithms then instruct the computer's actions.

For example, you might search for information about seasonal allergies. The computer can compile and compare information it received from your query with that which it received from other similar searches. In performing this analysis, the algorithm can determine that you might most likely also need to find an allergist or purchase an over-the-counter allergy medication. Under the guise of helping you quickly locate the information that is most relevant to your query, it will present you with options it determines would be most helpful for you. Those suggestions are based on the behaviors of the hundreds of millions of other similar data searches. With a high and ever-increasing degree of accuracy, it will likely be helpful to and welcomed by you.

Passion, when not tempered, obscures rational thought

In this manner, the computer fed you more of what you wanted to hear or view based on its algorithms. Artificial intelligence permits computers to more effectively predict human interests, passions, and behaviors. Information as simple as the amount of time you spent researching a red pick-up truck versus a blue sedan reveals information about your personality and passions that can be exploited by marketers in unrelated fields. These marketers can then recognize you as one who fits the profile of consumers for their product, and they'll cause that product to appear more prominently and frequently before you whenever you access your computer again.

Paul forewarns the disciples, *"For the time is coming when people will not endure sound teaching, but having itching ears they will accumulate for themselves teachers to suit their own passions, and will turn away from listening to the truth and wander off into myths"* (2 Tim. 4:3-4 ESV). The thing about biblical warnings is that when they come to fruition, it is often not exactly how we might have naturally expected it. Jesus put it this way, *"if the master of the house had known at what hour the thief was coming, he would not have left his house to be broken into"* (Luke 12:39 ESV).

Our vulnerabilities will not be immediately obvious to us. This is why God instructs his prophets to discern the times and to issue the warnings, to those who would listen. Surely, it would be easy for us to avoid turning away from the truth, if only had to just not seek out false profits. Here, we don't have to seek teachers; they are selected for and deployed to us by algorithms that know our passions based on our patterns of behavior.

For this reason, we must be ever vigilant to guard our responses to the information that we consume. Some of it is brought to us of our own pursuits, but others are sent to us. 1 Peter 5:8 says, *"Be sober-minded; be watchful. Your adversary the devil prowls around like a roaring lion, seeking someone to devour"* (ESV). Sober-minded in this context advises against drunkenness, but as importantly, it is an admonishment to be calm, rational, temperate, and dispassionate. Passion, when not tempered, obscures rational thought. In an earlier chapter, I discussed how passions become vulnerabilities for manipulation. We are to be moved with compassion, not by the human emotion of passion.

Being sober-minded also means to be circumspect. That is to be careful to consider all circumstances and possible consequences (Merriam-Webster Dictionary). In this age where truth is endangered of extinction, we should circumspectly evaluate all information that is presented to us, regardless of the content and source. I fear that the motivation to evaluate information on the internet in this manner has waned because the information we receive has been custom-tailored to scratch the itch of our ears.

The COVID-19 pandemic revealed just how insidious the pollution of information sources is. It underscored how easily the American people can be deceived by the masses. Deception was accelerated through a tool of Democracy we call 'free speech.' Social media effectively utilizes this instrument to rapidly disseminate false information to hundreds of millions of people in a matter of hours. At no time in history have we been more freely and readily able to spew the toxin of misinformation to those vulnerable to its seduction.

Hosea 4:6 says, *"My people are destroyed for lack of knowledge"* (KJV). In this context, knowledge also means skill, perception, discernment, understanding, and wisdom. God is speaking to his priests and places the responsibility of this ignorance squarely on the shoulders of the priest. He said, *"Because you have rejected knowledge, I reject you from being a priest to me"* (Hos. 4:6 ESV). In this dialogue, we can surmise that God holds those whom he has given authority to a higher standard of accountability than those who are charged to follow. *"But the one who did not know, and did what deserved a beating, will receive a light beating. Everyone to whom much was given, of him much will be required, and from him to whom they entrusted much, they will demand the more"* (Luke 12:48 ESV). Clearly, if the leaders reject knowledge, the probability that the people will reject knowledge increases. Because of their dereliction of duty to inform the people, God rejected the priests.

In March 2019 (before the pandemic), Representative Adam Schiff wrote a letter to Amazon owner Jeff Bezos to implore more responsible promotion of products and information.[37] He was concerned that *"the algorithms which power social media platforms and Amazon's recommendations are not designed to distinguish quality information from misinformation or misleading information and, as a result, harmful anti-vaccine messages have been able to thrive and spread."* He continued, *"The consequences are particularly troubling for public health issues."*

Much of that information promulgates myths that have been repeatedly debunked by valid scientific investigation. Further, the information contradicts historical demonstrations of the safety and efficacy of vaccines to eradicate diseases such as smallpox and polio almost completely from the face of the earth. Yet, the repeated exposure of parents, who are desperate for answers to

---

[37] "Schiff Sends Letter to Amazon CEO Regarding Anti-Vaccine Misinformation," House.gov, March 2019, https://schiff.house.gov/news/press-releases/schiff-sends-letter-to-amazon-ceo-regarding-anti-vaccine-misinformation.

why their child might have certain medical problems, to this misinformation reinforces their distrust of valid scientific research.

A CNN investigative report found that on Amazon, searches related to vaccines often led users to publications or videos that provided medically and scientifically inaccurate information. Some of these included misleading titles that purport to be medically accurate or neutral on the topic.

Consequently, when Amazon's consumers see the same information presented by several apparently legitimate sources, they are more inclined to believe it.

Sadly, but predictable in a capitalistic society, organizations are financially incentivized to promulgate false information. Like many other online platforms, Amazon will give prominence and search result priority to paid advertisers, regardless of the scientific veracity of the publication. Consequently, a new parent who might simply be searching for parenting tips may readily be fed books containing misinformation about vaccination. In fact, the first several they receive might be of such nature.

The scientific community has inadequate resources to combat this misinformed bombardment of the internet because, unlike the vendors who promote their myths using paid advertising, they have no financial incentive to do so. Moreover, most people will not take the initiative to read a boring and sometimes confusing scientific publication that refutes the falsities espoused in materials distributed for profit. On whom, then, does the responsibility for informing the public fall? Rightly so, it should be the government, responsible media, and community/religious leaders. Failing to do so, as we see in Hosea, will be met with a stern rebuke and rejection by God.

The media historically has attempted to validate the information that is presented to the public. But now, people are becoming more distrustful of the media. This is in part due to their own failures. It is also due to a systematic attempt to discredit the media for the personal gain of those who seek to deceive a large swath of the public who are vulnerable to their wiles. In their quest to be the first to break the story and not be late in reporting, the media undermines its own credibility. In pursuit of ratings, news media have resorted to presenting information that they know their viewers and subscribers want to hear, whether it is truthful or not. And because the media has historically been controlled by a relatively small group of wealthy individuals, they have always been subject to the purse strings of the owners and shareholders.

These vulnerabilities are exploited by those who desire to corruptly attain power while subverting the accountability imposed by a free press. The mantra "fake news" has become an integral part of the lexicon of the corrupt and has become quite effective at shutting the ears of passionate individuals, who listen with itchy ears, to the truth.

The only truth that will then remain will be Jesus

The open access to the internet with little regulation of the information that is placed on it provides an opportunity to easily mislead consumers who purport to have 'done their research.' Unfortunately, most of such alleged research is performed, of course, on the internet. Because most people are not trained to critically evaluate data and frankly would do almost anything to avoid the need to, they allow repetition to be their assessment of validity. If they see multiple articles from various sources stating the same information, it is deemed more credible.

The truth is that most of the information they consider validated is not a repetition of the data but rather a recycling of it. It is not that the data has been interrogated by multiple sources and found to be veracious. Rather, it was duplicated by multiple sources and posted on the internet, often without having been evaluated at all. And guess what the motivation is... money. Advertising dollars for websites incentivize the posting of these unvalidated results.

Soon, we will be unable to determine what is truth or what is not. For decades, we have been able to fabricate printed documents. The ability to produce fake audio tapes has also existed for decades. Now, deep fake videos can make anyone appear and sound like they are saying or doing anything. As technology advances and we gain more knowledge, it will become increasingly difficult to distinguish the truth from a deep fake video. This technology has been and will continue to be used for nefarious purposes. Some people will intentionally create such videos to disparage political opponents and other leaders. Others, who will legitimately have been caught on video committing some deplorable act, will be able to dismiss the video as a deepfake.

This underscores the necessity of always being circumspect and not being easily moved by the reporting of information. While the erosion of trust in consumable information is an intentional goal of some corrupt individuals, organizations, and countries, it is also a tactic of spiritual forces that seek to divide humans into sects. That which we presumed to be truth in the past will no longer exist. It will be indiscernible to those who are too motivationally crippled to uncover the truth. The only truth that will then remain will be Jesus – *the way, the truth,* and the life (John 14:6).

The truth can never be discerned without a prerequisite love for the truth

---

Paul, in his second letter to Timothy, admonishes us to *"Study to show thyself approved unto God, a workman that needeth not to be ashamed, rightly dividing the word of truth"* (2 Tim. 2:15 KJV). We must work diligently to uncover the words of truth (Jesus). He goes further to give examples of Hymenaeus and Philetus, who have erred concerning their understanding of truth and caused others' faith to be overthrown.

We are in a time when the love of the truth is not being received, and *"... for this cause God shall send them strong delusion, that they should believe a lie: that they all might be damned who believed not the truth, but had pleasure in unrighteousness"* (2 Thes. 2:11-12 KJV). The truth can never be discerned without a prerequisite love for the truth. We must love the truth, even when it contradicts and disables many of our most affectionately held paradigms.

When truth is not affectionately embraced, it becomes impossible to distinguish it from a lie that happens to affirm our misguided beliefs.

The Rebellion Comes First

On August 10, 2017, I had a dream. In the dream, our country had deteriorated to an almost state of anarchy. A faction aligned itself to execute police officers. It was unclear to me the reasons why they had this goal. But today it is becoming more evident to me that this is the next front of those who believe strongly that this country and its attendant rights of citizenship belong to only certain groups of people. It is this passionate belief that compels individuals to subvert legal authority and processes to implement their wills, protecting what they believe is their birthright.

In my dream, the police represented all legal and judicial authority. The efforts of these factions were widespread and successful at instilling fear among these legal authorities. Rather than exercising their occupational duties, police officers would only engage in and stop these actions when threatened under penalty of failure to act.

I was a passenger on the metro bus. The driver rode past a scene where the factionalists were engaging in their murderous activities. The bus driver, who obviously was aware of the mandate for officers to engage actively, pulled over a short distance beyond the site of the altercation to allow an officer who was on the bus to deboard and engage. The officer refused and subsequently received a call, with an apparent mandate from his superior to engage, or his job would be jeopardized, or he might suffer some other punishment. Nonetheless, he refused.

In another scene, I was in the police locker room. The tension from the societal unrest was palpable in the room. A gentleman entered the locker room with a priest's collar. I presumed he was there to pray for the force and to encourage them to continue with their honorable duty. Suddenly, the man in the priest's garb pulled from his jacket a gun and started shooting at the officers in the locker room. Afraid of being hit in the crossfire, I hid under one of the benches and immediately awakened from the dream.

This dream particularly disturbed me because various factions are developing within this nation and across the globe (particularly in democratic nations), each with its own motives and tactics to rebel against established authorities. Some have very laudable goals, at least by human standards. Others have motives that are only justifiable to those who promote them, and that would otherwise be broadly rejected by society. These various small groups of people garner much influence through a variety of means. Some will blatantly induce violence and use terror to execute their wills. Others are more insidious and will exploit laws and intimidate lawmakers to implement theirs. The end result is the same: rebellion.

America was founded on and has always operated under a White patriarchal system. To perpetuate this hierarchy, those in positions of power and with wealth have intentionally implemented mechanisms and policies that ensure minorities and women would never rise to power. Many of the tactics were covert and were hidden from history books. Often, evidence of their malicious and self-serving tactics was destroyed. Nonetheless, through time and education, minorities and women have acquired knowledge and power. As they've acquired wealth, they've acquired even more power and education.

Now, in this information age, investigative journalists are uncovering truths that past paternalists desired to keep secret indefinitely. The media is then strategically vilified as peddling false narratives and being provocateurs of civil unrest. The opponents of truth presume that if the media can't be silenced, it can at least be discredited. Despite a vicious smear campaign, the eyes of the masses are now being opened. The American spirit that abides within true patriots who believe in life, liberty, and justice for all now demands that America finally live up to its promise.

The heavy and partial hand of justice is stubborn. It is unyielding. But it has given birth to a generation of compassionate people who refuse to be intimidated at the expense of justice. They are arising and demanding that justice flows like a river, drenching all those who come in its path regardless of race, gender, religion, orientation, or creed. This challenges the establishment of the patriarchs and in their minds, it must be dominated and squelched before it gets out of control.

To aid their attempts to silence the voices of those who demand equality, the children of compassion and justice will be vilified. Anarchists are what they will be called because they demand justice and refuse to be intimidated by or back down from those who abuse the power of the badge or military command. A show of unfettered solidarity is the biggest threat to the established patriarchy and will eventually provoke a home-grown assault of American military might on its own citizens. Liberty will be bought but with the price of blood.

It is the nature of man to seek better when he learns that better exists

---

America was born through rebellion and protest. Today, we call it the American Revolution and look upon it with great honor and gratitude. We understand, in hindsight, that the oppression imposed on the occupants of this land was sufficiently burdensome to warrant an outright rebellion from the authority of Britain. One might even call it anarchy. Certainly, King George III and the British Parliament viewed it that way, as evidenced by their issuance of "A Proclamation for Suppressing Rebellion and Sedition."[38] Anarchy is a state of disorder, often temporary, due to the absence or nonrecognition of authority.

Today, when Americans make the same demand as was made then by the White Patriarchy that founded this country, no taxation without representation, they are labeled anarchists. The only difference is that those who were formerly the oppressed have become the oppressors. An attempt to be freed

---

[38] "'By the King, a Proclamation, for Suppressing Rebellion and Sedition' (1775)," Encyclopedia Virginia, n.d., https://encyclopediavirginia.org/primary-documents/by-the-king-a-proclamation-for-suppressing-rebellion-and-sedition-1775/.

from oppression is likewise considered rebellion or sedition. The true target of the resistance is not authority but resistance to what is perceived as corrupt or unjust authority.

The word oppression is itself incendiary and evocative of immediately dismissive responses. The Oxford Dictionary defines oppression as the state of being subject to unjust treatment or control. It does not mean that you have no liberties or benefits. It simply means that you remain under the influence or control of an unjust authority. In America, that unjust treatment often disproportionately impacts the poor, minorities, and members of the LGBTQ+ community.

Understand clearly that I do not advocate violent protest by any means. However, I offer a warning like the one Dr. Martin Luther King, Jr. issued in 1967 during his "The Other America" speech at Stanford University. He said:

"... it is as necessary for me to be as vigorous in condemning the conditions which cause persons to feel that they must engage in riotous activities, as it is for me to condemn riots. I think America must see that riots do not develop out of thin air. Certain conditions continue to exist in our society, which must be condemned as vigorously as we condemn riots. And in the final analysis, a riot is the language of the unheard."[39]

It is the nature of man to seek better when he learns that better exists. This is not a new human flaw. It existed in the Garden of Eden. Genesis 3:6 says, "When the woman saw that the tree was good for food, and that it was a delight to the eyes, and that the tree was to be desired to make one wise, she took of its fruit and ate, and she also gave some to her husband who was with her, and he ate."

I submit, as Dr. King intimated, that rebellion does not occur in a vacuum. It does not occur because people suddenly awaken one day and determine that they no longer like the status quo. It occurs because those who rebel perceive

---

[39] "The Other America Speech Transcript - Martin Luther King Jr.," Rev, n.d., https://www.rev.com/blog/transcripts/the-other-america-speech-transcript-martin-luther-king-jr.

the forces placed upon them (often governmental) to be oppressive. They feel that the systems to which they are subject are unjust or unfair. If another or better way is not known, ever seen or imagined, the people relegate their situation to that of normalcy. However, when a better way is discovered, and it is perceived that other people discriminately enjoy this better way, those who are forbidden from such enjoyment (e.g., the oppressed) pursue or demand access to the enjoyment of the similar.

Using the temptation of Eve as an example, I propose that there are at least four steps that lead to rebellion:

1. **Discovery of the better way's existence:** Someone external to Eve, who knew something she didn't know, made her aware of what might be perceived as a 'better way.' In this case, it was the serpent. It is possible that the one who exposes you to the better way could have earnest or malevolent intent. It is prudent that we determine the intent when such information is brought to us. There's no scriptural indication that prior to her being shown the supposed goodness that the tree offered, Eve was ever tempted by it. However, after the serpent suggested to her that a better way existed, she was open to further exploration.

2. **Determination of the better way's viability:** The Bible says that Eve looked at the tree and saw that it was good for food. She had no idea, at that time, whether she would like the food or not. She only saw that it produced fruit. In that regard, she saw that the 'better way' was viable. Just because an alternate way exists and is functional for some does not mean that it would be desirable for the individual who inspects it.

3. **Recognition that the alternate way is desirable and not just viable:** Eve perceived that the fruit not only existed and was viable, but it was tempting or desirable to her.

4. **Recognition of the enduring benefit offered beyond the appearance:** Having a desirable appearance alone is not sufficient to

warrant rebellion. To rebel against an authority, the alternative way must promise a future benefit we currently do not enjoy.

At this point, the individual is ripe for rebellion, as Eve was.

As mentioned previously, we have never had such free access to information as we have today. Even in poor and underdeveloped countries, people have at least access to information about what happens in free countries. When they consider the poverty and oppression they witness in their own countries, comparing it to the images of liberty and freedom that they see people enjoying in other countries, they will eventually contemplate the existence, viability, desirability, and enduring promise of a better way. They will then pursue or demand the same treatment for citizens in their country.

An authoritarian regime can try to suppress an uprising under threat of force for a period, but eventually, the masses of people will rise and rebel against their government. This is why authoritarian countries such as China and Russia closely restrict the access of their citizens to information. They receive only that which their leaders feel is beneficial to maintaining their harmonious and submissive existence.

In the United States, we have unfettered access to information. Poor people are becoming increasingly aware of how they are exploited to further enrich the wealthy. Black people and other people of color have always recognized the unjust treatment that they have historically received in this country and are now discovering even more that had been hidden from the history books. An exploration and education of such information is now perceived to be divisive. There are all-out political assaults on and demonization of scholarly expositions of such, called Critical Race Theory.

Entire political campaigns have been organized to prevent information about past systemic oppression and its current residual effects from widespread exposure. I believe it is not because of an embarrassment of the past actions of this nation's forefathers but rather because it will reveal that the more subtle tools of oppression still exist and thrive. With such exposure, the Judeo-Christian White patriarchal system that still controls most of the power in this country will be weakened.

As we see more, we demand more. People of color and people of other disenfranchised groups in America are gaining political and economic might. As such, they rebel against the oppressive forces that seek to deny them their rights as citizens. At times, it manifests as a violent or riotous expression. Other times, it manifests as political influence. Violent acts are easily condemned and dismissed as barbaric. However, political influence is hard to ignore. It must, therefore, be subverted. In this regard, those who have presented themselves as the higher moral authority but who also seek to maintain their governing authority will subvert even the systems they've instituted when they seem to no longer be working in their favor.

In my dream, a priest entered the police locker room under the guise of one who sought to divinely advocate for the police. Instead, he was there only to eradicate even their authority. Sadly, we are now witnessing Evangelicals who have long advocated for the rule of law subvert the very processes they previously heralded. Why? Because the democratic process no longer favors them.

Much like when Blacks in America obtained the right to vote, and many were being elected to Congress by a sheer number of Black residents in certain districts, they devised strategies to disenfranchise Blacks from their voting rights. In the past, it was through the institution of poll taxes. Today, it continues to be through the restriction of access to voting rights and through gerrymandering of voting districts. When these tactics become less effective, they resort to more deplorable methods. They demonize the systems of law enforcement that have existed initially in their favor but now seem to treat them as citizens equal to the people they previously oppressed. Those systems then must be neutralized at all costs, they reason.

Evangelicals and conservatives, in a desperate effort to maintain governmental control, have aligned themselves against the justice department, local law enforcement, and intelligence agencies of the United States. They convince themselves that these entities have been hijacked by the 'woke' mob and, therefore, must be rendered impotent. What is really happening is that these systems are no longer preferentially serving their needs but trying to live up to the mandates of the Constitution.

An equitable distribution of rights and power among all citizens of the United States is not a desirable outcome for them. There is no way that they would ever want a gay couple to enjoy the same rights as they do under the Constitution. Although they would not admit it, many of them also do not want a Black person or naturalized immigrant to have the same privilege as a 'pure blood' White American. Consequently, like the other groups that feel as if their interests are inadequately represented, even those who profess to be Christ's ambassadors find themselves rebelling against the authorities they established.

2 Thessalonians 2:3-4 says, *"Let no one deceive you in any way. For that day will not come, unless the rebellion comes first, and the man of lawlessness is revealed, the son of destruction, who opposes and exalts himself against every so-called god or object of worship, so that he takes his seat in the temple of God, proclaiming himself to be God."* When we see the rebellion against authorities of all types, we can be assured that the man of lawlessness will soon be revealed. The information age and access to various forms of information (truthful and untruthful) have made conditions ripe for further rebellion, and the man of lawlessness is revealing himself.

In 2016, I wrote a blog exploring the attributes of the antichrist and Donald Trump. Many people have wondered and wrongly presumed why I have been so vocal and publicly critical of Trump. It is not because I vehemently disagree with his policies. In fact, I personally agree with many of the moral conservative issues and have personally benefited from some of his enacted policies. However, neither of these clouds my recognition of the potential underlying truth of his purpose in being elected President of the United States of America.

From the beginning, my sharpest criticism has always centered around Donald Trump's faith or lack thereof, not his policies. Moreover, I've been particularly critical of Evangelicals and Christian leaders who vociferously support Trump despite his unashamed proclamation that he has NEVER asked God for forgiveness. The impetus for my criticism is a charge to sound the alarm for Christians to be on alert for the manifestation of the antichrist. While I am not suggesting that Trump is the (or an) anti-Christ, I am cautioning us to be alert and discerning of scriptural references to the manifestation of the antichrist. Clearly, if the antichrist came and identified himself as such, most would outright reject him. However, when he comes with power, signs, lying wonders, and *"all deceivableness,"* as the Bible says he will (2 Thes. 2:9-10), we can and will easily be misled.

The antichrist is one who denies that Jesus is the Christ and he who denies the Father and the Son (1 John 2:22). The anti-Christ is described as a deceiver, and we are warned that if anyone comes to you and does not bring the doctrine of Christ (e.g., redemption through forgiveness and the blood of Christ) to not welcome them in our homes and don't even wish them well or we'll become partakers in their evil (2 John 1:9-10). For this reason, and despite having done so with other presidents for whom I didn't vote, I have not wished President Trump success, or even prayed for his success. Rather, I pray for his genuine salvation. The success of an unrepentant leader is, in my opinion, empowering to a potential anti-Christ. I don't intend to be insulting in my exposition here, but we need to critically evaluate each leader for the things they do and say.

In two separate interviews during his candidacy, Donald Trump admitted that he never asked God for forgiveness. If he did something wrong, he would try to make it right himself. In saying this, he is essentially saying that he is his own redeemer. The second interview was even more troubling because he doubled down on his ideology of self-redemption. He admitted that he could have lied to the Christian conservative crowd, saying that he had asked God for forgiveness, but what would it benefit him? The people wouldn't want him to lie about that, he suggested.

When I saw that dialogue, my spirit was deeply troubled. Truly, an antichrist could not or would not acknowledge the redemptive work of Christ for their own lives. He wouldn't even lie about it. Remember, in a dream I previously shared, the Lord confirmed to me that an anti-Christ could not submit to the sovereignty of God because he is not the god of the anti-Christ. In the Christian faith, salvation is based on the confession of one's own mouth, compelled by the belief in their heart (Romans 10:10). The profession from the mouths of other Christians is wholly insufficient to produce salvation for an individual, no matter how fiercely those Christians might desire it to be so.

The ardent support of Trump by Evangelicals and Christian Leaders does not reassure me. Rather, it makes me more cautious. The scriptures warn us, *"For false christs and false prophets will arise and perform great signs and wonders, so as to lead astray, if possible, even the elect"* (Matt. 24:24). I believe many of these leaders are misinterpreting signs and wonders and consequently are being deceived. They celebrate greatly and proclaim that God allowed Trump to overcome what was perceived to be a certain defeat to emerge victoriously.

In 2016, he seemed to be the most unlikely of all Republican candidates to be the nominee for the party. Despite an overwhelming number of polls that predicted Hillary Clinton would win by a landslide, Donald Trump won the presidency. His 2016 presidency was marked by repeated investigations into his behavior, which many claimed were politically motivated. Investigations by Mueller resulted in no prosecutable charges, which was interpreted by many Trump supporters to be an exoneration, although the report explicitly stated that it wasn't. He received incessant negative coverage by the media, for good reason. His behaviors were so undiplomatic and atypical of a President of the United States that the media needed to report it. Besides, it was good for their ratings. Because Trump relentlessly and boisterously decried that the investigations were a witch hunt, his supporters readily agreed. His presidency culminated in two house impeachments. He survived both because the Republican-controlled Senate refused to remove him from office. Together, these strengthened the resolve of his supporters and solidified their perceptions that he must be the chosen one of God.

Although he lost the 2020 presidential election, which I believe was spiritually strategic, he is now emerging as a formidable 2024 presidential candidate. Federal and state criminal charges and civil suits have been filed against him. Some have resulted in convictions, and others are now being dismissed and/or slow-walked by judges, which many presume to be partial and subservient to Donald Trump. Even the Supreme Court of the United States issued rulings that confound legal experts, but seem to add more wind to the sail of the presidential campaign of Donald Trump. And Evangelicals celebrate exuberantly, proclaiming, "God be praised!" God is finally hearing and answering their prayers, they presume.

Again, I caution us all to discern the process, not the product. If any of these apparent victories are secured through malevolent means, chances are it is not the divine endorsement many might presume it to be. Even still, it does not preclude Donald Trump's ascent from being a part of the plan of God. Revelation 13 warns us that the anti-Christ will suffer what seems to be a mortal wound to the head and will recover. At this many will marvel and will follow him as a result. What the apparent mortal wound to the head is, we do not know. It could be metaphorical and refer to the rise and return to power of one who people presumed to have suffered certain political death. It is also possible that it could be a physical wound from which this person might recover.

In July 2024, there was an assassination attempt on the life of former President Donald Trump. During a campaign rally speech, a sniper apparently aimed and fired a gun at the head of Donald Trump. Fortuitously, Trump turned his head sharply to his right side while speaking to the crowd. At that moment, the bullet missed his head and only grazed the top part of his ear. He was quickly protected by the Secret Service until the assassination threat was neutralized. Trump arose from the podium and threw his fist in the air, shouting to the crowd, "Fight! Fight! Fight!" This show of strength and resolute fortitude invigorated an already faithful crowd of adoring supporters. Moreover, it solidified the image of "Teflon Don." The implication is that he cannot be stopped regardless of which tactics the opposition employs.

Could a gunshot wound to the ear be suggestive of a mortal wound to the head of the beast referenced in Revelation 13? Perhaps. It is important to recognize that at the time John saw the vision, he would not likely have interpreted it as a gunshot wound. Because prophecy is always in part and often without explicit clarity, it remains possible that what seemed like a mortal wound might not have actually been a mortal wound to the head. But it might still have the same awe-inspiring effect of engendering undying fealty to one who would later rise to power. It certainly had that effect on Trump's supporters who are even more resolute about their allegiance.

Another thing that has concerned me about Trump is his boastful demeanor. He often seeks and seems to feed off the praise and adulation of his supporters. The more exuberant they become, the more Trump is emboldened to be open about who he is. At this point, he has little motivation to be deceptive before his supporters. He stated once that he could stand on Fifth Avenue and shoot a person, and he still would not lose support. This proclamation is proving to be frighteningly accurate. Adulation and worship appear to be high priorities for Trump. If no one else gives it, he'll lavish it upon himself.

Trump repeatedly makes claims of victories he never accomplished and asserts himself to know more than various experts who actually were appointed to his cabinet or who served his administration. This included economists, military generals, scientists, and various others. Any speech he gives is laden with self-adulation, and yet, it doesn't seem in the least to be alarming to his Evangelical base. He claims to have subdued various world dictators, a claim to which there is no valid evidence of the sort.

In 2017, under what I believed to be the inspiration of the Holy Spirit, I predicted that he would enjoy economic success as a president and would establish relations with Russia, North Korea, and Iran (and possibly China). It was not because I felt his policies were phenomenal or that he was the great negotiator and strong man he purports himself to be. It was not even that I believed God's hand was upon him to bring blessings to the American people. To the contrary, I recognized that his inherent need for idolization and the desperation of conservatives, who were growing weary of the seemingly slow progress of spiritual methods of warfare, would position him to be elevated as a divine figure in the eyes of many. This is an integral part of God's end-time plans; if not with Trump, then with someone who apparently behaves like Trump.

The following is the blog that was posted at the time:

On the world stage Trump will be successful in subduing world leaders who are a threat to America. Daniel 7:24 states that the anti-Christ will subdue three major kings. I'm thinking of Russia, North Korea, and Iran (maybe China). But we should watch closely and prayerfully with great discernment. As many Christians pray for the success of Donald Trump, their prayers might just be answered as the fulfillment of prophecy. It would potentially be for our good if he were truly a Christian. This is why I am so adamant about watching for his profession of faith. He who starts as a 'friend of religious liberty' shall not always remain such.

"He shall speak pompous words against the Most High, shall persecute the saints of the Most High, and shall intend to change times and law. Then the saints shall be given into his hand for a time and times and half a time." (Daniel 7:25)

Character still matters! That Christians are so ready to give a 'baby Christian' (if he even is one - which remains arguable) this much credence is highly concerning for me. We know how easily power corrupts. We've all preached at some point to not let your talent, ability or charisma take you places your character can't keep you. There is not among those leaders who support Trump, one who would authorize a baby Christian to assume pastoral leadership in their mega church. Why should it be so for our country?

"For the love of money is the root of all evil: which while some coveted after, they have erred from the faith, and pierced themselves through with many sorrows." (1 Timothy 6:10)

I hate to say it, but some of our most trusted Christian leaders have (or will) succumb to the temptations of prosperity. Some have been led astray by the allure of affiliation with Trump, which ensures the promise of wealth for them. Others will see a thriving economy and align with his precepts. Don't be deceived! GAIN IS NOT GODLINESS! (1 Timothy 6:5)

"And he was given a mouth speaking great things and blasphemies, and he was given authority to continue for forty-two months." (Revelations 13:5)

The next 43 months of Trump's 48-month presidential term will be crucial. He will not be impeached, but rather, the decision of the special prosecutor will grant him the opportunity to complete his term. He will be further emboldened by this victory and the several others to follow. The allegiance of prior reluctant followers will fertilize his arrogance, which, with rapid growth, will compel him to seek worship as a god himself. The one who was first perceived by many to be a "friend of religious freedom" will become its foe. "He shall speak words against the Most High, and shall wear out the saints of the Most High, and shall think to change the times and the law; and they shall be given into his hand for a time, times, and half a time." (Daniel 7:25)

I recognize that many will disagree with my assertion, but you must first recognize that Trump is a deceiver, above all. He is cunning in his ways and with his words. He "speaks like you and I, not like a politician," is the foolish exclamation of the deceived. What he really says is exactly what you want to hear for that moment.

"For the time will come when they will not endure sound doctrine; but after their own lusts shall they heap to themselves teachers, having itching ears; And they shall turn away their ears from the truth, and shall be turned unto fables." (2 Timothy 4:3-4, KJV)

He will say, promise, or do whatever is expedient at the moment to accomplish his goal. His supporters defend this and characterize it as "flexibility." Some even excuse it as inexperience and grant him immunity as he finds his presidential legs. I call it double-mindedness, which is the hallmark of instability (James 1:8).

I realize that many of the things I've stated herein seem a bit emphatic. The truth is, I really don't know for sure and could very well be wrong. However, this I know for certain. There will be many led astray because they are witnessing the miracle but not discerning by whom the miracle is wrought. I am persuaded by the many dreams (and the prophetic gift) God has given me that these events will happen, and the litmus test will be, "Can they proclaim that Christ is Lord?" To date, Trump cannot with his own mouth. That causes me great concern. His eventual goal will be to magnify the voices of those who praise him and silence the voices of all who oppose him.

Consider how effective Trump has, in a short period of time, been in discrediting the media. The Bible encourages us to watch and pray (Mark 14:38). I understand the context was different, but it is still imperative that we have a source for fact-gathering. Admittedly, much of the media has its bias, in either direction. However, I have confidence that the vast majority of the media still have some modicum of integrity and verify their sources, hopefully through at least 2 or 3 witnesses (Matthew 18:16). Trump has been so effective at alluring the hearts and minds of his supporters that they will choose not to acknowledge even the potential veracity of facts that have been verified by multiple witnesses. It is a tactic to silence his opposition and to allow his agenda to proceed unchecked. Not so Mr. Trump!

We must continue to gather facts and discern the truth from therein. It is imperative now, more than any time in history, that Christians put on the whole armor of God, including the helmet of salvation (e.g., that which protects the head). Currently, the head of our country is not protected by the blood of Jesus, and that should cause us great alarm! Don't be deceived by 'miracles' and unprecedented victories. Don't be enticed by the appearance or the promise of financial liberty. Don't be ensnared by the promise of policy (letter of the law) to

deliver what only the spirit of the law can produce. Don't be mesmer-
ized by the charisma or art of deal-making with foreign rulers. Know
that our head is still uncovered, and the season is ripe for the manifes-
tation of the Antichrist.

This blog was written in 2017, and many of the prophecies mentioned therein have come to pass. I am particularly concerned by the reference in Daniel 7:25, wherein we are warned that the deceiver would try to change the times and laws. This has been the highest priority for Evangelicals, at least since the 1980s. Donald Trump provided them with their greatest victory in appointing conservative judges and Supreme Court justices. Now, what has been accepted law for generations is being overturned in the name of righteousness. Remember, righteousness is not accomplished through the law. Paul renounced such efforts, saying, *"For his sake I have suffered the loss of all things and count them as rubbish, in order that I may gain Christ and be found in him, not having a righteousness of my own that comes from the law, but that which comes through faith in Christ, the righteousness from God that depends on faith."* (Phil. 3:8-9)

It is the charge of Christians to influence the heart of a nation, not its laws

---

By August 2024, at least three states with conservative-majority legislative bodies have enacted laws that challenge the separation of Church and State. Louisiana passed a law mandating the posting of the Ten Commandments in each public school classroom. The Oklahoma School Superintendent has mandated that the Bible be specifically taught in public schools. Texas, Florida, and Louisiana have passed laws that allow schools to hire religious chaplains to counsel students. They have struck down restrictions that prevent these chaplains from proselytizing or that require parental consent before permitting their children to be counseled by the chaplains.

At least 18 states have instituted laws that either require or permit the posting of "In God We Trust," the nation's motto, on the walls of classrooms. On their face, these should be considered victories for those of the Christian faith. However, these feats are misguided in their impetus and method. It is the charge of Christians to influence the heart of a nation, not its laws. This is only accomplished by changing the hearts of its citizens.

Together, these actions of Evangelicals and other Christians to change the laws of this land while using manipulative tactics is a flagrant rejection of God's way. In this way, it is a rebellion against the mandates of God as conveyed through the teachings of Jesus and his apostles. Thus, the rebellion is not just among those whom Christianity would call 'unsaved' or 'lost', but it also reveals the rebellion of those who have allegedly received the truth of and salvation in Jesus Christ.

The rebellion mentioned in 2 Thessalonians 2:3 is interpreted in other versions of the Bible as a 'falling away,' an apostasy, or a departure from the truth. I submit that it is not simply a rejection of facts in favor of indulgences of one's own paradigms, but it also means a departure from The Way, The Truth, and The Life – Jesus Christ (John 14:6). It is not just a rejection of The Truth, but also his Way – his methods for conducting life and extending his kingdom. In this way, those who reject the Truth and his Way, will never enjoy the Life he offers to those who do not fall away from such.

Persecution Must Come

Perhaps one of the most potent motivations for the 'falling away' is the fear of persecution. It is for this reason that Peter denied Jesus three times. It is also the reason why many of his disciples hid themselves after Jesus was crucified. One thing is certain; that is the word of God is true. Everything God, through Jesus and his servants, said in his Holy Word will come to pass. No intervention by humans will delay or thwart the execution of God's plan. What we see now taking place is multiple seemingly unrelated events working synchronously to fulfill the prophetic word of God and his plan for end times.

Jesus spent a considerable amount of time warning his disciples and us what fate would befall us as followers of Christ. He said, *"If the world hates you, know that it has hated me before it hated you. If you were of the world, the world would love you as its own; but because you are not of the world, but I chose you out of the world, therefore the world hates you"* (John 15:18-19). This followed an exhortation he gave to them, encouraging them to abide in him (e.g., stay connected to him) and to always bear fruit. The latter could not occur unless they first remained connected to Jesus. A connection to Jesus, in this context, was not merely a profession of a relationship or affiliation. Rather, he uses the analogy of vegetation wherein he considered himself the vine and his followers, the branches (John 15:5). That means that all that flows through the vine penetrates the branches and enables it to bear fruit.

Jesus describes how a connection to him and his love is first keeping his commandments (John 15:12). The first of these is to love one another, just as Jesus has loved us. With the growing divide in our country and the preponderance of hateful rhetoric espoused for people who believe or live differently than we do, it seems increasingly difficult to show this type of love. Even when one blatantly expresses hatred for us, Jesus' expectation is that we reciprocate with love. Early in his ministry, Jesus urged his disciples not to respond to hatred according to their natural inclination but rather to love those persons who hate them and to pray for those who persecute them (Matt. 5:43-44).

Jesus knew the response his presence, words, and actions would have on those who would rather persist in their own wills and traditions than submit to his teachings, which would challenge their tightly held paradigms. In the aforementioned passage, he shares this information plainly with his disciples, encouraging them to continue in their expressions of love.

Jesus continued then, explaining a few circumstances his followers could expect to endure. He prefaced his warning by saying, *"I have said all these things to you to keep you from falling away"* (John 16:1). Again, Jesus knew the intense persecution his disciples would experience could greatly tempt them to fall away from his ways, teachings and example. He continued, *"They will put you out of the synagogues. Indeed, the hour is coming when whoever kills you will think he is offering service to God. And they will do these things because they have not known the Father, nor me. But I have said these things to you, that when their hour comes you may remember that I told them to you"* (vs. 2-4).

I submit that many Evangelicals have not remembered what Jesus told them. Their memories have been blunted by the allure of schemes and benefits that a democratic process offers. Some argue that Democracy, as we know it today, did not exist at the time when Jesus walked the earth. At that time, aristocracies predominated. Consequently, the people had no way of enforcing their wills above that of the government. By contrast, and especially in the United States, the Constitution affords 'We the People' the opportunity to establish laws and rules that we hope might subvert or at least deter the persecution that we see brewing for Christ followers. Some reason that the voices of Christians are increasingly being silenced and those of sinners are being amplified, all in the name of constitutional rights. They assert that our governmental system allows for the righting of this great wrong.

Indeed, we are blessed to live in a country where the voices of all citizens can be heard, and each duly authorized citizen can influence the writing of the laws of this country. There are two caveats to consider in making this assertion. The first and most important is that no law that We, The People advocate for or write will be sufficient to pause or delay the persecution, as previously stated. The second is that in recent generations, We The People's voice has been progressively hijacked through the exploitation of the laws that were originally intended to protect it.

Since the founding of this country and our electoral process, only four Presidents have won the electoral votes and the presidency without winning the popular vote. Two of those occurred in the 21st Century: George W. Bush in 2000 and Donald J. Trump in 2016. These are both Republicans and increasingly, Republicans are given a slight electoral college advantage because of how the electoral votes are determined.

Regardless of the population, each state receives one electoral vote for each U.S. Senator and House Representative elected to Congress for that state. While the delegates to the House of Representatives are determined by the population of the state, each state receives two Senators regardless of the population size. Many of the more rural states have a lower population of citizens and tend to vote Republican. In contrast, more populous states tend to vote Democratic but still only have two electoral college votes for their Senators. This allows the disparity between popular and electoral college votes to favor Republicans.

In fact, Bush's 2004 win was the only time in the last six presidential elections that a Republican candidate took more than 48 percent of the popular vote. However, for a Democrat to win the electoral vote and presidency, he/she must receive about 53-54% of the popular vote.[40] This advantage is not new to Republicans and is craftily utilized by Republicans to win presidencies and appoint conservative Supreme Court Justices, who interpret the law not based on the popular opinion or the will of the people but rather based on their own paradigms and sometimes only those of the person who put them into that position. Thus, the argument in support of We The People is moot as a justification for how Christians can or should influence the law of this or any other secular nation.

I am convinced that sinners don't or won't merely hate Christians simply because they follow the mandates of Christ. It strains credulity to make this assertion. I believe, rather, that the reason Christians are hated is two-fold. First, those who truly follow the instruction of Jesus will be hated by the religious establishments of this world, most of whom, like the Pharisees, seek power, control, and domination. Their end goal is to force their wills upon the people who are subject to their authority. When those who truly follow Christ, The Church, speak out against this hypocrisy, much like Jesus did, they will be

---

[40] Amy Walter, "The Republican Electoral College Advantage," Cook Political Report, July 22, 2022, https://www.cookpolitical.com/cook-pvi/2022-partisan-voter-index/republican-electoral-college-advantage.

hated by those who stand to lose power because of the liberating power of the Gospel.

I believe the second group of people who will hate the True Church will be sinners who have misappropriated the actions of Pharisaical Christians toward them. As the Impostors, as I choose to call them, succeed in their manipulations of the levers of government to impose restrictive laws on an unwilling and unwelcoming group of people, resentment for all of Christianity will grow. Those who have not fallen away from the ways of Jesus, but remained connected to him, will recognize that there is a separation between State and Church. Jesus intimated that separation when he said, *"Therefore render to Caesar the things that are Caesar's, and to God the things that are God's"* (Matt. 22:21).

In governments, particularly where citizens enjoy numerous freedoms and rights, citizens don't respond very well to the forceful restriction of those rights, especially when the rights have been enjoyed for many years prior to the change of guard. This is why our focus should be to change the hearts, not the laws, even though we can. Even when we do change the laws, we must be careful not to employ unjust (or what is perceived as unjust) schemes.

The overturning of Roe vs. Wade, after over 50 years will be deemed an act of hatred by many who have appreciated the liberty afforded them by the previously upheld decision. Citizens are not ignorant of the mechanism by which it happened. They recall that the Republicans denied President Obama his right to appoint a Supreme Court justice during his term. They witnessed the hypocrisy of the Republican Senate when they afforded President Trump the latitude to appoint Amy Coney Barrett, ignoring the very rationale they used when they denied Obama his right. More ominously, they observed how the Impostors applauded and celebrated these underhanded tactics. They also watched how Republicans gerrymandered state congressional districts to completely further deprive their citizens of the right to abortion and voting rights. For clarity, I need to restate that I am not advocating for abortion. I'm merely bringing to light, the hatred that is brewing for Christians and how it is brought about by the despicable conniving of those who profess to be Christian.

Those who choose not to follow Jesus are watching how supposed Christians scoffed at the equal treatment of persons who embrace different gender identifications or sexual practices than Christians. While The Church would approach these issues with the love Jesus commanded them to, the Impostors seek to restrict the liberties afforded them under the Constitution. They find themselves under an all-out assault against their existence and expression. And who do they identify as the culprit for their disenfranchisement? Christians! Yes, The Church will suffer an embarrassment of favor and a growing hatred from those whom we seek to evangelize simply because Evangelicals have abandoned the ways and tactics of Jesus for the methods of this world.

Although Jesus warned that the persecution and hatred would come, he never gave the method by which it would come. Persecution from the religious and world governmental system is likely unavoidable, because it is inspired by our obedience to Jesus' precepts. However, I suspect the persecution by the unsaved could be avoidable if we remained connected to Jesus and followed his example. Because so many, under the influence of Evangelicalism, fail to love like Jesus loved, the hatred of the whole body of Christians will likely occur. This is what Jesus meant when he said the leaven of the Pharisees ruin the whole lump. They think with a carnal mind and resort to carnal strategies to execute what they suppose is the will of God. In the process they create enemies and then devise strategies to shield them from the persecution they've provoked. Almost laughably, they don't see their role in causing the animus. But with pious indignation, they suppose they are hated only because they are righteous. These people, my friends, are deceived!

The notion that through legislation or via any other strategy, Evangelicals can 'protect religious liberty' is carnal at its core. It was never the intention of Jesus to evade his own persecution. It should therefore not be our aspiration. *"From that time Jesus began to show his disciples that he must go to Jerusalem and suffer many things from the elders and chief priests and scribes, and be killed, and on the third day be raised. And Peter took him aside and began to rebuke him, saying, 'Far be it from you, Lord! This shall never happen to you.' But he turned and said to Peter, 'Get behind me, Satan! You are a hindrance to me. For you are not setting your mind on the things of God, but on the things of man'"* (Matt. 16:21-23).

Jesus understood that his persecution would come from the religious and political leaders of his time, not the sinners. Peter, thinking that he would be doing a noble thing, emphatically asserts that he would never let Jesus be persecuted as such. Jesus quickly rebuked Peter, stating that he is thinking with a carnal mind, which was an offense to Jesus.

Wisdom of God confounds the wisdom of man

A second time, Peter attempted to prevent Jesus' persecution, as Jesus was being apprehended by the Roman soldiers. Again, Jesus rebuked Peter, saying, *"Put your sword back into its place. For all who take the sword will perish by the sword. Do you think that I cannot appeal to my Father, and he will at once send me more than twelve legions of angels? But how then should the Scriptures be fulfilled, that it must be so?"* (Matt. 26:53-54). In this very emphatic statement, Jesus makes clear that although he has mechanisms or tools at his disposal to subvert the prosecution that is ordained, the scriptures would not be fulfilled if he used them. It should be concluded from this that even though it seems that we can exercise and/or manipulate many tools of Democracy to rescue us from persecution, how will then the scriptures be fulfilled? Moreover, Jesus warned that he who tries to save his life will lose it, but he who willingly loses it for His sake will gain eternal life (Matt. 16:25)

It deeply pains many Christians to succumb to the notion that, as Jesus did, we are to lay down our lives and not resist those who seek to kill us. We certainly are not justified in putting up a carnal fight, whether it be militarily or legislatively. The idea of being led as sheep to slaughter (Isa. 53:7; Psa. 44:20; Rom. 8:36) is utterly foreign and to some offensive. It goes against everything that we're taught about how we should defend ourselves. Are we not called to be the head and not the tail, above and not beneath? These thoughts are carnal in nature, but the wisdom of God confounds the wisdom of man (1 Cor. 3:19).

In the economy of God, the first shall be last, and the last shall be first (Matt. 19:30). Jesus, admonishing his servants not to do as the Pharisees did, said, *"The greatest among you shall be your servant. Whoever exalts himself will be humbled, and whoever humbles himself will be exalted"* (Matt. 23:11-12). Yes, it is the expectation of Jesus that if we are to remain connected to him, we produce the fruit that he himself produced and that is not a forceful or legislative opposition to the persecution that is foretold. Rather, in order that scripture be fulfilled, Jesus urged his disciples, *"If anyone would come after me, let him deny himself and take up his cross and follow me"* (Matt. 16:24). Following after Jesus means the full adoption of his love and methods.

So, what is it that we can expect to suffer and endure? John 16 tells us that we can expect to be put out of our temples. I was amazed at the outrage and flat-out defiance that Evangelicals and other Christians exhibited during the COVID-19 pandemic when the governments prevented gatherings at church. The disdain, in my opinion, was clearly uninformed and more a demonstration of lack of faith. If Jesus told you to expect these things, why would any of us be surprised or offended when it happens? Jesus warned that we would be put out of the synagogues (John 16:2). In the modern context, this could be interpreted as being prevented from gathering in our places of worship. The pandemic-related restrictions on church gatherings could be seen as fulfilling this prophecy and many Christians were unprepared for it.

In the same scripture, Jesus further warned that *"the hour is coming when whoever kills you will think he is offering service to God."* This is a sobering prediction of severe persecution. It's important to note that Jesus said these persecutors would believe they were serving God through their actions. This suggests that the persecution may come not just from secular sources but potentially from misguided religious zealots as well. A heathen has no desire or motivation to please God. Doing service to God is reserved for those who consider themselves faithful servants of God. But, Jesus explains, *"they have not known the Father, nor me"* (John 16:3). This lack of true knowledge of God and Jesus leads to misguided actions, often committed in the name of religion.

Jesus provided these warnings not to frighten his followers but to prepare them. He said, *"But I have said these things to you, that when their hour comes, you may remember that I told them to you"* (John 16:4). He intended to strengthen their faith so that when these tribulations occur, they would know that Jesus had foreseen them and had already prepared a mechanism for deliverance. Jesus concluded his foretelling of the impending persecution, saying, *"I have said these things to you, that in me you may have peace. In the world you will have tribulation. But take heart; I have overcome the world"* (John 16:33).

> ### *The testament of our faith is our willingness to face persecution with grace and love*

It's crucial for Christians to remember these warnings and not be caught off guard when persecution arises. Instead of reacting with surprise, anger, or attempts to legislate protection, believers should see these events as confirmation of Jesus' words. Such a resolute faith instructs a response that is consistent with His teachings of love, forgiveness, and perseverance.

Considering these teachings, we must also carefully contemplate our response to societal challenges to our faith. Are we truly following Christ's example and teaching, or are we reacting out of fear and a desire for worldly power and protection? The testament of our faith is our willingness to face persecution with grace, love, and unwavering commitment to the Gospel, not in our ability to subvert it.

The notion of protecting religious liberty through legislation or other political strategies is fundamentally antithetical to the teachings of Christ. Jesus never sought to avoid persecution, nor did He instruct His followers to do so. In fact, He repeatedly warned them that persecution would come and that they should expect it as part of their faith journey.

When we examine the early Christian church, we see a group of believers who thrived under persecution rather than seeking to avoid it. They understood that their suffering was a testament to their faith and an opportunity to demonstrate the power of the Gospel. The apostle Paul, who endured numerous hardships for his faith, wrote, *"For I consider that the sufferings of this present time are not worth comparing with the glory that is to be revealed to us"* (Romans 8:18).

The modern evangelical approach of using political power to shield Christianity from perceived threats is a departure from this biblical model. It suggests a lack of faith in God's ability to preserve His church and a misunderstanding of the role of suffering in Christian life. When we rely on legislative protections for our faith, we risk becoming the very thing we claim to oppose. In a zealous and misled effort to make Christianity and its values a legislative priority, we impose our values on others. The other end of that imposition doesn't perceive our efforts as noble or righteous but as oppressive. This approach will inevitably backfire and create resentment and hostility towards Christianity. Instead of drawing people to Christ, it pushes them away, making the task of evangelism even more difficult.

We must also consider the global perspective. Christians in many parts of the world face severe persecution without the luxury of legal protection. Yet, in these places, the church often grows stronger and more vibrant. This should cause us to question whether our pursuit of legal protection is truly necessary or beneficial for the health of The Church.

Instead of seeking to avoid persecution through worldly means, we should focus on preparing ourselves and our fellow believers to face it with grace and steadfastness. This involves deepening our faith, strengthening our communities, and developing a robust theology of suffering that aligns with biblical teaching.

Ultimately, our goal should not be to create a comfortable Christianity that fits neatly within the confines of secular society. Nor should it be an intrusive faith that abuses ill-gotten political and legislative might to trample over people of other faiths or none. Rather, we should strive to embody a faith that is transformative, counter-cultural, and willing to pay the cost of discipleship. Our energy would be better spent preparing for persecution rather than trying to avoid it, trusting in God's sovereignty and the power of the Gospel to prevail even in the face of immense opposition.

A Nation Divided

Solomon is credited with being the wisest king to ever live. This was not by happenstance. Rather, he was granted wisdom far beyond any king because his greatest desire was to know how to rule over God's great people. He recognized that his birthright did not automatically grant him the ability or wisdom to rule in all if any, matters. He did not take privilege in the heritage of his legacy to indulge in self-gratification. Rather, his personal desire and entitlement were altruistically subjugated to that of the people over whom he ruled. God, being so pleased with this heart and request, granted him the great wisdom he requested. Additionally, Solomon was granted what he did not request, which many others in his position would have first requested - wealth and riches.

Evidence of his wisdom was quickly displayed when two women, whom the Bible refers to as harlots, brought a matter before Solomon. The two women gave birth to children around the same time. They stayed in the same home. While they slept, one woman's child died. She swapped her dead child out for the live child of the other woman while she slept. The mother of the live child recognized that the dead child was not hers when she awakened, but there were no witnesses. When the matter was brought before King Solomon, he determined that in the absence of a witness, he should order the child to be cut in half. Immediately, the true mother pleaded that he spares the child and gives the child to the other mother. In contrast, the false mother was willing to have the child slaughtered to satisfy her aspiration, with no concern for the life or health of the baby. In this action, Solomon deciphered the true mother.

In America, we are at an impasse. Unlike Solomon, who refused to ask for long life, riches, or the destruction of his enemies, our leaders seem to place high emphasis on longevity in their appointed positions, riches, and, above all, political annihilation of the opposing party. There is little genuine and selfless concern for the well-being of our country.

In the passage of scripture, the two women were harlots, women of loose values. I would like to, for the purpose of illustration, equate the two women with our two political parties, who battle over the possession of the baby - the nation. One harlot (or political party) is hardened by the death of their beloved child. They lament the changing demographic and the seeming death of their moral heritage. They obviously believe that the other harlot is less deserving of such a precious possession, so they compromise their own moral base to devise a strategy to take the baby from the other harlot.

They have determined that by any means necessary, they will recover their lost possession. The worst-case scenario in their mind is that neither harlot would be left with a baby. In desperation, they suppose they have no alternative other than to lay it all on the line for their last-ditch effort to reclaim that which they feel they had lost. They are so committed to reclaiming what they believe is their right or entitlement that they are willing to risk the division of the baby (nation), which would undoubtedly result in its demise.

Our country, at least in recent generations, has never been so visibly divided. Each political party claims to have the best interest of the country at hand. The defining or revealing question is, "How far are you willing to go to achieve your goal?" The mother whose baby died had already suffered a grave loss and saw no harm in compromising her already loose morality in deciding to move forward with the false claim. If the other child dies in the process, so be it because she has nothing left to lose.

There was, however, a possibility that if the king ruled in her favor she has everything to gain. In contrast, the other mother has everything to lose. She's faced with making the decision of whether she'd rather lose her possession of the child versus the life of the child. Loving the child more than her own personal desire, she determines that she is unable to suffer the loss of the child's life and willingly surrenders the child to the other mother.

America is now like the child on the chopping block. We are on the verge of irreparable division and yet one party seems to be so hell-bent and focused on the prospect of finally achieving their desired political and legislative end that they are willing to sacrifice the life and spirit of the nation to see it come to fruition. While both parties have engaged in questionable political maneuverings to accomplish their legislative agenda, the Republican Party appears to have forsaken their standing as the 'party of Christian values' in their desperate attempt to pass conservative legislation.

From brazen hypocrisy in blocking the appointment of a Supreme Court justice during the last year of Barack Obama's presidency to manipulating voting districts to their favor, it seems that nothing is off limits to them. The hypocrisy was on full display when they rushed through a conservative justice with even less time remaining in Trump's presidency than was left in Obama's. The standard they allegedly righteously established only four years prior was now null and void.

After the January 6th insurrection at the Capitol building, many Republicans publicly denounced Donald Trump for not attempting to end the riot and others for his stated role in inciting it. Yet, in the 2024 presidential race, the very same people have fully unabashedly endorsed Donald Trump. They have fully embraced the by any means necessary dogma. While this behavior can be expected from political figures, it should never be endorsed by the church, much less the leaders of the church. I'm reminded of a graphic dream I had in August, 2017, which I believe will elucidate the harm of maintaining silence about matters that clearly require attention and correction.

I dreamed that I was performing surgeries as usual in the operating room. It was a very busy day for me. I do not recall the details of the conversation, but I had finished one surgery and asked the question, "How long have you stayed in a relationship that you knew was bad for you because the person was attractive, they had money, or for some other reason." One lady chuckled and quietly said I stayed in a relationship for some other reason. Although not explicit, the implication was that she stayed in the relationship for sexual pleasure. Without much further elaboration, we moved on and awakened the patient from anesthesia. We transferred the patient from the operating room and began preparing for the next case.

Between surgeries, a gentleman who worked at the hospital pulled me to the side to ask a very private favor of me. This man had apparently been a friend of my father and I vaguely recognized him. Due to some hard times, misfortune, and bad decisions, he had a hard time keeping a job and presumably staying out of jail. He asked me to examine a mass that had been growing in his groin. Clearly ashamed to ask an Ear, Nose & Throat surgeon to examine his genitals, he finally determined it had grown out of control enough to inquire.

I was quite reluctant to examine him at first because it was beyond the scope of my expertise. I wondered why he would ask me and not someone with expertise in the field, like a urologist. I knew I was unqualified to assess a mass in this region. Certainly, I thought he would know this as well. Further, I was concerned about how it would look to people who passed by the operating room and saw me, of all surgeons, doing a genitourinary exam. Nonetheless, discerning his desperation and final mustering of courage to bring it to attention, I agreed to examine him.

As soon as the man began unfastening his pants, another male employee entered the room. At first, it seemed that he would impede the examination, but after a quick explanation of what was going on, he discerned the urgency of the situation and wisely suggested that the patient lie on the operating table. This made the examination easier and made it more obvious to passersby.

As I examined the man, people passed by the operating room and knocked on the window in disapproval of the care I offered him. I feared that they would report this to the hospital administrators and potentially jeopardize my hospital privileges and the job of the man who assisted me. Nonetheless, we proceeded with the examination.

Uncomfortable with performing the examination but somewhat reassured by the other gentleman's presence, I proceeded to examine the least intrusive, embarrassing, and sensitive regions. I began palpating the patient's abdomen and quickly noted some abnormalities that would not be immediately obvious to the patient or any other casual Observer. I felt dilated loops of bowel as if the man had been constipated. It caused me to wonder whether the patient had cancer with metastasis to his pelvis and his abdominal cavity. I asked the patient first if he had been constipated or noticed that he had difficulty moving his bowels. I do not recall that he answered.

I then continued my examination of his groin and inguinal regions. There he had two hard masses, one on each side. It then became clear to me that cancer had grown and spread to the lymph nodes in his groin. Growing even more concerned about this person's prognosis, I continued my examination and noted a fungating, erosive lesion on his scrotum. On further examination, this lesion extended to the undersurface of his penis. The mass was so extensive that it had eroded away most of the substance of the undersurface of his penis.

I thought this man clearly had to know he had cancer here. There was no way that this mass could be ignored. Even if he urinated, he had no way for urine to normally come out of the penis without spilling over himself due to the extensive erosion. Surely, he would frequently soil himself due to incontinence, which should unquestionably have caused him concern. He would have to take deliberate and laborious action to keep this problem hidden from public view or suspicion.

Very disheartened, but in empathy, I strongly urged the man to seek medical treatment as he donned his clothes again. Fearful that he would continue in his denial, I attempted to be as frank as possible and told him that I was certain that he had cancer that had spread. If he does not seek appropriate medical care, he will surely die from this. The man gave me a perfunctory nod as to suggest that he would seek care,

both of us discerning that he really wouldn't. The man walked away,
and I awakened from the dream.

It was not until I wrote this book that I completely understood this dream. Clearly, there is cancer growing among this body of believers we call the church. Refusal to address it, for whatever reason, simply enables its growth. Eventually, it will result in the death. In the dream, the man who hid the cancer once knew my father. It seemed that I once knew him, but he was hardly recognizable at the time of his presentation. He seemed to have been beaten down by various hardships and now found himself in desperation. I believe this man is like many Evangelicals who once knew my Father. However, they are hardly recognizable now because they have subjugated the power of their faith to carnal systems. Even though they unquestionably recognize their perishable state, they still refuse to seek the spiritual care they require to address the cancer. The cancer site impacts their virility – their influence on the earth, their witness. Still, they seek no true remedy.

I am an Ear, Nose & Throat Surgeon. Some might argue, including myself, that I am not qualified to do the prophetic assessment required to diagnose and treat this cancer that is growing in Christianity. But this person who once knew my Father was directed to me for some reason. I dare not presume to be alone in this endeavor. I know there are many others who cry out against the hypocrisy that is growing in Evangelicalism. Realizing the potential jeopardy my involvement might have on my career, I am compelled by the urgency of the matter to expose the cancer, along with my co-laborers. I implore my Evangelical brothers and sisters that you've stayed in this relationship too long. Forsake whatever benefits it offers and get out for the sake of your witness and the sake of your spiritual life.

I believe many evangelicals recognized early that their endorsement of a morally destitute candidate for the highest office of the land was not a sound or godly decision. With honorable legislative intention and promise, they believed that perhaps God would change his heart. That was respectable, I guess. However, when it became evident that the evil that had seemed to drive many of his past behaviors persisted after his election, they continued to put a little salve on the cancer, hoping and praying desperately that the lesion would resolve. All the while, the cancer continued to grow.

There remains room for redemption for those who humbly acknowledge their fault and seek it. For the sake of our country and the sake of God's name, be bold and courageous. Repent and denounce the divisive politics that seek to destroy this nation. Privately, many of them will give a perfunctory nod as if they will take redemptive action. However, we both discern that they will not have the courage to seek the required remedy. The consequence of their neglect is a growing divide in this nation, fueled by a 'Divider-In-Chief.'

This nation has many divisions. Historically, they have been based on race. Today, they have many appendages that are consolidated by political affiliation. We are often divided along political lines on matters of civil rights, patriotism, abortion, religious expression, humanitarian and military aid to national allies, vaccination and mask use, and racial justice/equity.

The Bible is clear in its mandate that God's people advocate for justice. In recent years, advocacy for racial justice has gained tremendous national and international support. Following the death of George Floyd at the hands of a Minneapolis police officer on May 25, 2020, widespread and international protests erupted in opposition to police brutality and racial injustice. In large part, the Black Lives Matter (BLM) movement was responsible for organizing the protest events.

The US Crisis Monitor — a joint project between ACLED and the Bridging Divides Initiative (BDI) at Princeton University — collected real-time data on the trends of organized protests. They sought to provide timely analysis and resources to track, prevent, and mitigate the risk of political violence in America. They found that demonstrations surged in 2020. Between May 24th and August 22nd, ACLED recorded more than 10,600 demonstration events across the country. Fewer than 570 (approximately 5%) involved demonstrators who engaged in violence, while over 10,100 (nearly 95%) involved only peaceful protesters.[41]

It seemed that peaceful protests were making headway in garnering support for legislative change and just treatment for people of color. But you wouldn't know it if you listened to conservative media, legislators, and President Trump. They asserted that Antifa (a nebulous, poorly organized, anti-fascist group) was in cahoots with BLM to destroy the country. Despite there being no evidence that BLM had any association with Antifa, the false narrative propagated on conservative news stations strategically linked the two inextricably. The goal was to villainize the entire movement. Among the consumers of this hit job were White Evangelicals who joined in the mischaracterization of the whole movement by the actions of only 5% of the events. This was a coordinated effort to prevent the growth of efforts seeking racial justice. Moreover, it became an important topical basis for the 2020 re-election campaign of Donald Trump.

It is not my prerogative to litigate the legitimacy of BLM as an organization. I simply point out that the goal of achieving racial justice in America should be championed by those who purport to be ambassadors of God. At the very least, these efforts should not be thwarted by this group. However, the leaven of Evangelicalism saw fit to make it a political issue and exploited it for the advancement of an overall political agenda.

Shortly after the surge in support for racial justice, there was a push for uncovering the truth of America's sordid history concerning racial injustice. An academic exploration of how the residue of these past atrocities undoubtedly still impacts the economic and judicial systems today, Critical Race Theory, was again mischaracterized by those who identify as Evangelical. It was villainized and consequently used as a political weapon to unify a group of

---

[41] Roudabeh Kishi and Sam Jones, "Demonstrations & Political Violence in America: New Data for Summer 2020," ACLED, September 3, 2020, https://acleddata.com/2020/09/03/demonstrations-political-violence-in-america-new-data-for-summer-2020/.

people who have increasingly begun to feel disenfranchised by the extension of equality to other people groups.

Diversity, Equity, and Inclusion (DEI) arose in recent years as a collective goal of various corporations and institutions to improve ethnic and racial diversity, particularly in their leadership. The organizations recognized the productivity and morale benefits of having a diverse leadership team. This growing trend swiftly elicited backlash from a group of people who felt that they were then being disenfranchised by the efforts. They misrepresented that the inclusion of diversity as a company goal somehow lessened the qualifications for the position.

The presumption that the recruitment of minorities was synonymous with recruiting lesser qualified candidates is beyond inaccurate. Moreover, the assertion is insulting. Nonetheless, the reaction to DEI was a vigorous campaign to end such activities that seemed to disfavor White people. Conservatives and Evangelicals rushed cases to their tailor-made, strategically appointed Supreme Court and succeeded in getting Affirmative Action overturned. This made it illegal for companies to use race as a priority in increasing diversity. Companies are now dismantling their DEI divisions and efforts, an initiative deemed laudable by conservatives who collectively denounce efforts to produce equality and equity as 'wokeness.'

Let us explore what is considered wokeness. Oxford Dictionary defines it as the quality of being alert to and concerned about social injustice and discrimination. In a nation whose constitution purports that all men are created equal with certain inalienable rights, wokeness should be an aspiration, not a pariah. The slang term originated in African American vernacular in the 1930s as a reference to awareness of social and political issues affecting African Americans. In the 2010s, it resurged as a broader reference to include awareness of social inequalities such as sexism and denial of LGBTQ+ rights, in addition to racial injustice. Perhaps the expansion of its references engendered even more vitriol in those who opposed efforts to prove, but ironically tout, their support for the Constitution. Apparently, that support is only for those who conform to or subscribe to their ideologies.

Equality, equity, and justice are key priorities for God. Proverbs 11:1 tells us, *"A false balance is an abomination to the LORD, but a just weight is his delight."* The battle between equality and equity is pervasive. In terms of resources and opportunities, equality means providing the same resources and opportunities to everyone. It disregards the historical impediments that were placed upon particular people groups that prevent them from benefiting equally from opportunities and resources that are now given to them with a pre-existing deficit. Equity, on the other hand, recognizes that the success of people who have been unjustly disadvantaged is hindered by the created by the imposed deficit. Considering this, Equity gives them what they need to reach an outcome equal to those who have previously enjoyed privilege over them. Anything less than equity is a false balance and, as such, is an abomination to God.

Psalms 99:4, referring to God, states, *"The King in his might loves justice. You have established equity; you have executed justice and righteousness in Jacob."* We've previously discussed the first church in the Book of Acts, where the people had all things in common. I've engaged with Christians who purport that this referred only to the church and not the government. But, another Old Testament scripture specifically tells us that after God caused David to be victorious in every battle in which he engaged, *"... David reigned over all Israel. And David administered justice and equity to all his people"* (2 Sam. 8:15).

Perhaps the most illustrative example of equity in the Bible is the parable that Jesus told concerning the workers in the vineyard (Matt. 20:1-16). Jesus tells the story of a landowner who hires workers early in the morning to work in his vineyard for a daily wage. He then goes back out later in the third, sixth, ninth, and eleventh hours of the day and hires more workers who are unemployed. When the landowner asked the people why they were not working, they replied, *"Because no one has hired us"* (vs. 6).

The Bible doesn't say why no one would hire them, but at least in American society, we are keenly aware of why certain people suffered economic, occupational, and professional disenfranchisement of a group of people. The landowner hired these disenfranchised workers, promising to pay them "whatever is right." When evening came, the landowner told his foreman to pay the workers, starting with the last group hired and working their way back. To the surprise and dismay of the first group of workers, everyone received the same amount of pay, even though some worked longer and harder. Angrily, they questioned the landowner who replied to them, *"Friend, I am doing you no wrong. Did you not agree with me for a denarius? Take what belongs to you and go"* (vs. 13).

What is most striking in the parable of the vineyard workers is that the parable begins with the phrase, "For the kingdom of heaven is like..." Whenever Jesus began a parable with such a phrase, it was a foreshadowing that what follows is contrary to our carnal paradigms. According to our human estimations, if I worked longer or harder, I should receive greater compensation. This would be considered equality – compensation should be commensurate with the work performed. But the Kingdom of God considers more than equality. It seeks equity!

The workers who were neglected, overlooked, discriminated against, or were otherwise forsaken or disenfranchised were deemed worthy of the same resources and opportunities as those who first enjoyed preferential treatment. The natural response of the originally privileged when they witness others receive equitable resources is to feel as if they have been wronged. The Bible clearly states in this example that no wrong had been done to them. It can be inferred that the wrong had been done to the ones who stood idly by, not by choice but because they were not given an opportunity.

If the landowner paid the workers who came on later in the day the same hourly wage, he would have exercised equality. However, the workers who were subsequently hired would have had fewer resources, not by any fault of their own but by the nature of the system that worked against them. The landowner instead sought to produce equity by providing those who were previously forgotten and discriminated against with the same opportunities and resources as those who were favored in the beginning. The Kingdom of Heaven is like this.

Today, our Evangelical friends still have not comprehended that the Kingdom of God favors equity. Instead, they rebuff the efforts of corporations and institutions that seek to mimic this Kingdom principle. This causes me to question whether they truly desire to establish God's kingdom or one that serves their preferences and comfort. I fear the latter further divides not only the country but also the Church.

There remains a remnant of Believers who still seek to follow Kingdom precepts and methods. They still believe that the power of prayer is greater than that of the voting booth. They have resolved to the notion that the world will continue its moral decline as prophesied in the Bible, which will eventually result in their inevitable persecution. Rather than exploiting the levers of democracy in a futile effort to protect their 'religious freedoms,' they vigorously prepare their faith to endure until the end. This remnant of people will not stand silently while the Christian faith is misrepresented. The consequence is that it appears that not only is the nation divided, but the church appears to be also. About this, many are disheartened. I'm not!

Jesus warned his disciples, *"Do not think that I have come to bring peace to the earth. I have not come to bring peace, but a sword. For I have come to set a man against his father, and a daughter against her mother, and a daughter-in-law against her mother-in-law. And a person's enemies will be those of his own household"* (Matt. 10:34-36). Jesus understood that there would be a time when those persons whom we once considered our brothers and sisters would become our enemies. The dividing factor would be those who loved their relationships, liberties, and life more than they loved Him.

Today, we see clearly a group of Christians who love the accouterments of democracy more than they love Jesus. They are unwilling to take up their cross of persecution to follow Jesus. They will follow Him as long as it doesn't inconvenience their comforts of living. However, to follow Jesus means to do and respond as Jesus did, including in persecution. Rather than calling twelve legions of angels, which were at his disposal, to rescue him, Jesus submitted to his apprehension and persecution so that the word of God might be fulfilled (Matt. 26:54).

No, I'm not disheartened by what seems to be a division among Christians. I believe and am encouraged by the Bible. In Matthew 13:24-30, Jesus tells the parable of the weeds. He states that the Kingdom of God is like a sower who sowed good seed in the ground, and later that night, his enemy came and planted weeds next to them. When the wheat grew and began to make grain, it became apparent that weeds were growing amongst them. Baffled by this, his servants inquired, *"Master, did you not sow good seed in your field? How then does it have weeds?' He said to them, 'An enemy has done this'"* (vs. 27-28).

The master instructed his servants to let the weeds grow next to the wheat so that the wheat would not be mistakenly removed while attempting to remove the weeds, which deceptively resembled the wheat. But when they had reached maturity, it became evident which was which. He said, *"at harvest time I will tell the reapers, 'Gather the weeds first and bind them in bundles to be burned, but gather the wheat into my barn'"* (vs. 30). It is harvest time, and the impostors are being identified. Soon, the harvest will come, and God will remove those who have feigned the faith and, in so doing, have defamed the faith.

In 1998, the Lord showed me a dream concerning this. In this dream, he presented me with the most beautiful bush I have ever seen in my life. I'm not sure what the great appeal of the bush was, but just being in its presence brought comfort, peace, and a sense of serenity. Then suddenly, as I admired the beauty of the bush, what seemed to be a broomstick started beating the bush. Immediately, swarms of pests, insects, and other vermin flew from within the bush. What started as serenity quickly evolved into a horrific fear.

The voice of the Lord said to me, "Don't Run!" He explained to me that the bush was his church that was beautiful on the outside but was filled with vermin that would pollute it. The broomstick was His spiritual stirring that would evict the vermin from the bush so that his church would be as beautiful on the inside as it is on the outside. "When you see it happening, resist the urge to run," the Lord warned me. Today, we see it happening. The wooden rod of God is exposing the ugliness hidden behind The Church's beauty for centuries. Sadly, many who have witnessed this have run and left the organized church. Much of the impetus for this departure was the witnessing of Evangelical hypocrisy. I believe in this season God is calling them back. I pray that he is using the writing of this book to help them see that there remains a remnant of The Church who have remained connected to Jesus and have not fallen away. They are equally disturbed when the weeds are mascaraed as the wheat. God knows the difference. He will not suffer those who genuinely desired to know him but, because of the leaven of Evangelicalism, were obstructed to remain separated.

Several decades ago, the Lord gave me a prophetic word that there would be two harvests. The first harvest would be those who were once connected to the Church but have left because of offense, neglect, or abuse. Like Peter, Satan has desired to sift them as wheat (Luke 22:31). But Jesus is praying for them as he did for Peter so that when they return to themselves, they will go and strengthen their brother.

The second harvest the Lord showed me consisted of those who we would consider the 'unchurched' – people who have never accepted Christ or his Gospel. God intends to use those who, like Peter, returned to the calling of their faith to disciple the unchurched without perpetrating the same offenses that drove them away.

Jesus is praying for all those Christians who have been discouraged by the hypocrisy and leaven of Evangelicalism. In John 17:9, he states, *"I am praying for them. I am not praying for the world [kosmos] but for those whom you have given me, for they are yours."* After God has completely exposed the hidden vermin in the church, he will reclaim those who ran, horrified by what they witnessed. God will use these to build The Church that he desires to receive when he returns – one without spot or blemish. Until then, like the nation, Christianity will appear divided but divided according to those who remain deceived and those who walk in The Truth.

DR. MARK WILLIAMS

Merging Music, Medicine & Ministry

Dr. Mark Williams, a native of Cincinnati, Ohio, is one of 10 sons born to Charles and Mary Williams. His journey from a young boy fascinated with surgery to a renowned otolaryngologist, gospel artist, and author is a testament to his faith, resilience, and diverse talents.

Early Life and Education

Williams' childhood interest in becoming a surgeon manifested in playful "operations" on bumblebees. At age seven, he embraced his faith, which would become a guiding force throughout his life. He attended the University of Cincinnati on a full academic scholarship, initially majoring in Biology.

A tragic turning point came at age 19 when his father and brother died in a boating accident. This devastating event led to his exposure to the funeral industry, prompting him to change his major to Mortuary Science. He graduated as salutatorian from the Cincinnati College of Mortuary Science.

Medical Career

Williams later returned to his original passion, attending the University of Cincinnati College of Medicine. He became only the second African American to complete the Physician-Scientist Training Program, earning his doctorate of philosophy (Ph.D.) in Pharmacology & Cell Biophysics as well as his medical doctorate (M.D.). He then completed his residency in Otolaryngology – Head & Neck Surgery at the same institution.

After his training, Dr. Williams moved to Nashville, Tennessee, where he founded Ear, Nose & Throat Specialists of Nashville and the Voice Care Center of Nashville. His surgical practice focuses on treating voice disorders in singers and other ear, nose, and throat problems.

Music and Ministry

An award-winning Gospel recording artist and songwriter, Dr. Williams brings a unique perspective to his medical practice, understanding the medical, psychological, and spiritual impact of voice disorders. He is a sought-after speaker and educator on voice care and worship.

Dr. Williams has released two nationally acclaimed Gospel albums: "Everything" and "When A Man Worships." A third album is slated for release in 2025.

Author and Thought Leader

Weekly, Dr. Williams co-hosts a live podcast, "RoundTable Consult," with Attorney Sonya Madison. Together, they discuss current social/community issues from a medical, legal, spiritual, and political perspective. No topic is off-limits.

In 2020, Dr. Williams published his first book, "When A Man Worships," a compendium to the same-titled music recording. With prophetic insight, his second book, "DECEIVED! The Poisoned Fruit of Evangelicalism," explores the intersection of faith and politics.

Personal Life

Dr. Mark Williams has been married to Darice Williams for 31 years. They have three adult children together and will soon welcome their first grandchild.

A true renaissance man, Dr. Williams seamlessly combines his roles in music, medicine, and ministry, making a profound impact in each field.

Videos:

Weekly Podcast:

Book Dr. Mark Williams

Speaking, Singing, Book Signing

ATAP Music Group

P.O. Box 110793

Nashville, TN 37222

(615) 724-0131

booking@atapmusic.com

For Medical Care

Voice Care Center of Nashville

341 Wallace Rd., Suite D

Nashville, TN 37211

(615) 333-2222

www.entson.net

www.drmarkwill.com